KILIMANJARO

TO THE ROOF OF AFRICA

KILIMA

ANJARO

TO THE ROOF OF AFRICA

AUDREY SALKELD

NATIONAL GEOGRAPHIC

WASHINGTON, D.C.

CONTENTS

At the edge of Kilimanjaro's crater, with the Furtwängler Glacier, 18,700 feet; Preceding pages: The shining dome of Kilimanjaro, 19,340 feet, towering above the savanna; Pages 6–7: Two giants of Africa: elephants under Kilimanjaro; Pages 8–9: The film team hiking from the Great Barranco toward Kibo, the main summit of Kilimanjaro; Pages 10–11: Flamingos taking flight from the Empaki Crater on the eastern edge of the Ngorongoro Highlands; Pages 12–13: Filming the giant Breach Wall on Kilimanjaro at 13,800 feet

DAVID BREASHEARS

There, ahead, all he could see, as wide as all the world,
great, high, and unbelievably white in the sun,
was the square top of Kilimanjaro.

ERNEST HEMINGWAY, "THE SNOWS OF KILIMANJARO"

I FIRST ENCOUNTERED KILIMANJARO from an unusual vantage point—cruising toward 19,000 feet strapped to the outside of a wicker basket suspended from a hot-air balloon. I had placed my feet flat against the basket and straightened my legs in a sturdy V-shaped stance, which helped steady my nerves as well as the camera. While balloonist Ben Abruzzo worked the controls of the twin propane-gas burners, I recorded his efforts, and the 360-degree panorama, with an unwieldy video camera.

As we drifted eastward, the view, more than three miles straight down to the farmland bordering Kilimanjaro's southwestern slopes, was stupendous. But it wasn't until we had floated past a clump of cumulus clouds that the mountain revealed itself. The sight was spellbinding—in a single majestic sweep the solitary giant rose straight up above the flat grassy plains of the East African savanna. It was also overwhelming. I had never seen another mountain like it: There were no surrounding peaks or river valleys to provide scale, and I realized immediately that it would be impossible to capture the vastness of Kilimanjaro with the camera balanced on my shoulder.

Our intent that day in 1983 was to ascend vertically, as fast as possible, from a soccer field near the forest's edge outside the village of Mweka in Tanzania, and then float over Kilimanjaro's 19,340-foot summit. We wanted to skim across the Roof of Africa with camera rolling, finally landing just inside Tanzania near its border with Kenya. The two countries were fighting a small war and we were warned not to fly over Kenyan territory or risk being shot at.

From my precarious, creaking perch I peered through the swirling clouds and tried to close the gap between the mountain of my imagination and the mountain before me. Unfortunately, the winds in the upper atmosphere didn't favor us. We couldn't get close to the summit or the broad glaciated crater just below it.

I was startled, though not alarmed, when Ben abruptly turned to me and said: "Come on David—get back in the basket. We're out of propane." I wasn't ready to go, and was just beginning to grasp the dimensions of this legendary mountain. But we had lingered too long, spellbound by the mountain's great expanse and the glinting glaciers wrapping its summit. Reluctantly, we descended quickly, with barely a whisper. The light was fading as we scanned the terrain below for a landing zone free of obstacles. We couldn't find one. Ground winds pushed us along and the red earth rushed up too fast. We crashed. The first impact drove me to my knees and broke the camera in half. Ben valiantly pulled on the cord that releases the balloon's hot gas as the basket whacked, thudded, and ripped its way through the African bush. We finally came to rest upright and unscathed in a swirl of dust. Later, as we sat recounting the day's events, and our good fortune at surviving uninjured, the last pink rays of a dazzling African sunset blinked off the summit of Kilimanjaro.

Two months earlier I had climbed Asia's highest peak, Mount Everest. The sky-scraping massifs of the Himalayan range brought to mind the epic struggle of mountaineers at high altitude. For me, Africa's highest point held a different fascination. The name Kilimanjaro conjured up scenes of wonder and mystery, of faraway places and eternal snows. I was eight years old when I first heard of the mountain. I had watched the movie, *The Snows of Kilimanjaro*, starring Gregory Peck, based on Hemingway's famous short story. The movie left me with indelible images of Africa, in particular the vultures patiently waiting in the trees for death against the imposing backdrop of the white mantle of Kilimanjaro.

Looking back I see plainly that it was the contradictions of Kilimanjaro that fascinated me as a boy staring, transfixed, at the movie screen. I was awestruck by the great snow-capped peak rising above the dry savanna where wild herds roamed, pursued by hunters on safari. But it wasn't until 1988, when I first climbed to its summit, that I witnessed firsthand the astonishing diversity of Kilimanjaro's terrain. Its lower reaches are blanketed in dense, humid rain forest; its summit slopes are capped by the icy remnants of Ice Age glaciers. Where else on our planet can you journey from the Amazon to the North Pole in less than a week?

My interest in taking others along on this remarkable journey and in capturing the mountain's stupendous scale are what inspired me to make a large-format film on Kilimanjaro. My earlier experience as co-director, cinematographer, and expedition leader on *Everest*, a large-format film released in 1998, had already impressed on me the unparalleled power of this format to transport viewers to far-flung regions of the planet.

We all experience the world through the prism of our own perspectives, a prism that is sharpened and transformed by age. The five trekkers you will come to know in these pages and in our film set off for Kilimanjaro's summit fueled by their own aspirations. Nicole and Hansi brought the enthusiasm and expectations of youth. Hansi was eager to climb the mountain he could see 40 miles away from his own backyard. He also wanted to make his family proud, and to touch snow for the first time in his 13 years. Inspired by her father's stories of his own ascent, 12-year old Nicole had to see for herself the summit plateau and the glaciers.

In contrast, Audrey Salkeld, the oldest climber on our team, had already established a distinguished career writing and researching mountaineering books. Yet she had never climbed a mountain as high as Kilimanjaro. For Audrey, the journey became a test of heart and spirit as she found the inner strength to reach the top of her first big mountain.

Part of the joy in making this film, and exploring Kilimanjaro again, was to watch all of the team members learn to cope with adversity, discovering that the rewards of the heights lie in the exertion required to attain them. The insights we gain about ourselves, and the wonders of our planet we experience, are what make the journey memorable. Hansi, Nicole, Audrey, Heidi, and Roger all came to understand the wisdom of Jacob Kyungai, their guide, who said to me before the tough, final push to the summit: "The climb tomorrow is the biggest hurdle, and it requires stamina and strength of heart. They won't know if they have it until they need it."

After reading this book, and going to see our film, *Kilimanjaro: To the Roof of Africa*, some of you may decide to experience the mountain firsthand. If you go, remember to take your time. Kilimanjaro's treasures and secrets reveal themselves slowly, to the careful observer.

And remember also to take care of the mountain. There is an irony in making a film showcasing Kilimanjaro's wonders. The more people that are exposed to the glories of this mountain, the more people may want to climb it, and Kilimanjaro is already a mountain under tremendous pressure. Despite its seemingly pristine, limitless slopes, Kilimanjaro is fragile and can bear the traffic of only so many footsteps. We worked closely with officials of Kilimanjaro National Park, encouraging them to uphold their preservation policies, which limit visits to the park to current levels.

Tanzanians are justly proud that Kilimanjaro, the icon of Africa, lies within their borders. The park officials we spoke to wish to preserve this national treasure. But in a country dependant on tourism for much of its revenue, limiting the number of tourists is not an easy choice. The officials face the dilemma of making decisions of short-term benefit to the country that could hurt the mountain in the long term. I hope the guardians of Kilimanjaro will decide that preserving their incomparable national treasure is not only good for the mountain but also good for the country.

Eighteen years after my ballooning adventure, Kilimanjaro still maintains a firm grip on my imagination. I have climbed the mountain eight times, crisscrossed its slopes dozens of times, traveled hundreds of miles over its terrain, and ascended and descended countless thousands of feet along its slopes. Yet even now I hardly know Kilimanjaro. Every journey I've made there has brought surprises.

I had heard rumors that an elephant had died high on the slopes long ago, far across the mountain from our camp. Curious, I set out in search of its remains, eventually discovering the sun-bleached bones resting near 15,000 feet, in the desolation of the alpine desert. I marveled at the elephant's perilous journey and contemplated the purpose of the difficult climb it had made. What was it looking for? What drew it to this cold inhospitable place many thousands of feet above its comfortable habitat on the savanna?

In making the film documented in this wonderful book, I found that the Kilimanjaro I've experienced firsthand has far exceeded the Kilimanjaro of my imagination. You will find that in telling the story of the great and mysterious Kilimanjaro, Audrey Salkeld has managed to stir the ageless yearning we all share as human beings: to press beyond the confines of our daily lives, to discover more of our planet and ponder our place in it.

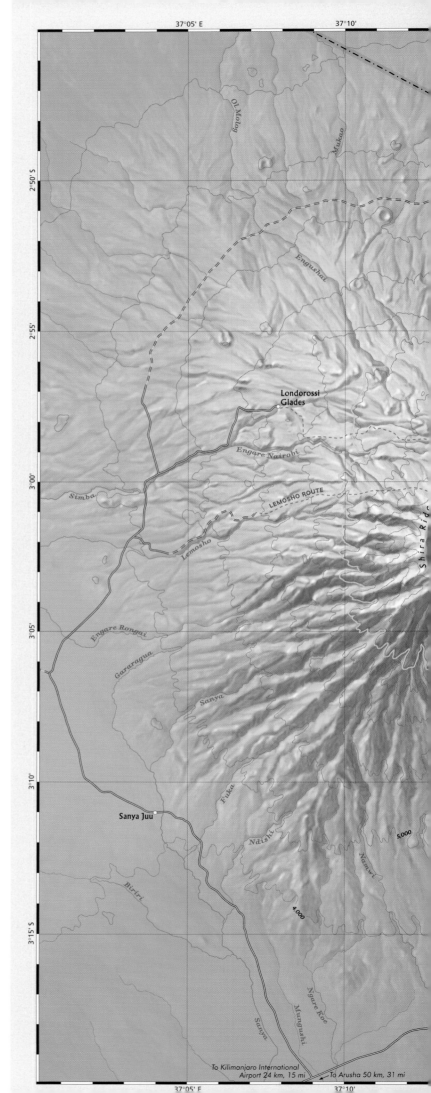

KILIMANJARO

Transverse Mercator Projection
SCALE 1:223,404
1 CENTIMETER = 2.26 KILOMETERS; 1 INCH = 3.57 MILES

KILOMETERS

STATUTE MILES

elevations in feet ; contour interval equals 1,000 feet

○ Populated place
△ Hut
— Kilimanjaro National Park Boundary
— All weather road
- - - Dry weather road
- - - Hiking trail
- - - Breashear's Expedition route

To Nairobi
259 km, 161 mi
To Namanga
96 km, 60 mi

KENYA
TANZANIA

Loitokitok

Rongai

To Tsavo
130 km,
81 mi

Tarakea

To Taveta
48 km, 30 mi

Moir △

Shira △

KIBO
Western Breach
Reusch Crater
Gillman's Point
18,650 ft
5,684 m
Outward Bound

Lava Tower △
Arrow Glacier
Uhuru Peak
19,340 ft
5,895 m
Kibo

The Saddle
MARANGU ROUTE

Mawenzi Tarn △

Hans Meyer Peak
16,896 ft
5,149 m

Heim Glacier
Barranco
Barafu △

Mawenzi △

MAWENZI

Machame △

Horombo △

Mweka △

Mandara △

Umbwe ●
Mweka ●

Park Headquarters ▢

Mango ●

Marangu ○
Mwika

Mkiashi ●

To Moshi 7 km, 4.3 mi
To Moshi
2 km, 1.25 mi
To Himo
4 km, 2.5 mi

CHAPTER ONE

MOUNTAIN OF EDEN

There is the grand dome or crater of Kibo, with its snow cap glancing
and scintillating like burnished silver...on its eastern flank, rise the jagged
outlines of the craggy peak of Kimawenzi. What words can adequately
describe this glimpse of majestic grandeur and godlike repose?

JOSEPH THOMSON, EXPLORER, ON FIRST SEEING KILIMANJARO IN 1883

FROM THE DOOR OF MY tent I have a magnificent view of Kilimanjaro and its massive Breach Wall, which rises in an almost vertical sweep for several thousand feet. Minute by minute, as the light changes and clouds drift across the mountain face, the mood in this high valley subtly changes. In the mornings everything sparkles and it is impossible not to feel high spirited, but when the mists roll in, usually toward midday, an open paradise becomes transformed into something mysterious. You sense the mountain walls huddling around you and boulders and trees loom like strangers in the shadows. Sometimes the clouds fray for a moment to reveal distant glimpses of snow and ice, and later in the afternoon they vanish altogether. Evenings have been golden and calm and, just when the sun slips over the valley wall, the rocks glow a bright, rusty red and the snow flushes pink. But at night, when the temperature dips below freezing, seen by the light of stars and moon, the mountain acquires a brittle clarity, and you feel it could shatter at the slightest sound. ∾ The Breach Wall is broken just above half-height by the Balletto Icefield and is surmounted by the Diamond Glacier, from which tongues of ice overflow as permanent icicles to give the upper tier of the face the

PRECEDING PAGES: THE MASAI TRADITIONALLY INHABIT THE FLATTER STEPPES AROUND KILIMANJARO. LEFT: HELICHRYSUMS
LOOK ACROSS THE SHIRA PLATEAU TOWARD THE GLACIERS ON THE WESTERN SIDE OF KIBO AND THE GREAT WESTERN BREACH.

look of a shark's gaping jaws. At the foot of the cliffs, overlapping fans of scree butt against giant moraines from earlier glaciations. For climbers, the Breach Wall offers the most serious challenges on Kilimanjaro. No one attempted it at all, even by the easiest glacier traverse, until the late 1950s. Its major routes remained untried for a further two decades. The giant icicle toward the top, which mountaineering's top men regarded as the last tantalizing "plum" on this mountain, was the scene of bitter struggle and one of the most dramatic epics ever to have taken place on the mountain.

This is the wildest side of Kilimanjaro—or, more correctly, of Kibo, Kilimanjaro's higher, western summit. The lesser peak, Mawenzi, is rugged too, particularly its eastern face, which has been dubbed the Eiger of Africa. But at two and a half thousand feet lower, Mawenzi no longer carries permanent snow and ice.

We are camped in the extraordinary Great Barranco, a deep, steep-sided valley gouged from the southern side of the mountain with the Breach Wall at its head. Here, at its upper end, this valley is broad and stepped. High, steeply angled cliffs continue around to the east, though it is possible to make out a narrow track zigzagging up them. From time to time, we have seen figures laboring up this path, which leads toward the Heim Glacier and forms part of the mountain's southern circuit trail. The western side of the valley, the way we approached from the Shira Plateau, is less steep with much loose scree, but it completes the sense of enclosure. So, we are in an amphitheater. Below our camp the terrace ends abruptly and the valley plunges downhill as the gorge (barranco) of the Umbwe River.

It is a magical place. The first thing that strikes you, dropping into this Great Barranco, is its primeval-looking vegetation, dominated by giant groundsels and giant lobelias. At a height of almost 13,000 feet, you might expect plants to grow low and compact as protection against the extreme environment. But in the mountains of East Africa some species have taken the alternative

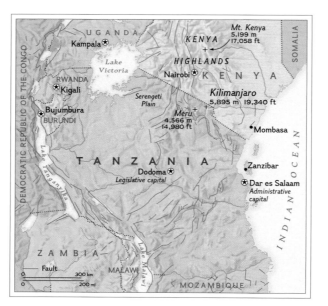

route of gigantism; it helps them absorb more heat in the daytime that can be relinquished slowly at night.

The commonest form of lobelia cultivated in Western gardens is a dainty edging plant, no more than a few inches high; here lobelias push out hefty columnar flowerheads from stiff, spiky rosettes several feet across. And the groundsels, or senecios, familiar to us as lowly weeds in the vegetable plot, have representatives here that have grown into bizarre trees 20 or more feet tall, with thick corky trunks and contorted limbs, each bearing a lax mop head of leaves. When in flower, it's as if another, altogether different, plant has sprouted atop the parent: Vast inflorescences of daisy-like flowers borne on thin, branching stalks explode from the leaf rosettes. As one botanist remarked, "these giant groundsels would feed all the canaries in the world for a time approaching all eternity." We haven't spotted any canaries, but the giant groundsel's mustard-colored flowers are popular with the scarlet-tufted malachite sunbird, a creature every bit as exotic as its name suggests. At least, the male is a thrilling sight with his coat of iridescent green and foot-long tail streamers. You see him hovering like a hummingbird over the groundsels or gathering nectar with his long, curved beak from lobelia spikes. Generally, he'll fly off before you can get your camera trained upon him. Mrs. Scarlet-tufted malachite sunbird is dowdy by comparison, a mud-colored little thing, with no fine tail streamers, let alone a metallic sheen or scarlet tuft.

Rising abruptly from the dry, open plains of East Africa, Kilimanjaro presents an island of difference, a self-contained ecosystem, you might say, entirely unlike its surroundings. Anyone climbing the mountain becomes aware that this ecosystem is made up of altitudinal layers, reflected in the vegetation. The ascent is often described as a condensed journey from the tropics to the poles. If a little romantic, this description neglects only to point out that this journey is also an upward one, from 6,000 feet through increasingly thinner air to 19,340 feet.

NEAR ARUSHA, ENTREPRENEURS USE PLASTIC CONTAINERS TO TRANSPORT WATER, COOKING OIL, OR KEROSENE TO CITY MARKETS.

From the dry savanna and thornscrub of the plains, you pass first through a cultivated zone—which for the most part conceals the original transitional plant cover—to reach the montane forest, the point at which most of the trekking routes start. The forest in turn can be subdivided into rain forest and cloud forest before it opens out onto the alpine zones above. These, at first richly vegetated, become increasingly barren as you climb higher, leading ultimately to glaciers and the summit ice cap. The uneven distribution of rainfall gives an asymetrical pattern to the "zonation." On the much drier north side the forest belts are narrower and don't extend as high, with the consequence that different trees are found there than on the wetter southern slopes.

Botanists over the years have struggled with applying a nomenclature to these vegetation intervals, and indeed in deciding precisely where they start and finish. It varies from one study to another; this valley where we're camped now may be identified as being in the Afro-alpine, Afro-montane, Altimontane, Subalpine, or Moorland Zone. Doubtless, the question will be chewed over for some time, but there is call for standardization.

A BRITISH PRIME MINISTER in Queen Victoria's England could not imagine why anyone should be interested in that "mountain country behind Zanzibar with the unrememberable name" and was astounded that his soberest advisors recommended colonizing it. Today there can be few people who do not recognize the name Kilimanjaro, and most can put an image to it. Books, films, and photographs have familiarized us with the elysian view of elephants and giraffes grazing against a backdrop of Kilimanjaro's shimmering dome. This is Paradise garden, the icon of Africa—the way we imagine the world was in the beginning. Floating over the plains, more mirage than mountain, Kilimanjaro ranks among those universal dream locations whose names echo like spells—Samarqand, Xanadu, Marrakech—places so special you are almost frightened to go and see them, in case reality proves a disappointment. But Kilimanjaro does not

OSTRICH, ZEBRA, AND WILDEBEEST KICK UP THE DUST.

disappoint, neither in beauty nor in its rich mystery—something reflected in its recognition as a World Heritage Site.

KILIMANJARO LIES 3° south of the Equator. It is contained entirely within Tanzania, although its northeastern flank abuts the Kenyan border. Looking on a map, the border runs in a straight line, apart from where it loops around the foot of Kilimanjaro, thus avoiding any of the mountain spilling into Kenyan territory.

The mountain covers an area of over 2,000 square miles, set in an elongated oval, lying on a northwest/southeast axis. Thrusting into the sky to a height of more than three miles, Kilimanjaro is often described as the largest freestanding mountain in the world. This implies that other, higher mountains are clustered in ranges, or built one upon another. Yet Kilimanjaro, too, is a composite: three volcanoes, superimposed. First there was Shira, which today remains as a weathered-down caldera on the mountain's western flanks. No point along what remains of Shira's shattered rim rises much above 13,000 feet, yet originally its cone would have stood between 16,000 and 17,000 feet. Close by, to the east, another volcano erupted—Mawenzi. This was similar in height and stature, and the tops of the two peaks would have been only 18 miles apart. Kibo appeared last of all, thrown up from a vent midway between the others. Its lavas piled upon the slopes of its neighbors, pushing its crater higher than theirs, and its outpourings welded all three peaks together.

That is a simplification. There would have been other emissions in between and afterward. Many satellite cones bristling over and around Kilimanjaro are proof of protracted activity, but the main dome of Kibo was erected, so geologists believe, about half a million years ago, and this is the summit we see today. Elevated plateaus separate it from its brothers: Shira Plateau on the west and, to the east, the Saddle, a 14,000-foot col between Kibo and Mawenzi. Kibo alone retains the characteristic volcanic cone—Mawenzi, much like Shira, having been reduced to a deeply serrated ridge whose highest point is 16,896 feet.

KILIMANJARO IS one of the youngest volcanoes in Africa. Shira's eruption from the African Plate was no more than a million years ago, the result of cataclysmic Earth movements associated with the formation of the Great Rift Valley. That is very recent, geologically speaking, well within the timespan of hominids on Earth. Our early ancestor *Homo erectus*, as well as *H. ergaster*, forerunner of the Neandertals, would have been roaming the surrounding plains when Kilimanjaro went through its birth pangs. They certainly would have seen fire and lava shooting into the air, experiencing its fallout and some pretty extreme effects on the weather. Some may have been forced to migrate and give the mountain a wider berth as rocks and ash rained down; others, less fortunate, could have been crushed beneath the massive lahars, or mudflows, that coursed down the mountain's flanks to blanket a wide area.

Our even earlier ancestor, *Homo habilis*, whose fossilized remains have been found in Olduvai Gorge within 120 miles of Kilimanjaro, would not have seen the fireworks, since he is presumed to have died out before the arrival of Kilimanjaro. Another significant eruption is believed to have occurred within the past 20,000 years when *Homo erectus*, too, had long passed from the Earth and the comparatively advanced *Homo sapiens* was hunting and foraging widely. The most recent eruption of all, though a minor one, took place only about 400 years ago, well within the folkloric memory of the Chagga living on Kilimanjaro's lower slopes today and the Masai from the steppes around.

Various local myths and legends persist that appear to be referring to this and earlier volcanic activity.

This means that Kilimanjaro, even inhabiting only the most recent epoch of geological time, will have been seen by at least four different *Homo* species. Indeed, there are scientists today who feel that the tectonic movements and volcanism associated with the rifting process did not merely provide the geographic backdrop to hominid development, as has been widely accepted, but actively favored that development. It is no accident, they say, that so many of man's ancestors have been found in and around the Great Rift Valley. They don't mean simply that the manner of sediment deposition there serendipitously lent itself to the preservation of fossils; the complex topography produced by rifting, with its lake basins, valleys, fault scarps, lava flows, and caves, would have been highly attractive to early man and given him an edge when it came to interacting with other animals. Landscape structured in this way "may have exerted selective pressures favoring bipedalism, the exploitation of animal foods, and evolutionary divergence," according to Geoff Bailey, Geoffrey King, and Isabelle Manighetti in a paper on the subject. The very patchiness of this highly dynamic environment would have made potentially fast-moving or elusive prey more easily accessible to an intelligent predator who did not share the biological advantage of rapid movement. It has been something of a puzzle in the past for paleoanthropologists to explain how, when the forests began to dwindle, vegetarian tree-dwelling primates could so successfully evolve into meat eaters of the highly competitive open savanna. This offers one seductive expla-

moving south to settle the plains and highlands of northern Tanzania. They were agriculturists and may have been the first to develop irrigation channels on the mountain. Within the last few thousand years, Nilotic people also started arriving from the Nile Basin, and Bantu migrated in from western Africa. These are represented today by the Masai and the Chagga, respectively. The Chagga—formerly known as the Wachagga (the prefix *Wa* indicating the men or people of), were diligent farmers and took possession of the fertile mountain slopes, building up an intricate irrigation system. The Masai, by contrast, were seminomadic pastoralists and remained mostly on the plains, their life and wealth dependent on the size of their livestock herds. The 19th century was one of great strife among the Masai and, during the years running up to European colonization, tribes were ravaged by smallpox and cholera while their animals fell to rinderpest and bovine pleuropneumonia. As a result, the Masai were in no position to challenge the territorial seizures made by

WEDNESDAY All my adult life, I've been in love with mountains, I've walked in them, written about them, collected books about them, but I don't find myself on top of mountains very often, except at home in Britain. So it's hard to imagine myself on the summit of this one. Still I dream.

nation; the relative security of the basalt lava flows and their potential for ambush and containment would assist such a transition.

LITTLE OF GREAT anthropological or archaeological antiquity has been found on Kilimanjaro itself, for the simple reason that the mountain will be sitting on top of any fossils, tools, or footprints left by man's earliest ancestors. Stone bowls and rings recovered from Kilimanjaro's western slopes and fashioned from local lava are thought to be around 2,000 years old. Some flakes and tools of obsidian have also been reported and a polished stone axe, which could be older, has been found.

With its numerous springs and streams, its soft mountain climate, and its rich wildlife, the Kilimanjaro area would have supported early (Holocene) hunters and gatherers as soon as it became safe to live there. Later, waves of Cushites from the southern highlands of Ethiopia began spreading across northeastern Africa, some

their new masters. Relegated to reserves, they lost the best of their traditional grazing lands and drought-retreat areas. Things improved somewhat after Independence, but many now see diversification as the only way forward. Some still live a traditional life on the homelands, but increasingly the young are drawn into cities, seeking better opportunities. It is nothing to see a Masai warrior in full plaid wrap and beaded decoration, staff in hand, riding a bike or a motorcycle around town.

TANZANIA IS East Africa's largest country; it is also one of the poorest nations in the world, with a growing population and expanding cities. Four times as much is spent per capita in servicing debt than on basic education. Tourism assumes increasing importance, but agriculture is still the main industry and the majority of Tanzania's 31 million inhabitants remain on the land, many as subsistence farmers. The main cash crops are coffee, cotton, tobacco, cashew nuts, tea, and sisal, but parts of the country, like Kilimanjaro, are so clement and fertile that almost anything can be grown there. With no winter and sufficient water, several crops a year can be produced. There are two rainy seasons, the Long Rains, which are expected from February to May, and the Short Rains in November to December. These can be erratic, however, and there are years when the plains experience great drought and some streams fail on Kilimanjaro.

KILIMANJARO, Kilima Njaro, Kilimanscharo—the name has flourish, but there is no consensus about what it means or how it came to be. When the missionary Johannes Rebmann approached the mountain in the late 1840s, he'd already heard about it from Swahili traders. The Chagga on the slopes of Kilimanjaro spoke of the mountain's two main summits separately, as Kibo (or Kipoo) and Kimawenzi, and, so far as Rebmann could discover, had no singular term in their language for the massif as a whole. Through trading they became familiar with the Swahili word and in time adopted it.

Rebmann made a study of the various coastal dialects and thought that the most probable interpretation of Kilimanjaro was "Mountain of Greatness." But he threw in another suggestion as well: If one considered *njaro* as a corruption of the Chagga word *jaro*, then the translation might be "Mountain of Caravans." Visible from afar, and a watering stop for the caravan traders, this seemed to him an apt name for the peak. Few agreed. A name hybridized from two languages is always uncomfortable. A straight combination of *kilima* and *njaro* in Swahili would seem far more likely, as it produces "Mountain of the Cold Devils"—or, more precisely, "Little Mountain" of the same, for the prefix *ki* generally indicates a diminutive form of the subject word. Why *mlima* should be rendered as *kilima*, demoting an obvious monster into a mere hill, can perhaps be explained as affectionate irony.

Njaro, too, presents problems. It can mean the demon or djinn responsible for manufacturing coldness, but another Swahili word, *ngara*, translates as "shining," and you'd be hard put to choose which of these descriptions best fits the summit of Kilimanjaro. To complicate matters further, a Masai word, *njare*, "the fount of water," has also been promulgated, though in association with *kilima* this again would constitute a hybrid. In any case, the Masai have a perfectly good name for it themselves, Ol Donyo Ebor, "The White Mountain." Snow-streaked Mount Kenya, by

comparison, is Ol Donyo Egeri, "The Striped Mountain." To the Masai, most mountains are sacred, and the holiest of all is Ol Donyo Lengai, "The Mountain of God," which, unlike Kilimanjaro, has erupted in recent years.

The Chagga, too, attach great spiritual significance to mountains. Even now, when many are Christians, like their ancestors they respect Kibo as the home of gods. And, as one would expect, they have their own variations on the name Kilimanjaro. My friend Freddie Munna, from Moshi, went around the towns and villages talking to the elders. He found alternative origins for the name, or perhaps evidence of local wordplay on the existing Swahili word. Kilimoroyoo, for instance, which is heard in the area around Marangu and Kilema, literally translates as something that is impossible to climb, and it is said to date back to when the first Europeans entered Chagga with the ambition of scaling the peak. There are plenty of old men in these villages today, Freddie says, who like to tell you that the word Kilimanjaro was simply the result of the Europeans' inability to pronounce what the porters were trying to tell them. Another designation one may hear is Kilimakyari, "Mountain of Heaven," a description particularly appropriate, he thinks, when the peak alone stands clear in the sky and the bulk of the mountain lies hidden behind white clouds. And Kimawenzi? Freddie says that means "a gap" in Chagga—and so could refer to the Saddle.

In the 19th century Doctor Krapf picked up yet another variation. The Wakamba, who live around the upper Tsavo river, called Africa's highest peak Kima ja Jeu, he said. Like the Masai name, this again translates as "Mountain of Whiteness"—but then so too does their name for Mount Kenya, Kima ja Kegnia. In early writings, Kilimanjaro was sometimes also known as Kilimangao where *ngao* means a tribal shield. Whereas the armchair geographer William Desborough Cooley convinced himself in 1845 that the commonest rendition was Kirimanjara, which he took as a reference to red matter on the mountain—carnelian perhaps. Certainly the mountain glows red at sunset, yet *kirira* is a word for snow in Masai. Although the permutations seem endless, the Swahili view of Kilimanjaro as the home of the cold-genies remains perhaps the most logical of them all.

Endless, too, are the myths and legends. In the folklore of the local Chagga population, a story recurs, with slight variation from place to place, telling how Mawenzi came to be so broken and jagged.

BANANAS, HERE BEING SOLD AT MARKET, ARE A STAPLE FOR CHAGGA WHO LIVE ON KILIMANJARO'S SLOPES. FOLLOWING PAGES (32-33): FLAMINGOS FEED ON ALGAE OR TRAWL FOR TINY CRUSTACEANS IN THE MOMELA LAKES, ARUSHA.

When the Earth was young and unsteady, it goes, these two giant volcanoes were neighbors and similar in shape, although "Kipoo" was always the taller and more important of the pair, a fact which racked "Kimawenzi" with jealousy. Kipoo was also very diligent, not like Kimawenzi who got by so far as he could by sponging off his neighbor. One day Kimawenzi let the fire go out in his hearth and begged live coals from Kipoo to restart it. Kipoo was pounding dried bananas with a pestle and mortar, but he stopped his work to gather some coals, giving Kimawenzi as well some bananas for his supper. Now Kimawenzi was a poor cook and he loved the food Kipoo prepared, so he kept letting his fire go out in order to be able to go back at mealtimes and ask Kipoo for more coals. Always his generous friend sent him away with something tasty, though the wretched Kimawenzi never thought to thank him for it. Sometimes he'd let his fire go out three times in a row, testing Kipoo's patience to the breaking point.

One suppertime when Kimawenzi called around as usual, he found Kipoo away from home. What would he do for a meal now? He couldn't be bothered to wait until Kipoo came back, so he carried the burning logs and coals from Kipoo's hearth across to his own, grumbling that he was going to have to cook for himself. It was dark and from a distance the returning Kipoo saw the blazing logs crossing the high plateau toward Kimawenzi's home and he was furious—especially when he arrived home to find Kimawenzi had left not a single spark in the grate. Grabbing up his pestle, he rushed across to his neighbor and smashed him over the head. This, the people say, is how Kimawenzi came to have such a jagged crown.

In some versions, the story goes further, indicating that the people of Chagga recognized the volcanic origins of their landscape: Kimawenzi sees the enraged Kipoo coming for him, roaring and brandishing his pestle. In a panic, he throws out the burning logs, which fall with a noisy splash into a pool, extinguishing the precious fire. After bashing Kimawenzi, Kipoo, still fuming, has to work hard to start a new fire for cooking his supper. It takes hours, and he works up such a frenzy that streams of lava and molten rock spew from his giant belly. When Kipoo

wakes, he is surprised and chastened to see so much damage, and especially to see Kimawenzi a shattered relic of his former self. But there was relief, too; he would no longer be plagued by an uninvited guest. As his temper cooled, Kipoo vowed never to erupt with such violence again. For many years, he has lived up to that promise.

The Chagga have always been believers of folk magic. Kibo represents their good fortune. All the streams that make the land so green and bountiful flow from this mountain. If you meet someone on the slopes of Kibo, the person highest on the mountain has to give the first greeting, for he is coming from the fortunate side. The uphill side of a house and its compound is more

esteemed than that looking away from Kibo. This is the men's side, where feasts and councils are held. Bruno Gutmann, who recorded Chagga folklore in the early years of the 20th century, was told that a young man whose father was still alive may not, while washing or bathing, turn his face toward the plain, but must face Kibo. Anyone breaking this rule demonstrates an unloving disposition. People say "He casts his father out on the plain," which interpreted means he causes his early death. The same applied to girls and their mothers.

WE ARE HERE on Kilimanjaro to make a movie. Director David Breashears has assembled an experienced team of filmmakers, which includes the Austrian mountaineer-cameraman Robert Schauer who worked on his groundbreaking Everest film in 1996. Because an expedition to Kilimanjaro doesn't involve the expense of a lengthy walk-in and eight-week stint on the mountain of a major Himalayan climb, David hasn't had to be so spartan this time when choosing and outfitting a crew. He can enjoy the luxury of not one, but two IMAX cameras. Over his many filming trips in Nepal, he's built up a team of Sherpas proficient in film work; he was not prepared to contemplate an ambitious project using large-format cameras without them. Four Sherpas have joined us in Tanzania for this shoot and are already

Continued on page 34

EAST AFRICAN RIFT

ROGER BILHAM
PROFESSOR OF GEOLOGY, UNIVERSITY OF COLORADO

SOON AFTER the giant southern supercontinent, Gondwanaland, fell to pieces about 180 million years ago, Antarctica, India, and South America went their separate ways. In contrast to their vigorous progress and collisions, the remaining African plate led a long sedentary life. True, its northern margin crumpled as it bumped into Europe (forming the Alps and Atlas Mountains), but compared to India's eventual collision with Asia to form the Himalaya, Africa was parked over the Earth's mantle, forgotten by the world of active tectonics for a hundred million years.

A result of this lethargy is that the African continent acted as a blanket that prevented the escape of heat from the Earth's deep interior. Elsewhere, heat is transported from the Earth's core by convection currents, which splay out at the surface beneath the crusty plates we live on, jostling and rearranging them. Eventually, as heat is lost, cold, dense streams of rock plunge back to the core, where they are reheated for another 8,000-mile journey to the surface and back again. In the absence of this convective cooling, the Earth's mantle beneath Africa has become unusually hot. Hot rock expands, and some scientists believe this may explain Africa's average surface elevation being hundreds of feet higher than that of other continents.

About 40 million years ago volcanoes began to puncture the ancient surface of the African plate. Accompanying this rude awakening, a broad and subtle bulge appeared in the continent's northeast corner, which at that time included all the lands of Arabia. Compared to a volcano, a bulge on the Earth's surface is almost invisible; its geological calling card is the diversion of river channels. We see this in the river Nile: Instead of draining a few hundred miles into the Indian Ocean, which it may well have done prior to the arrival of the bulge, the Nile now heads northward for a thousand miles to the Mediterranean, not even attempting a shortcut to the Red Sea.

Despite its innocuous appearance, the bulge announced the return of the drastic events that 140 million years before had broken up ancient Gondwanaland.

Beneath the bulge in Ethiopia and Yemen was a vast quantity of hot rock delivered by the arrival of what geologists call a hot spot. Although there is some debate about the nature of a hot spot, it is often thought of as a plume of hot fluid rock no wider than the City of London, rising straight from the Earth's core. Imagine a narrow plume of smoke rising from a cigarette and spreading out when it encounters the ceiling. Although hot spot plumes were possibly responsible for all the little volcanoes puncturing the African surface at this time, by far the largest delivery of hot material occurred beneath what is now Ethiopia and Yemen. In fact, some geologists conjecture that this hot spot may have fed all the other volcanoes in Africa. They envisage rivulets of hot magma trickling darkly throughout the underbelly of Africa seeking to escape to the surface through thin parts of the African crust.

The bulge in Ethiopia eventually burst in a flurry of volcanic eruptions. When the dust settled 10 million years later, three gigantic radiating cracks had been created in the African crust. One pointed toward Suez, one toward India, and the other southward into the heart of Africa. The two northern cracks are now 150-mile wide, one-mile deep oceans that continue to widen: We know them as the Red Sea and the Gulf of Oman. At the intersection of the three cracks occurred one of the world's largest outpourings of volcanic lava. These lavas flowed hundreds of miles, some of them more than a hundred feet thick, like sloppy cement, forming a flat-surfaced pile that almost blocked the Red Sea between Yemen and Djibouti.

The runt of this family of cracks was the African Rift. Although potentially a new ocean, the separation of Arabia from Africa had left relatively feeble forces at work to pull it apart. Satellite geodesy (GPS) reveals that points on either side of the rift in Ethiopia recede by an inch every five years—four times slower than the widening rate of the Red Sea—but speed is not a requirement for a crack to rip apart a continent. The rift's passage through Africa is marked by a series of deep valleys flanked by faulted blocks rising several thousand feet above sea level. Volcanoes form hills both within the valleys and on their sides. The rate of opening of the rift slows as it progresses southward. The tip of the crack is now in Botswana, but as with all cracks it is not expected to stop there. On its way south the East African Rift branches several times. The largest of these forks occurs in northern Kenya where one branch heads west around Lake Victoria and another east and south to Tanzania. From the numbers of earthquakes in each section of the rift the western branch is known to be more active, with the eastern branch being almost a dead end, apparently unable to rip through the tough old rocks of central Tanzania. It is here that we find Kilimanjaro.

Earthquakes and active volcanoes are the smoking guns of active rifting. Volcanoes signify the delivery of magma through cracks deep into the Earth. It is estimated that 100 cubic miles of once molten rock now surface the floor and edge of the rift system. Earthquakes are caused by the flanks of the rift sinking in response to slow stretching of the African crust. The energy released from the rocks in these earthquakes is akin to the response of a stretched rubber band snapping when pulled too far.

In the western branch of the rift near the great lakes of Albert, Tanganyika, and Malawi, earthquakes are common and in some cases severe. Several earthquakes exceeding magnitude 7 have occurred this century, and one prehistoric earthquake in the Malawi rift may have approached magnitude 8. A fresh-looking vertical wall of rock 100 miles long and 30 feet high testifies to a crack that may have ripped right through the African crust, here believed to measure more than 30 miles thick. The wall represents the line between the base of the rift and the active edge of the rift valley.

Why the rift has not broken through Malawi into the ocean lies in the strength of the ocean floor, which is largely formed from the strong mineral olivene. Continents consist primarily of weak (and lightweight) quartz crystals, that are easier to break. It is thus rather likely that the rift will extend eventually southwest through Botswana and into South Africa. But this will take a long time because the crack-widening rate at this latitude is less than an inch per century, slowing to nothing at a point a few hundred miles from the southeast shore of South Africa. East Africa is rotating away from the rest of the continent about this imaginary pivot in the southern oceans, with the fastest separation presently occurring where it all started—in northern Ethiopia.

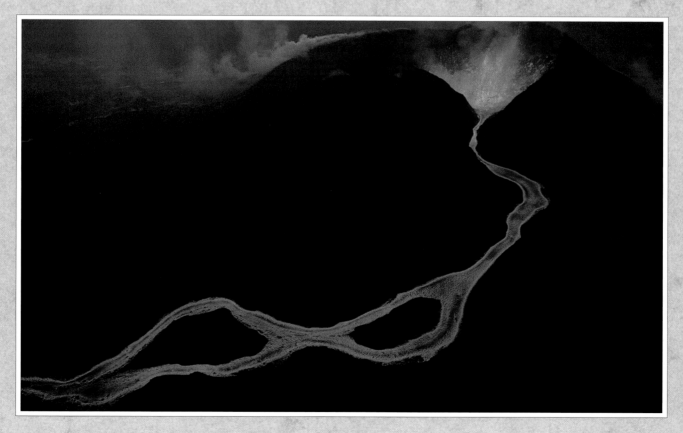

AN ACTIVE FISSURE SPILLS FOUNTAINS OF LAVA. VIOLENT ERUPTIONS ARE A BY-PRODUCT OF RIFTING.

invaluable. They anticipate David's every requirement. Before he's determined what lens or other equipment is needed for a shot, they are beside him assembling it. Organized, nimble, and incredibly strong when it comes to portering, they are unvaryingly cheerful; no matter how absorbed in film detail, they remain alert to the well-being of everyone around them. Someone stumbles, out goes a hand to steady them. I wondered beforehand if their presence might be resented by the African staff with us, but nothing of the sort. The locals are as interested in them as the Sherpas are delighted in every new thing they're seeing here. Wongchu, the senior among them, I know from earlier expeditions. He'd been a teaboy on Everest in 1986, but by 1996, when I again visited that mountain, he was sirdar to several of the expeditions in base camp. Of few words and great

Denmark, but since winning a modeling contract at 17 has worked out of New York. She is tall and athletic, but this is her first big mountain climb.

Roger Bilham is a geophysicist, one of the world's leading authorities on earthquakes and the subtle movement of tectonic plates; his work takes him around the globe looking at volcanoes and other hot spots. The great thing about Roger is his enthusiasm and boundless curiosity. He rarely gets bored, except perhaps when waiting around for cameras to be set up; even then, it's not for long. After the first five minutes he'll have set up some puzzle for himself. Out will come the pocket computer and an amazing scientific discovery

WEDNESDAY Everyone's in high spirits. We've spent free time patching each other up and every tent is festooned with stuff hanging out to air. Roger is rummaging in his gizmo-boxes. He has the difficult task of deciding what is essential, to reduce his equipment by one box-load as porters cannot be spared to carry it all. Hansi has borrowed a video camera and is wandering around making a film. He's been gaining in confidence every day. From the first days, when he was rather overwhelmed by many new white faces, he's now full of questions. He's taken a shine to Roger and keeps asking what he's doing; he'd like a box of toys like that himself.

resourcefulness, he commands wide respect. Our African porters and kitchen staff quickly formed the impression that he has the powers of a witch doctor.

Our trekking party spans the generations. Youngest is Nicole Wineland-Thomson, a self-possessed 12-year-old from Boston. She is here with her father, Rick, who was in a bad automobile accident shortly before the expedition when his hip was broken. He is still in a lot of pain, but can walk, stiffly, with two ski poles. Tanzanian Hans Robert Mmari, Hansi, is slightly older than Nicole—he had his 13th birthday on the day before we set out. He lives within sight of Kilimanjaro at Tengeru, right at the foot of Meru. He speaks English as fluently as Swahili and tells us his ambition is to go to Los Angeles. When he grows up, he says, he'd like to design cars. Twenty-three-year-old fashion model Heidi Albertson grew up in

will follow shortly afterward. Kilimanjaro is not just one more volcano to Roger, but a laboratory and library combined, stuffed full of interesting science.

And then, there's me: As a sexagenarian, my role in the film is to show that the roof of this continent is not simply the preserve of the young. Though I'd always longed to, I'd never seen Africa until six months ago when I visited Zanzibar with my family. Flying into Dar es Salaam, we'd seen the twin peaks of Kilimanjaro floating ethereally in the distance. That was as close as I ever expected to get to this mountain until I received an invitation to join the expedition. Being here is fulfilling a lifetime's ambition for me—even if I could wish I'd made it a lot earlier. I'd love to be scampering around and exploring like Nicole and Hansi instead of puffing along in the rear. But I count my blessings.

CHAPTER TWO

SNOW ON THE EQUATOR?

I deny altogether the existence of snow on Mount Kilimanjaro.

WILLIAM DESBOROUGH COOLEY,
CELEBRATED ARMCHAIR GEOGRAPHER, IN *ATHENAEUM*, MAY 1849

THE FIRST EUROPEAN

To see Kilimanjaro at close quarters, certainly in modern times, was the German missionary Johannes Rebmann in May 1848. He was making an exploratory journey inland from the East African coast when he was transfixed by what he at first took to be a dazzlingly white cloud on a high mountain ahead of him. ⟨ Rebmann worked at the Rabai Mission, which had been set up four years previously on a hillside outside Mombasa by his countryman, Ludwig Krapf. This was the first Christian mission on the East African mainland. At the time Mombasa was an established port for slaves, ivory, and the many other goods brought to coastal markets from the heart of the continent. The two missionaries taught themselves Swahili, the language of the coast that had become also the language of trade, and they made a point of conversing with merchants and caravan leaders to learn all they could of the hinterland and its peoples. In this way they had picked up talk of a great mountain in Chagga-land, some 200 miles to the west, which served as a landmark for caravans plying the long-distance routes. This peak's name—Kilima Njaro—was familiar, but they could make nothing of the often-told stories that it was decked in gold and silver and guarded by evil spirits

PRECEDING PAGES: DAWN BREAKS OVER KILIMANJARO, SEEN FROM THE NORTH. LEFT: A CHAGGA VILLAGE, IN 1908, AMONG BANANA TREES, WOULD HAVE CHANGED LITTLE SINCE THE FIRST EUROPEAN TRAVELERS ARRIVED THERE HALF A CENTURY EARLIER.

so fierce that they killed anyone bold or foolish enough
to venture near.

It may seem curious that, notwithstanding the caravan traffic, the interior of central Africa remained virtually a mystery to outsiders in the first half of the 19th
century. That is to say, the area was unmapped and
unvisited by Europeans. In truth, less was known then
than had been in classical times when Herodotus
described the sources of the Nile as three great fountains astride the Equator in what he called the Mountains of the Moon; Claudius Ptolemy, in his *Geographia*
recorded snowcapped mountains in the interior.

Phoenician sailors are believed to have circumnavi-
gated the African continent in 600–597 B.C., from the
Red Sea to the Nile Delta. Good harbors on the east coast
served traders between Arabia, India, and even the Chinese Empire over centuries. From the shores of the Red
Sea, King Solomon's ships sailed around the Horn of
Africa to the port of Kilwa, returning with precious car-
goes of gold, silver, ivory, and apes. So the coast was well
mapped, but it was also known to be pestilential and we
can assume that few of the early traders ventured far
ashore. One interesting account has survived, however.
During the first century A.D., a Greek by the name of Diogenes claimed to have traveled inland from "Rhapta,"
reaching (after 25 days) two great lakes and a snowy range
of mountains from which, it was claimed, "the Nile draws
its twin sources." There has been much speculation as to
where this Rhapta could have been; possibly it was today's
Pangani or even Dar es Salaam. In either case Kilimanjaro
could have been one of the mountains Diogenes
described. The Portuguese established themselves along
this coast in the last years of the 15th century to be dis-
lodged by Arabs from all ports north of Mozambique by
1729. In a book published in Seville in 1519, the Spanish
scholar Fernandez de Encisco recorded that "To the west
of this port [Mombasa] lies the Ethiopian Olympus,
which is very high, and further inland lie the Mountains
of the Moon, from which the Nile flows."

In 1832, the Sultan of Oman, Seyyid Said, moved his
court to Zanzibar, taking control not only of that island,
but also of the mainland coastal towns. As he consolidated

his grip, backed up by military force, the caravan trade—
which till then had operated mainly from the interior to
the sea—changed direction and tempo. Traveling inland in
search of ivory, and later also slaves, Arab and Swahili
merchants tempted the chieftains with manufactured
goods, most notably muzzle-loaded, flintlock guns that
were in great demand for hunting and intertribal warfare.

This was the stage at which Rebmann launched into
what was for him the unknown, his journey of discovery
predating those of better-known explorers such as David
Livingstone, Richard Burton, and John Hanning Speke.
And he did so independently of the Royal Geographical
Society, which had been founded in 1830 to promote geographical research. The Society's interest in the Dark
Continent centered upon unraveling the mystery of the
source of the Nile; it seemed unthinkable to its Victorian

members that this great river could rise, as Herodotus had told, from snowcapped mountains astride the Equator.

It is hard at this distance to gain a sense of what the young Johannes Rebmann was like, this accidental adventurer who had come to Africa without thought of making geographical discoveries. We know he was scholarly, shy, intense, and, in those early days at least, quite energetic. For a long time I thought no portrait of him had survived, but missionary archives in Switzerland finally yielded up two pictures: one of a clear-eyed, solemn youth, another showing a bulky, bearded, middle-aged figure with a chillingly dead air of resignation. Whatever had happened to the ardent young traveler of his Kilimanjaro days?

Rebmann's evangelical highlights are recorded cursorily by his missionary superiors. "His career is soon told," declared an article after his reluctant retirement

from East Africa in 1875. "His work has been mainly a preparatory one; he has reduced three East African languages to writing, and compiled a dictionary of each—labors of which future missionaries will reap the benefit." The great traveler Richard Burton, who was happy enough to pick Rebmann's brain before embarking on his own East African travels, left an unkind portrait: "an honest and conscientious man, he had yet all the qualities which secure unsuccess."

In the early days of the Rabai Mission, Krapf was the higher profiled of the two laborers. For the most part Rebmann was content to leave it that way. Krapf, as senior man, handled most of the correspondence with their employers, the Church Missionary Society (CMS), and it was he, in his autobiography, who detailed their mission

helper was as committed to the project as himself. As a preliminary step, the two embarked on a series of reconnaissance expeditions to gain a feel for the land.

Rebmann ventured as far as the mountain "Kadiaro" in Taita (Kasigau), "some thirty-six leagues from the seacoast." Apart from feet sore from the unaccustomed marching, Rebmann returned euphorically convinced that the inhabitants of these uplands would be receptive to the Christian message. Encouraged, he set out six months later to extend the journey as far as Chagga ("Jagga, the Snow Country of Eastern Africa"), which he estimated to lie 100 leagues inland. He was at this time 28.

From the outset he kept his eyes skinned for Kilimanjaro, which had captured his imagination. As his small caravan trailed over the thorn-clad ranges of

> **THURSDAY** When Johannes Rebmann walked to Kilimanjaro from the East African coast, it took him several weeks to get there and his fate throughout the whole journey was uncertain. Today, with Kilimanjaro International Airport in place, in theory you can reach the mountain within a day of leaving London, or two days from most places in America. I say in theory because while the dangers may now be minimized, the frustrations of travel cannot be eliminated. My flight missed its Amsterdam connection and I was rerouted to Nairobi, where I arrived ten hours late and without my luggage. This delay had more than doubled before I reached Arusha. But by then, I was at African pace and all irritation and stress had melted away.

work and exploratory travels, though drawing heavily on Rebmann's spare accounts when it came to describing his friend's travels. Krapf seems to have edited these freely; the writing style fits so seamlessly with his own.

Like Krapf, Rebmann came from Württemberg in southern Germany, but the two had never met until Africa. Both trained at the protestant Basel Seminary, a regular source of able and faithful recruits for the London-based CMS, which experienced difficulty in finding British candidates prepared to take up such thankless and unhealthy postings. Krapf's vision was to forge a chain of mission stations across the continent, linking the east and west coasts of Africa, spreading the gospel, and fighting the slave trade. He was relieved, he wrote to a colleague after Rebmann's arrival, to discover that his new

Taita, some 12 days into the journey, he would clamber to high points along the way to see if the great mountain was yet in view. When the horizon revealed nothing, he felt sure his chronic shortsightedness or his failure to bring a strong enough telescope must be to blame. But his disappointment would be short-lived for he found he loved being on the move and away from the humid coast. This rugged landscape exhilarated him. As acacia scrub gave way to more luxuriant vegetation, "so beautiful was the country so delightful the climate," he could fancy himself back in the Jura Mountains where he'd hiked in his student days, "or in the region about Cannstadt in the dear fatherland."

Rebmann was traveling with nine hired porters and his personal guide and assistant, an experienced Muslim caravan leader by name of Bana Kheri. By accounts, Bana was a great "fixer," but he had his work cut out smoothing Rebmann's relationships with tribesmen and chiefs along the way. Although a kindly man, brimming with curiosity, and one who'd gone to great lengths to pick up a working knowledge of local languages and customs, the missionary could never put from his mind that those he encountered were heathen and that his duty was to redeem them. By reading every situation from his staunch Lutheran viewpoint, he would misinterpret overtures of hospitality for ungodly customs and his eyes were sealed to cultural richness. Naked flesh unsettled him, though paradoxically he was no more comfortable when people more modestly adopted decorated "aprons" and body jewelry. The beads around their necks, feet, and loins served only to remind him of the rosaries of the "Romanists" (Catholics), who in his eyes were barely less misguided than these heathen.

Rebmann's obsession to wrestle with "contamination" wherever he perceived it drove Bana Kheri to distraction. In Bura, suspecting witchcraft, Rebmann protested against the ceremonial inspection of the intestines of a goat. Similarly, while admitting his response was probably unwise, he refused to have a small portion of the animal's hide put upon one of his fingers. "It's only a token of goodwill," Bana insisted, "not sorcery." At last, Rebmann was persuaded to place his hand on the creature's head and swear that his journey was well intentioned and the chief his friend, but only with the deepest unease. It didn't matter how much Bana Kheri railed; Rebmann confided to his journal, "I told him that the light needs to reprove darkness," adding soulfully, "Oh, how is the whole land groaning in expectation of its Christian cultivation!" [Yet it would be delivered, he comforted himself, and soon.]

Provoking local chieftains was only one of many risks run by the expedition. When Rebmann elected to stop for the night at a place where earlier caravans had been ambushed by fierce Wakuafi tribesmen, his horrified guide remonstrated in vain. Before they set out, Bana Kheri had pleaded for the expedition to arm itself with at least 10 firearms, telling Rebmann that other caravans regularly carried as many as 500. Brushing Bana's misgivings aside, Rebmann replied that the hand of the Almighty would serve better than "fleshly arms." It looked as if the missionary's simple faith was well founded when the only disturbance that night came from

hyenas trying to raid the expedition's fresh meat stores. Nevertheless, Bana Kheri—who had an outstanding quarrel with the ruler whose country they were to pass through next—played it safe next morning by leading them off the trodden path and into the bush. Or, in this instance, into tall, sharp elephant grass, which, "full of needles," shredded the missionary's feet in a couple of hours. Wild animals were becoming numerous now, and Rebmann's diary records "large herds of giraffes and zebras, and in the evening also a rhinoceros."

The following morning, May 11, they were away by daybreak. The countryside was dry and dusty, but rising in the distance could be seen the mountains of Chagga. Toward what he estimated to be 10 o'clock—he carried no timepiece—Rebmann's attention was caught by an apparition ahead:

I observed something remarkably white on the top of a high mountain, and first supposed that it was a very white cloud, in which supposition my guide also confirmed me; but having gone a few paces more I could no more rest satisfied with that explanation; and while I was asking my guide a second time whether that white thing was indeed a cloud, and scarcely listening to his answer that yonder was a cloud but what that white was he did not know, but supposed it was coldness, the most delightful recognition took place in my mind of an old well-known European guest called snow.

THAT WAS IT! All those strange stories about gold and silver, about malign spirits killing people, twisting and blackening their limbs, suddenly made sense. Snow. Of course! Snow and extreme cold—phenomena to which, as he supposed, the poor natives were perfect strangers. Rebmann could well see how quickly "half-naked visitors" might succumb to such conditions.

Elated by this enlightenment, he endeavored to explain the nature of the strange white substance to his party. He shouldn't be surprised, he supposed, that they had trouble grasping it, especially if it was true (as Bana Kheri assured him) that no name for snow existed, even in the language of the Chagga who lived at the foot of the white-topped mountain. Calling a rest stop, Rebmann retired under a tree to comfort himself with his daily Bible reading. His text that morning was the 111th Psalm. On coming upon the words "He hath shewed his people the power of his works, that he may give them the heritage of the heathen," Rebmann was fairly transported. It was a message for him. In granting him a vision of "the beautiful snow mountain so near to the Equator," his Savior was blessing his efforts and promising to open a way for His Gospel. Rebmann was still emotional when he came to write up the revelations in his diary later. It had been a day of wonders:

At noon my people saw again some rhinoceroses, which my own short sight could not discover at the same distance as themselves. I therefore went futher on to get a view of them; but the men who followed me cried so much out to me to make me stop, that I could not gain my object. The Natives are of no animal so much afraid as of the rhinoceros, and at its sight immediately look out for some trees as their refuge. In the afternoon we also saw some elephants, with their young ones, very near to us, which quietly went their way even before my guide had fired his gun to frighten them....

Incidentally, this passage also reveals that Bana Kheri was reluctant to rely solely on God's will and Rebmann's trusty umbrella for protection; taking matters into his own hands, he'd ensured the party had one weapon at least.

The scenery grew ever more grand the nearer they approached Chagga, and that evening, just after sunset, after two days in a barren landscape with no fresh water, the party came upon a pool in some rocks. Rebmann bathed his torn feet in the cistern before Bana Kheri and Loogo, a Taita man who was traveling with them, led him by the hand over steep and slippery boulders to an overhanging rock, under which they were to rest that night. Rebmann knew nothing more till he was woken next morning by the sound of Loogo communing with the Komas, or departed souls of his countrymen, who had been slain at this place in battle with the Wakuafi.

One more day and they at last entered Chagga. Here the vegetation was lush and of astonishing variety, and Rebmann was delighted to see beautiful, tall trees for the first time since leaving the coast. Before long, thick jungle enveloped them, through which the going was slow and painful until, some hours later, they entered a majestic valley grown over with waist-high grass. It burst with plenteousness. Thousands of cattle could be raised on

WORKERS UNLOAD A BRITISH STEAMER IN ZANZIBAR, AN IMPORTANT TRADE PORT, EARLY IN THE LAST CENTURY.

such abundant pasture, Rebmann mused and gave thanks, "Oh, what a noble country has God reserved for his people!" Now they were fording rivers so cold and clear that they could only have come down from glaciers. He gazed around rapturously at the dark green of perpetual summer before raising his eyes, as he put it, to "eternal winter." The snows of Kilimanjaro, apparently so close as to be reachable in a few hours of walking, were, he accepted, probably still several days' journey away.

Rebmann's arrival in the small Chagga kingdom of Kilema took the chief and his people by surprise. Where had the white man and his small party sprung from? Where were his soldiers and slaves, where the weapons? For his part, Rebmann eyed the inhabitants with a

sinking heart: They struck him as the most shameless of any he'd met. Were it not for the cold and a love of ornament, he believed they'd have done away with clothing altogether. Thank goodness he'd brought cotton cloth and beads as his gift for this young king, Masaki. By now, Rebmann was heeding Bana's advice on etiquette. When the king had a lamb slaughtered in his honor and offered him a ring of hide from its forehead, Rebmann knew to take this *kishogno* on his middle finger as a sign of friendship, and to reciprocate the gesture. Accordingly, he was declared "the son of the king," and he took the opportunity to demonstrate his Bible to the monarch and to explain the purpose of his journey.

This passed off well, but the king—or the *mangi*—kept

him waiting several days between audiences so that Rebmann was detained in Kilema for more than two weeks. He was glad of the break as the rains had started. He spent most of the time in the hut that had been put at his disposal in a quiet banana plantation, giving his sore feet a chance to heal and himself the opportunity to stitch some new shoes for the journey home. The king's steward called regularly with a string of questions about Rebmann's message, and in return Rebmann gleaned what information he could of Kilema and its surroundings. The people here had an ongoing feud with nearby Marangu, he learned. Masaki wanted to know if Rebmann's "magic" extended to calling up lions that would eat up all the bad folk of that village. Notwithstanding

PORTERS AND GUIDES

MOSES KAZIMOTO
KILIMANJARO PORTER

IT IS NO LONGER POSSIBLE to arrive at Kilimanjaro with a rucksack and climb the mountain on your own. These days climbers must first register with the park authorities, pay the appropriate park fee, and agree to observe certain rules and restrictions. For this reason most visitors choose to make their arrangements through a local tour operator or trekking agent, someone familiar with the formalities who will complete the necessary paperwork and hire the porters and guides required for the trek.

Kilimanjaro National Park recommends one or two porters per person on all routes, and each group is obliged to take a local guide. Remembering that it's very easy to get lost in the wilderness of Kilimanjaro and its frequent mists, part of a guide's job is to assist in route finding—but guides also organize porters and catering details and recommend itineraries. Most guides are well versed in natural history and local traditions and can assist the climbers in recognizing animals, birds, and plants. The guides are usually well informed about the country and the people who live there. A climber can expect his guide to be with him throughout the climb, encouraging and advising. The last stage of a climb, the summit, is where a guide's professionalism counts the most. If his client is flagging, he must decide whether it is because he or she is exhausted or sick, or just in need of some extra assistance.

Mountain porters are drawn from various sources. They may be native youths between the ages of 15 and 20 who have finished school and perhaps still live at home with their parents. Some are older and may have worked as a porter for 10 or 15 years. They may be farmers or small businessmen with families, who supplement their income on the mountain. Despite the number of tourists who come to Kilimanjaro, there is not enough work for everyone who needs it. Competition between guides and also between porters is high. Unless you are employed as a porter on a regular basis—perhaps because you have kinship with one of the resident guides or you come from the same village—it is hard to get work. Newcomers to the area may find themselves competing with well-established porters, making it difficult to get regular work even in the peak season. It is not unusual for some would-be porters to return, disappointed, to their homelands in search of other less adventurous jobs.

Porters who manage to get regular work can enjoy a good income, but there are pitfalls. Kilimanjaro National Park recommends a daily rate of 3,000 Tanzanian shillings (about $3.30) per day per porter. In practice this is considered the going rate for the popular Marangu route, but twice that is asked for the Machame/Shira Route, which is more strenuous and where the inherent risk of injury is greater. While this may seem like an adequate wage, especially as it's paid in cash with no declared taxes, if a porter manages only one trip a month on the Machame Route, he could expect to take home TS 60,000 per year, which is equivalent to what a schoolteacher earns for the same period for far less arduous work. In practice, however, it's not unusual for porters to be exploited by their guides, who may hire fewer porters than are actually declared on the park permits they file and pocket the salaries saved. Guides, who are responsible

> *...if a porter manages only one trip a month on the Machame Route, he could expect to take home TS 60,000 per year, which is equivalent to what a schoolteacher earns.*

for allocating work, may abuse their position by giving jobs to friends and relatives over more qualified individuals or taking a percentage of fees paid to anyone who gets hired through them.

The porters who work directly for tour companies are usually better organized and can expect a regular income. Some companies even offer instruction in the English language, guiding, first aid, and hygiene to their porters, and it's a great pity all do not follow their example. Porter compensation and training varies greatly from one tour company to another; it's something of a lottery how porters will fare. Standardized rates of pay are disregarded. Trekking is a lucrative business for the government and the tour companies but, though many porters and guides are able to support large families on their incomes, many remain poor.

On trek, the porter's food is usually the same day after day—a thick porridge (*ugali*), eaten with cabbages or *mchicha* (spinach), sometimes with a little meat in the mix. Tea, with a little sugar, is consumed in copius amounts, as it is important to stay hydrated at the higher elevations. A porter can expect 2 real meals every 24 hours. Some may supplement their diet with additional food, but this adds extra weight to their loads and becomes an additional expense most porters do not want to incur.

Most western trekkers come well provided with climbing gear—boots, gaiters, waterproof clothing, and high-altitude wear. Regular porters may gradually equip themselves with odd items gleaned from their different tours, but by and large the men and boys are dressed in whatever they can rustle together. Older hands know this should include woolly hats and socks, but these are by no means widely used. And the assortment of footwear ranges from flip-flops and canvas shoes to fine boots that may or may not be the right size. Trekking companies usually supply communal tents for porters. Sleeping in caves and rockshelters, as in previous years, is now outlawed on ecological grounds. So, too, are open fires. Even so, due to overcrowding, porters may still find themselves having to seek refuge in caves, where they huddle round the cookstove, smoking and talking.

CLOCKWISE FROM ABOVE LEFT: LHAKPA GELJE SHERPA, ESTOMY NKYA, REINATUS MJOMBAA, EXAUD NKYA, SHAFAEL MBOYA, GOODLUCK SWAI, NAWANG PHURI SHERPA, JACK TANKARD, GOODLUCK WILSON, BOB MASSAWE, JULIUS NKYA, DAVID BREASHEARS

Rebmann's response that such powers were not in the hand of man, the mangi expressed a desire for him or one of his fellow workers to return and teach his people more about God and the Great Mangi Jesus. But, he stressed with vigor, he did not want the missionary to take his magic to any other chiefdom.

Rebmann turned for home, his feelings for the Chagga much softened. He'd been shown a flourishing, organized society in a land of great beauty and perfect weather. The people were clean, healthy, industrious, and not at all inward looking. Swahili traders called regularly—in fact,

Bana Kheri must have already been known to them. It's easy to understand Masaki's surprise that Rebmann brought nothing to trade, only the magical power of his Holy Book. Buoyed by warm memories, Rebmann found the Taitas, when he reencountered them, dirty and sickly by contrast. Even so, they, too, declared themselves ready to receive teachers of the Gospel. Rebmann was jubilant. All that was needed now were individuals or, better still, pious Christian families—truly converted fathers and mothers with well-educated children—to carry on the missionary work in East Africa.

ABOVE: THE JUXTAPOSITION OF KILIMANJARO'S TWIN PEAKS, MAWENZI (LEFT) AND KIBO, PERHAPS IN 1854, SUGGESTS IT IS SKETCHED FROM THE NORTH, WHERE FEW VENTURED AT THE TIME APART FROM ARAB CARAVANS. RIGHT: REBMANN'S FELLOW MISSIONARY JOHANN LUDWIG KRAPF ALSO SAW KILIMANJARO IN THE 1840S; HE WAS THE FIRST EUROPEAN TO SEE MOUNT KENYA.

The first extracts from Rebmann's journal were published in the *Church Missionary Intelligencer* (No 1) in May 1849, along with a general account of the Chagga people. The article concluded with a story Rebmann had picked up from Bana Kheri about the "Madjame Tribe" and Kilimanjaro. It ran like this: The late powerful King Rungua of Madjame (Machame) was so intrigued by the white substance on towering Kilimanjaro that he "dispatched a large embassy of his own subjects to examine into the nature of that strange white guest." One man alone returned, his hands and feet destroyed. Bana had seen the poor fellow, he said, his extremities bent inward by the cold, and he had heard the story from his own lips. The man's companions had frozen to death, Rebmann surmised, or perhaps fled in sheer terror—which could prove equally fatal on a precipitous mountain.

IN NOVEMBER 1848, Rebmann trekked again to Chagga with Bana Kheri. This time the guide succeeded in bringing along some muskets and bows and arrows for protection, but the missionary was not happy. With 15 Swahili bearers they reached Kilema safely at the end of the first week in December, where Masaki welcomed them warmly. The chief's mood changed on learning that the men only intended passing through his domain on their way to Machame. Throwing every obstacle in their path, Masaki stepped up demands for calico and beads until Rebmann's remaining supplies, intended as gifts for the mangi of Machame, had trickled away. The missionary may never have escaped at all were it not for the support of some warriors who'd been sent to fetch his party by Mamkinga, the Machame chieftain. Mamkinga outranked Masaki. He was aware the visitor would be bringing no gifts for him, nonetheless, he was curious to see for himself this strange mzungu (white man) and to find out what he was about.

Striking northwestward, the escort party guided Rebmann around the forested foot of Kilimanjaro, scrambling in and out of the many deep valleys that radiated from the mountain's two summits. The track led at first

directly uphill, affording tantalizing glimpses of Kibo's majestic summit. Even by moonlight the snow-clad sight was impressive, though the temperature, Rebmann noted ruefully, was every bit as cold as southern Germany in November. He was certainly glad to sleep that night in a hut with a good fire. Another thousand feet of climbing took them above the limit of villages and banana cultivation before a descent westward through Uru brought Machame into view below. The village extended between the southwestern foot of Kilimanjaro and the northeastern foot of Shira. Rebmann was told that Shira, an old volcanic cone on Kilimanjaro's western slopes, was also sometimes covered with snow. On January 7, the king's brother welcomed them into Machame territory with a kishogno ceremony, and on the 12th Rebmann had his first audience with Mamkinga himself.

The two got on well enough, though Rebmann had to grit his teeth when it came to this king's kishogno. Medicine men had prepared an evil mixture of herbs, blood, and the contents of a goat's stomach, which without warning was flicked over Rebmann's face and chest with a cow's tail. He and the king were now blood brothers. Mamkinga had hoped his guest would prove a sorceror who could be inveigled to stay and boost his own power. In this he was disappointed, though he still invited Rebmann to settle and to instruct his son in the manner of a Christian. Someone would return, Rebmann assured him, but he could not say who or even when, for his own country was far distant and communications took a long time. They parted on good terms—or so it seemed to Rebmann. In all, the missionary had spent three weeks in Machame.

With better weather on his homeward trek, the summit of Kilimanjaro was completely free of cloud. For the first time Rebmann saw distinctly the mountain's full form:

There are two principal summits placed upon a basis some ten leagues long and as many broad, so that the space between them forms as it were, a saddle.... The eastern summit is lower, and pointed, whilst the western and higher one presents a fine crown, which, even in the

hot season, when its western and lowlier neighbor can no longer support its snowy roof, remains covered by a mass of snow. The snow of Kilimanjaro is not only the perpetual source of the many rivers (twenty at least) which proceed from it, but…is a continual source of rain, as may be daily observed….

Rebmann had heard the Chagga refer to Kilimanjaro's highest summit as Kibo. Subsequently he learned that this was also the local word for snow; Bana Kheri was mistaken in maintaining, as he had on their first journey, that the Chagga had no word for the white stuff. Not only had they

a name for it, but it was clear they understood that Kibo turned to water when put onto a fire and that the source of all the rivers of the region was Kibo. Rebmann suddenly grasped that it was the coastal Swahili who had difficulty with the concept of snow, not the locals, and once more he set about enlightening his porters. Silver couldn't come and go with the seasons like this white material, he told them. And all these rivers they were encountering, weren't they testimony, if such were yet needed, that the whiteness was just another form of water?

Rebmann returned to the subject in his letters home to the CMS and later in Krapf's book, asserting that the

pathetically received. With Rebmann concentrating on territories to the west, Krapf initially turned his attention southward, to Usambara and Zanzibar. These two devout travelers are frequently portrayed as naïve, which to an extent is true. Yet they were quick to recognize that their findings were potentially of great public interest, and they were worldly enough to see how publicity could benefit their cause. "We considered it to be our duty to make Christians at home acquainted with the unknown countries of the African interior," Rebmann declared, "that they might be stimulated to promote the Gospel more energetically than hitherto in that part of the world." He knew that to most people in Victorian England talk of the mission field conjured images of India or China—not Africa. At the end of February 1849, Krapf told the CMS that each of their journeys cemented their resolve not to rest until one nation after the other has heard of the Gospel.

Yet if their reason for travel was always to spread the word, it's easily seen that they became explorers by desire as well as obligation. At the beginning of 1849, at the height of their energies, both were so hooked on the romance of discovery that they'd consider almost anything to keep on the road. Krapf, when complaining to his bosses in England that shortage of funds was severely restricting their work, offered to go into the ivory trade on behalf of the Society to accumulate more funds. Unsurprisingly, the CMS failed to take up his offer, but a few months later two recruits were sent out from England to boost the strength of the Rabai mission. Johann Wagner would die of fever within weeks of arrival, but Jacob Erhardt, who brought with him useful medical skills, went on to become an important member of the team and another traveler in the coming years—until he crossed swords with Krapf on matters of policy.

Flying in to Nairobi was a bonus: I'd be seeing a chunk of Africa I hadn't expected to, and the only cost would be trimming any training treks. With a thrill of anticipation I clamber into a rickety bus. No sooner out of the airport than Africa swallows you. You know you are somewhere different, and it isn't just the heat: There are the flat-topped acacias and herds of zebra and wild asses. A flight of sunlit egrets rises against a dark sky. But though the clouds look stormy, no rain comes; from

Chagga were fully aware that "they could ascend the mountain, and descend again in safety, if they choose the right season." It was in knowing when precisely this season was that the problem lay: "Hence many have perished in the attempt."

Full of his discoveries, Rebmann returned safely to Rabai on February 16. In those days, he and Krapf were taking turns exploring. They still considered countrywide reconnaisance of vital importance if they were to initiate their hoped-for chain of stations. It was important to direct energies where they might be symthe look of things, there'd been none for weeks and weeks and weeks. The roads were everyone's thoroughfare and knots of red-clad Masai ambled tirelessly along, often driving their skinny cattle and goats ahead of them. Where villagers were repairing the road, a warning line of scrubby branches would be set out for some yards on either side to alert drivers to slow down.

Shortly after seeing my first antelope on its hind legs gnawing at a tree, the bus blew a tire and we all stepped out while the driver and one of the passengers changed the tire. We strolled into the scrub to investigate termite heaps, weaver bird nests, and the volcanic bombs that litter this scrubby plain. The repair completed, we resumed our seats and headed for the Tanzanian border, stopping first at a Masai trinket market set amid bouganvilleas of the most startling colors. Soon we were

Park, which incorporates Mount Meru Forest Reserve. The slopes of Meru are said to echo Kilimanjaro in some ways, though of course they are much more compact. Like Kilimanjaro, they support a few elephants that move around from area to area within the park on a daily basis.

My driver, Gabi, was anxious for me to see as much wildlife as possible and after we had in one morning observed colobus and green monkeys, baboons, zebra and giraffe, dik diks, water bucks and a number of other bucks, hippos, mongoose, buffalo and warthogs, and an astonishing array of birds, including soda lakes full of flamingos, it was a matter of pride to him that I should add elephants. He knew all the clearings frequented by elephant family groups and drove me from one to the next. In vain. We saw dung and freshly trampled undergrowth, but there were to be no elephants on my ticklist that day.

SATURDAY We've been in the area several days now and the weather has been bright and warm. Yet not once have we been granted that longed-for sight of Kilimanjaro soaring into the sky. Tomorrow we will see it, if only under our feet, for we're off into the rain forest that encircles the mountain. We've had an information briefing this evening, then turned in early because the wake-up call is to be 4:00 a.m. for the camera people and 4:30 for the rest of us. It's 10:00 p.m. now and the bad news is that it's absolutely teeming with rain. It sounds set in forever, and even if it stops later, it's going to be very, very wet in the forest.

seeing blue volcanic mountains on the horizon, though nothing that could be identified as Kilimanjaro. We reached crop fields, but they bore no more than scorched stalks. Nearing Arusha the vegetation became suddenly lush and tropical. As we swung into a hotel car park, I was relieved to see a young man waving a placard with my name on it. He whisked me off to meet the assembling film crew in a pleasant lodge on a coffee plantation. I still hadn't seen Kilimanjaro, but from the veranda its sister peak, Meru, filled the sky.

My first job next morning was to take a trip into town to buy some T-shirts and underwear to tide me through till I was reunited with my luggage. Mine weren't the only missing bags. It was fortunate we had a few days before starting the climb. Taking advantage of the lull, I hung on to the landcruiser and driver and paid a visit to Arusha National

WE HAVE OBSERVED that in the first half of the 19th century, outsiders knew little about East Africa beyond its coast. There was, however, a scholar in England who'd been diligently studying classical texts and Arab and Portuguese sources in an effort to fill out the map of East Africa. William Desborough Cooley produced major essays on the region's geography in 1835 and 1845, and was considered to be the leading expert of the African interior—without ever having been near that continent. The only opportunity he found to check his historical assumptions was when a Zanzibari Arab visited Britain on a political mission in 1834. Cooley quizzed this man, Khamis bin Uthman, and his servant exhaustively. The geographer knew perfectly well of the existence of Kilimanjaro and of Mount Kenya as isolated peaks in the interior of East Africa, but he believed them to be only one-fifth of the height required to sustain perennial snow at those latitudes. Ptolemy's Mountains of the Moon, to his mind, were not to be found in East Africa at all. When it came to the big question of the day—the source of the Nile—he championed a single vast inland sea, which seems to have been Lakes Nyasa and Tanganyika run together. Having made up his mind on these points, Cooley was not prepared to countenance any alternative interpretations.

To raise funds for its overseas work, the Church Missionary Society in London produced a number of publications for sale, documenting the endeavors of their men in far-flung mission fields. One was the *Church Missionary Record*, but when in 1849 a new editor, Joseph Ridgway, was appointed, he relaunched the periodical as the monthly *Church Missionary Intelligencer*. With an eye to boosting his circulation figures (and thereby CMS funds), he set out to appeal to an audience beyond normal missionary supporters. Travelers, geographers, ethnographers, and all sorts of general readers, he was convinced, would be excited by the exploits of the Society's pathfinders at the edge of the evangelized world. He was able to kick off with a real scoop. In his first issue in May of that year, Ridgway ran the story of Rebmann's amazing "discovery" of snow-capped Kilimanjaro. A giant snow-mountain so close to the Equator! Ridgway's public was incredulous.

Although snow-clad mountains were known to exist in the equatorial regions of South America, Cooley was not alone in doubting that any peak in East Africa rose high enough to hold perpetual snow. To do so would require "a stupendous mass" at least 17,000 or 18,000 feet high: The very idea seemed preposterous. Besides, it was patent that Rebmann was no scientist, nor did he reveal any geographical aptitude. Latitude, longitude, altitude, direction, and distances were all annoyingly vague in his writing, while his unsophisticated prose and the evident simplicity of his faith created an impression that he must be simple in his powers of deduction also. Scornfully, Cooley dismissed the missionary's supposed "ocular testimony" in the gentlemen's journal *Atheneum* for May 19. To see something white from a distance of 25 miles and conclude it must be snow, he declared, was merely the result of "a fortuitous combination of imagination and poor eyesight." The reverend gentleman deluded himself; he was having visions. No, he said, brooking no challenge to his authority, "I deny altogether the existence of snow on Mount Kilimanjaro."

The mountain in question, he had written in 1845, was known to Swahili traders not as the White Mountain, not the Snowy Mountain, but Kirimanjara, a name describing something red, like coral. "That mountain," he declared, "is famed for its great height and for the red carnelian strewed over it." This carnelian theory was presumably gleaned from his conversations with Khamis bin Uthman, and was in any case not new. Some years earlier Cooley had described the people of "Monomoezi" using translucent balls of a reddish color for money. He'd continued then by saying:

The most famous mountain of Eastern Africa is Kiriman-jara, which we suppose, from a number of circumstances to be the highest ridge crossed on the road to Monomoezi. The top of this mountain is strewed all over with red carnelian, the rounded pebbles of which were doubtless the money referred to. The importation of beads has probably caused the disappearance of the carnelian currency.

REBMANN HIMSELF was oblivious to the controversy over his discovery. No sooner had he returned from his second visit to Chagga and written up his reports than he was fretting to be on his way once more. He wanted to reinforce his relationship with Mamkinga in Machame, then push farther west to "Uniamesi" (Nyamwezi), where he expected to find one of the great inland seas (Lake Tanganika). He set off on this latest mission on April 6, 1849—in other words before the arrival of Wagner and Erhardt and before the *Church Missionary Intelligencer* was launched. He was not to learn of the widespread skepticism that greeted his findings until his return.

For some reason not revealed in his writings, Rebmann unwisely dispensed with the services of Bana Kheri this time. Maybe they disagreed over firearms once more, for the expanding caravan trade had brought with it a disastrous proliferation of weapons and lawlessness. Or perhaps Bana Kheri was already promised elsewhere, for his death at the hands of Masai warriors is recorded later that year. Rebmann hired 30 men, mainly Wanika from the Mombasa district, and loaded into his baggage rather more, and more varied, presents and trading items than before. He had once observed that in Chagga only the sorcerers had the measure of the seasons—knowledge they used to enhance their reputation for clairvoyance. Yet, in his eagerness to be off, Rebmann somehow overlooked the fact that this time he'd be traveling to that country at the start of the Long Rains. All the rivers would be swollen and there was no shelter to be had along the way for himself and his men beyond his ever present umbrella.

He would have liked to bypass Kilema and Mangi Masaki, but a shortage of supplies and the continual rain forced him "into the lion's den once more." Masaki put up a show of strength but eventually allowed the party to proceed. Damp and dispirited, Rebmann struggled through the forest on paths reduced to a thick mire. The only thing keeping him going was the prospect of the warm welcome he felt sure awaited him in Machame. Little did he anticipate that he was heading into an even fiercer lion's den. Mamkinga intended to make up for the meager gifts he'd received from Rebmann on his last visit. And he was equally determined to prevent him

sick with fever and dysentery, the missionary wanted nothing but to return to the coast. At last Mamkinga gave him leave, but not before a formal leave-taking, which took the form of being spat upon forcefully. "For this dirty expectoration with which, first the Wanika, then the Suahili, and last of all myself, were favored, a special favor was exacted from each," he told. His Wanika were forced to hand over beads that they were keeping to buy food on the way home; one of the Swahilis lost the clothes off his back. Rebmann cannot bring himself to tell what final possession was charmed from him by his acquisitive host. Without waiting for their promised escort, the party fled. "Right glad we were," Rebmann declared, "to exchange the company of such people, for the wilderness itself."

Taking no more chances, they avoided Kilema and kept to the forest. When their last beans were eaten, they relied upon wild honey and eggs from weaver bird nests to keep

> **SUNDAY** Under a gray, overcast sky, the drumbeats of rain continue on the thatched roofs of our huts. We won't be going anywhere today. The film crew has informed us that the ascent will be postponed. I am content to have an extra day to relax and prepare while the film crew continues to ponder the unusual twists in the weather and pace with impatience, frustrated by the delay. We can only hope for better weather on the mountain, that the weather gods will favor us higher up.

proceeding any farther. The chief's surprising attitude seemed to Rebmann treacherous, almost beyond belief. "Extortion followed upon extortion," he wrote later, smarting from the injustice. "I saw the stock of goods which I had intended for Uniamesi gradually melting away, and when by order of the king I was obliged to part with piece after piece of the calico which I had reserved for my further journey, I could not suppress my tears."

His weeping was not for the loss of the goods themselves, he was at pains to point out to the king, but because they had been furnished by fine folk at home who wished to send the Book of Life to all Africans. Any appeal to Mamkinga's finer feelings was a waste of time, if not a tactical error—as Rebmann should have known from his similar brush with Masaki. At the sight of his guest's discomfiture, Mamkinga took pleasure in tormenting him further. Rebmann crumbled. His health gave way along with his morale. Plundered, threatened, humiliated, and

alive until they reached friendlier territory in Taita.

This bitter experience changed Rebmann. Though he would work on doggedly at Rabai for a further quarter of a century till his health, spirit, and eyesight deserted him, he was through with exploration. Krapf and Erhardt could continue unraveling East Africa's secrets, but he doubted the value of attempting any new venture before Rabai was "consolidated." There was not yet enough "iron" in this first link, he told his CMS bosses, to fashion a transcontinental chain of a strength sufficient to bear the weight of East African heathendom. Only once more in his life did the romance of exploration momentarily tempt him. In 1856 it was proposed that he accompany Burton and Speke on their quest to reach the reputed great lake (Tanganyika) in central Africa. CMS gave permission for him to go, but Rebmann balked at being associated with explorers who carried weapons and let the opportunity slip by.

REBMANN RETURNED TO EUROPE IN 1875. ALMOST BLIND, HE WAS ACCOMPANIED BY HIS PUPIL, ISAAK NYONDO. A WIFE WAS FOUND TO LOOK AFTER THE MISSIONARY, BUT HE DIED THE FOLLOWING YEAR. ISAAK DID NOT SURVIVE HIS RETURN TO AFRICA.

CHAPTER THREE

LET
GEOGRAPHY
PERISH

Of Kilimanjaro we have little more to say:
its leading characteristics have been pointed out,
and its "eternal snows" must be regarded now as "eternal verities."

CHARLES NEW, AFTER HIS 1871 ATTEMPT ON MOUNT KILIMANJARO,
IN *LIFE WANDERINGS AND LABOURS IN EASTERN AFRICA*, 1874

B EFORE COMING TO Kilimanjaro I'd read of Rebmann's ventures and was thrilled that we intended to start our climb from Machame, the farthest point of his travels. That was not to forget this was also where he'd experienced his bleakest moments at the hands of Chief Mamkinga, moments of fear and despair. Machame was the source also of those stories about the fateful attempt to climb Kilimanjaro during the rule of Mamkinga's father, when all but one of the party died of cold, and this lone survivor—a man called Sabaya—returned with his hands and feet hideously frostbitten. I knew the village wouldn't look as it did when Rebmann was here a century and a half ago, yet I hoped to gain a sense of his perspective of Kilimanjaro—to see what he described to his unappreciative readership back in England. Actually, things have changed remarkably little. The range of crops has diversified, but Rebmann described huts among banana groves, and that is still the overall impression today. Machame lies in Moshi Rural District, a region where in some parts the population is currently doubling every decade or so. This means as many as 1,454 men, women, and children may be occupying one square mile of land. Although numbers of people walk along the road and

PRECEDING PAGES: LAKE NATRON REFLECTS OL DOINYO LENGAI. LEFT: BARON CARL CLAUS VON DER DECKEN MADE THE FIRST
ATTEMPTS ON KILIMANJARO—IN 1861 WITH BRITISH GEOLOGIST RICHARD THORNTON AND IN 1862 WITH OTTO KERSTEN.

children wave from the verges, you cannot gauge how many little farmsteads—or shambas—are hidden among the tall corn and banana palms on either side, nor how far the village extends back from the road.

TWELVE YEARS were to pass after Rebmann's third visit before another European approached Kilimanjaro, years in which the only corroboration of the mountain's ever-lasting snows came from his fellow missionary worker, Ludwig Krapf. As can be imagined—in view of the men's close association—geographical skeptics saw no more reason to award credibility to Krapf's "ocular testimony" than they had to Rebmann's, especially as his several reported sightings were all from a great distance. Yet he was able to give an accurate description of the mountain and even postulated that its origins were volcanic. He obtained his first view on November 10, 1849, while

traveling to Ukambani in what is Kenya today. Gazing westward from Mount Maungu, he "distinctly saw the snow mountain, Kilimandjaro, in Jagga," and his heart leapt. Krapf had been thoroughly disgusted that Rebmann's accounts were "unnecessarily assaulted by some people in England" and wasted no time in contacting the *Church Missionary Intelligencer* in defense of his friend. To clinch matters, he hoped, he threw in a startling further piece of information. "I discovered another snow mountain, of still greater height and extent," he announced. "It lies about a degree and a half south from the Line [the Equator], and contains the most probable source of the White Nile."

Krapf had become the first outsider to report first-hand on Mount Kenya, with its "two immense towers, or horns." This he'd seen from Kitui, after traveling some 300 miles northwest of his mission across arid steppe

GAZELLES FIGHT IN AMBOSELI NATIONAL PARK, KENYA.

Rebmann's various encounters with Kilimanjaro and Mount Kenya, as well as all the information they'd been able to glean about these peaks locally. He regretted that neither David Livingstone nor Burton and Speke could corroborate the existence of these mountains—having not passed close enough to see them for themselves—but Krapf couldn't believe such gentlemen would dismiss them out of hand as the academic world continued to do. Nor could he suppress his irritation with Cooley, who in his book reiterated the view that Rebmann's observations were "a most delightful mental recognition only, not supported by the evidence of his senses," and likened Chagga reports of frostbite to "fireside tales."

What stung Krapf most, however, was Cooley's gratuitous insult that he was "a man of vaulting ambition, whose taste for dealing with mighty problems was not accompanied by that mental acumen without which intellectual activity becomes to its possessor a highly dangerous endowment." The jibe was too personal for the missionary to address properly on his own behalf, instead he took up cudgels in defense of the trustworthiness of native testimony. "Had Mr. Cooley been accustomed to weigh and sift evidence more closely," he retorted, "he would have argued differently from that very fact; for by its own law evidence is always strengthened by the record of trivial and immaterial circumstances." And he couldn't resist one dig at the stubborn old codger:

The candid reader of Mr. Cooley's objections will not fail to see that in attempting to prove too much, he has managed to place himself out of court, and the presence of snow-capped mountains in Equatorial Africa will be credited notwithstanding the implied and open discredit which he attempts to cast upon the narratives of the missionaries of Rabbai Mpia.

Worn down by all the backbiting, Krapf, like Rebmann, was disillusioned with discovery. "Why should I endanger my mission for the sake of science," he wrote bitterly. "Let Geography perish!"

WITH EVEN THE PRESIDENT of the Royal Geographical Society believing the missionaries must have been "deceived by the glittering aspect of the rocks under a tropical sun," the only way armchair geographers were to

dominated by roving bands of Masai warriors and wild game. Without question this was an impressive and perilous journey for its day, but Krapf was mistaken in supposing the glistening giant on the horizon was higher than Kilimanjaro, mistaken, too, in his belief that its snows supplied the source of the White Nile. Cooley fired off another of his scornful missives to the *Atheneum* before settling down to write what he intended to be the definitive work on the subject, *Inner Africa Laid Open*, published in 1852.

By the time Dr. Krapf compiled his own *Travels and Missionary Labours*, the English version of which appeared in 1860, more was known of the African interior, and the White Nile question had been laid to rest for the moment by the discoveries of Major Richard Burton and Captain John Speke. In an Appendix dedicated to recent discoveries in East Africa, Krapf outlined his and

be convinced that Rebmann and Krapf were not credulous simpletons or hoaxers was for some other credible authority to confirm their findings. Such an authority would not put in an appearance until 1861, and even then would fail to satisfy the relentless hard-liners.

Despite British skepticism, it would be wrong to suppose that Rebmann and Krapf were universally disregarded. The French Société de Géographie awarded both men medals of honor for their achievements. "When the Geographical Society in Paris sent me a large silver medal for the dedication which I had shown in the promotion of geographical science," the modest Rebmann recorded, "I replied that my journeys were undertaken solely for the sake of the Mission. Hence the discovery of Kilimanjaro should in no way be regarded as something meritorious, but in the first instance as merely coincidental."

The reverend fathers were an inspiration to adventurous travelers, and their writings, along with those of Livingstone, Burton, and others, did much throughout the 1850s to stimulate a growing curiosity about the African interior. As the continent's secrets were relinquished, prospects of lucrative trade opened up. German businessmen in particular took a proprietary interest in developments; the Rabai missionaries were their countrymen after all, even if working under the umbrella of a British society. One German scholar wrote his university thesis on Ptolemy and the trade routes of central Africa. It caught the attention of exiled King Ludwig of Bavaria, who dispatched the young man to investigate the mysterious "inland sea" everyone was talking about. Albrecht Roscher was 22 years old in 1858 when he sailed to Zanzibar to undertake this quest.

At much the same time Baron Carl Claus von der Decken, a Hanoverian of considerable means, was so seduced by the Dark Continent as to abandon a promising military career in the hope of unraveling some of East Africa's secrets. He arrived in Zanzibar two years after Roscher, planning to waylay the younger man on his return and offer to underwrite further exploration, provided he could go along too. But bleak news greeted him: Roscher had been murdered by tribesmen at Kisunguni, near the eastern shore of Lake Nyasa. The baron at once dashed off to rescue Roscher's journals and avenge his death, but he succeeded in neither. His porters ran away with many of his possessions, the armed escort refused to obey his orders, and he found

it impossible to purchase food in the villages through which he passed. After penetrating 155 miles inland, von der Decken was forced back to the coast, convinced that Arab officialdom and tribal leaders were in league against him. But he wasn't ready to relinquish his dream. One way he could see of yet making his mark as an explorer would be to settle "once and for all, the still disputed question of snow in tropical Africa."

Back in Zanzibar he teamed up with a British geologist, Richard Thornton, who for a short while had served with Livingstone's Zambesi expedition. He'd been dismissed by the missionary—some reports say for laziness and "want of good sense," but others that Livingstone was acting on instructions from London after Thornton fell sick. Whatever the truth of it, Thornton was spurred to prove himself and went on to explore for 20 months on his own. He was 23, and the baron some four years older, when they set off from Mombasa on June 28, 1861, bound for Kilimanjaro. Missionary Rebmann walked with them for a few miles. Their caravan ran to over 50 porters and servants, among whom were the baron's Italian manservant and Thornton's "personal slave."

In Taita, they were threatened by 200 warriors—"roaring, howling, yelling, leaping," as Thornton recalled—who demanded immediate compensation for botanical specimens collected while "trespassing" in their territory. With no intention of paying up, the baron ordered his men to load their weapons, but the day was saved by their caravan leader who paid off the tribesmen from his own resources. A few days later, on July 14, the explorers caught a first tantalizing glimpse of the object of their quest. "Kilimanjaro," Thornton wrote in his diary, "shone out beautifully for a few minutes, showing streaks of snow running down its sides at the bottom of numerous ravines to nearly the base of the upper cone."

Climbing the mountain proved another matter. Local chiefs opposed the idea strongly, and the party's own porters balked at venturing above the rain forest. Von der Decken and Thornton spent 19 days on and around the mountain, basing themselves at Kilema and Machame, but the highest they managed to reach was a little over 8,000 feet. This was far from the triumph the baron had dreamed of, but it gave Thornton the opportunity to carry out an intelligent survey of the area. He became the first scientist to provide data that carried weight back home. Kibo's height, he estimated, was between 19,812 and 20,655 feet, somewhat high, as we

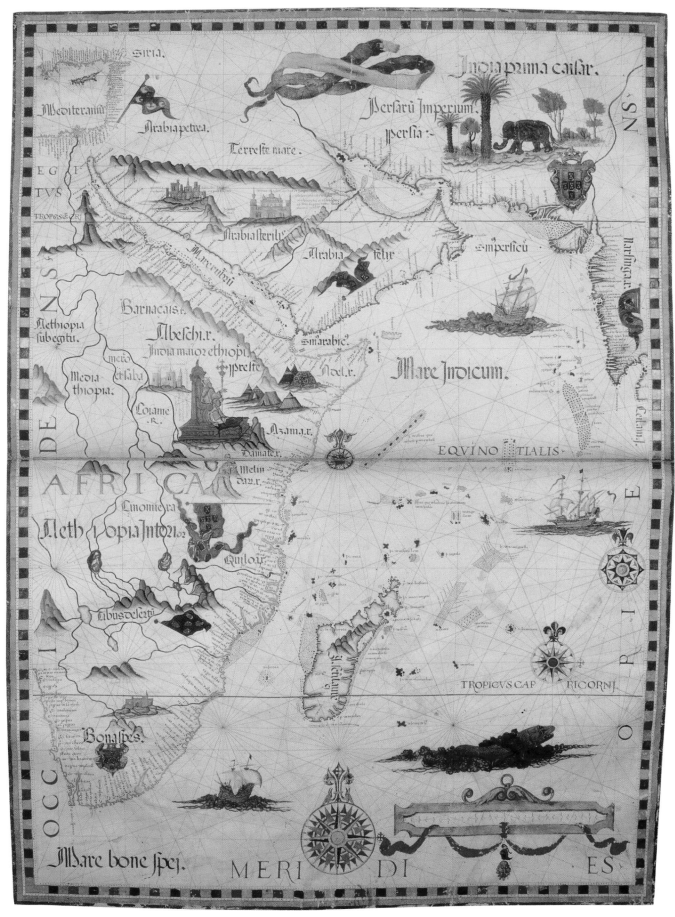

THOUGH THE COAST WAS FAMILIAR TO EUROPEAN NAVIGATORS BY 1558, KNOWLEDGE OF THE INTERIOR WAS HIGHLY SPECULATIVE. FOLLOWING PAGES: MASAI SURVEY THE HILLS BEYOND A HUT IN THE ARUSHA DISTRICT.

ABOVE: METHODIST MISSIONARY CHARLES NEW IS RECEIVED AT THE COURT OF MANDARA, THE QUICK-TEMPERED CHIEFTAIN OF MOSHI. RIGHT: NEW WAS THE FIRST TO REACH KILIMANJARO'S SNOWS IN 1871.

know now—the accepted height of Kilimanjaro is 19,340 feet—of which the top 2,200 feet carry permanent snow. The lesser summit, Mawenzi, he put at between 17,257 and 17,453 feet (today 16,896 feet). Geologically, the mountain appeared to be "composed of lava of subaerial origin"—that is, lava that had consolidated in the open air. Thornton added that on Kibo's northeast side "the rim of the old crater can still be distinguished, but on the southwest, which is considerably lower, it seems to have been destroyed." He had identified what we now know as the Western Breach, the way our party intended approaching the summit.

As events transpired, it was of no consequence that in a moment of thirst on the march-in the baron had prematurely consumed the bottle of champagne brought along to toast his summit triumph. He was determined to return the following year in full expectation of better

luck. Writing home to Germany to corroborate Rebmann's reports of Kilimanjaro's snowy crown, the Baron exaggerated the mountain's height to 21,000 feet. Thornton's more measured findings were published in the *Proceedings of the Royal Geographical Society*. Though nothing could sway Cooley, faced with this compelling evidence, others in Britain were forced to consider that the missionaries perhaps had been right all along.

Thornton was surprised on his return to be invited to rejoin Livingstone on the Zambesi; the great missionary's abrupt change of heart having been induced no doubt by Thornton's thorough and well-received Kilimanjaro report. Man enough to bury old differences, Thornton accepted Livingstone's offer—fatefully, as it would prove, for he died of fever during the trip in April 1863 before his 25th birthday.

In his place, von der Decken secured as his new partner the young German scientist Dr. Otto Kersten. He hoped, after they had tried their best on Kilimanjaro, to press farther to Lake Victoria and return via Mount Kenya. Wisely, these ambitions were trimmed in the face of risk of attack from marauding bands of Masai beyond Kilimanjaro. Instead, they would focus on climbing the mountain, which they reached in November 1862. Two attempts were made, but the baron failed to reach the snow line. He estimated his high point as 13,780 feet. One night on the mountain a heavy fall of snow left the ground around all white next morning. "Surely the obstinate Cooley will be satisfied now," von der Decken wrote.

Alas, no. Convinced that this latest "eccentric traveler" was interested merely in gaining acceptance for the "vascillating, inconsistent accounts" of his countrymen Rebmann and Krapf, Cooley reached for pen and ink once more. "The Sporting Baron did not experience a fall of snow," he proclaimed, nor had he succeeded in bringing back "a single particle of precise information of any kind." But Cooley's day was over; supreme pigheadedness had made him a laughingstock. *Inner Africa Shut Fast* was how his peers now referred to his great work. Rather late in the day, Sir Roderick Murchison, President of the Royal Geographical Society, admitted publicly that the missionaries had been right: there were indeed snow-mountains in Equatorial Africa. He saw to it that in 1863 Baron Carl Claus von der Decken was honored with the Gold Medal of the RGS for his contributions to the geographical knowledge of inner Africa. No retrospective awards were made to Rebmann or Krapf, however.

IN ZANZIBAR, one of many people Baron von der Decken met after his second Kilimanjaro expedition was a fresh-faced Methodist missionary. Fervent, impressionable, and devout, Charles New had only recently received his calling. His older brother was a missionary in Sierra Leone, but New never intended following in his footsteps until one day in July 1862 when he found himself involved in a serious rail accident. Sitting unharmed on the track as people around him lay injured, he was struck that it must be for some purpose. "A life thus spared should be devoted to God," it seemed to him, and later that day, on learning of the urgent need for a man to work for the Free Churches Mission in eastern Africa, he offered his services. Within months he was on his way, even though in the meantime distressing news of his brother's death had been received.

An avid reader, New had briefed himself on the state of East African exploration and the geographers' pontifications over Kilimanjaro and its ice cap. He was excited, soon upon landing in Africa, to bump into "that enterprising Hanoverian," Baron von der Decken, whom he eagerly plied with questions. On learning that the baron had failed to reach Kilimanjaro's snows, New's own mountain-climbing ambitions were kindled. "I would have proceeded thither at once," he wrote, "but for a while I had other work to do." Fighting fevers, picking up local languages, undertaking the "multifarious engagements" of mission life—all conspired to keep him from heading off for Kilimanjaro until the year 1871. By this time the sporting baron was dead—murdered by Somalis in the vicinity of the Juba River in October 1865, at the age of 33. He'd been attempting to reach Mount Kenya.

For all his reading, New failed to learn the lessons of African travel. Rebmann, Burton, Speke, and von der Decken all had bemoaned the necessity of carrying many goods for trade and tribute to chiefs. If coin would do, New thought, how the baggage could be reduced, how much trouble and inconvenience could be spared. Even in the knowledge that cloth, beads, and everyday items such as razors, scissors, knives, axes, looking glasses, thick iron wire, and "white-colored lead" (or pewter) were the only currency recognized in this "untamed" county, New decided to cut down on such encumbrances. Out of misguided frugality, he limited his purchases to stores worth $111.29, realizing soon along the way that he'd landed himself with far more trouble and inconvenience by not having what the Africans wanted most. By then it was too late.

The expedition's guide, Sadi, a tall, black-bearded man of about 45 years, had been to Chagga 8 years before with von der Decken. He was imposing, New tells, and "well-timbered." A Swahili with some Asiatic blood, he appeared half African, half Arabian, and he knew the Masai country and language as well as any man on the coast. Though New appreciated the breadth of his experience, he found he could not like Sadi.

The missionary's real sympathies lay with his sec-

travelers at infinitely more risk. Next morning, he and New prayed together before the latter stepped out into this unpredictable territory.

New describes his adventures in lively detail in *Life Wanderings and Labours in Eastern Africa*, published in 1874. He comes over as well meaning, but too ready to judge by his own British middle-class values. Finding in Kisigau that, although their dress was "very scant," the men appeared "on the whole, superior to the women." He labored the point to amuse his readers: "The poor women, how I pity them! Little as they would thank me for it. They are out in everything. In size, in figure, in feature, in dress, in ornaments, they are quite the reverse of what we desire to see in their sex." His intricate descriptions of their beadwork and dress—a "toute ensemble ...of the most unattractive kind"—were

MONDAY The roads were dry when we drove the 40 miles from Arusha to the mountain, which remained invisible. As we drove up the lush lower slopes, it began drizzling. Mist and cloud smothered everything. The higher we climbed, the grayer and gloomier everything became. Why did it have to do this today? The tracks will be rivers of mud. But, imagine our surprise and great delight when for a just a moment the clouds to the right of us ripped apart and we were treated to one shining glimpse of gleaming snow. Kilimanjaro at last.

ond-in-command, his cook and Man Friday, Tofiki, "a good looking African, with a muscular, strong, well-knit frame." Tofiki, to him, represented everything Sadi was not: "shrewd, thoroughly honest, courageous, and true as steel—a man to be depended upon: I knew he would stand by me to the last." In all, the party numbered 17, and this "unpretending little caravan" left Mombasa on July 13 to spend their first night away as guests of missionary Rebmann at the CMS station in Kisulutini, close to Rabai. As can be imagined, the two churchmen talked far into the night, calling Sadi to join them for discussions about the route ahead. The guide listened to the old explorer's recollections from 23 years before, but told both men curtly that those roads were now *kufa* (dead). A new way would have to be found. "So much has changed," Rebmann shook his head sadly, admitting that East Africa was far more unsettled now and

penned to convey what he saw as the barbarity of these people. Today, we can consider his observations sociologically valuable, one record at least of a period from which few accounts survive and fewer photographs.

Approaching from the southwest, New caught his first glimpse of Kilimanjaro from outside Taveta, its vast head enveloped in dense cloud. Even so, it could be seen that its eastern and western ridges fell steeply to the plain. New was impressed: The mountain filled almost one half of the horizon. As he drew closer to Moshi, at the southern foot of Kilimanjaro, his courage wavered. The region's warrior chief, Mandara, had a reputation for quickwittedness and cunning, which New's guide, Sadi, took every opportunity to reinforce. The one-eyed Mandara was unpredictable and dangerous, he warned New, and in constant conflict with his Chagga neighbors.

Known also as Rindi, and Mandikara, Mandara had

THIS 19TH CENTURY SKETCH DEPICTS A RIVER CROSSING. ALTHOUGH THE CLOTHING STYLE HAS CHANGED, MODERN KILIMANJARO PORTERS STILL PREFER THE TRADITIONAL TECHNIQUE OF BALANCING LOADS ON THE TOP OF THEIR HEADS.

grown up in violent times. When he was a child, his uncle murdered his father and assumed the regency. But one morning a herd of elephants trampled the tribal crop fields and this uncle, Silia, decided to scare them off. He was drying some gunpowder for his musket beside a fire when a spark flew into the explosive. Silia, along with 39 of his henchmen, went up in smoke—so the story goes. That was the day Mandara inherited the chieftainship of Moshi. With one brief interruption, he hung on to this power by a mixture of intrigue and intimidation. Within his domain his authority was absolute.

Coastal slave traders had been active within Chagga since the mid-1850s and it had become customary for these merchants to purchase captives taken in inter-tribal warfare along with plundered ivory and other goods. In return, local chieftains obtained guns and other arms and were able to build up warrior bands to perpetuate increasingly brutal raids upon their neighbors. Mandara hired Masai from the plains to fortify his ferocious army.

When New arrived in Moshi on August 6 he was shown to a site beside an irrigation channel where his party could pitch their tents. Moshi lies at a height of 6,000 feet above sea level. If he were to proceed farther up the mountain's forested flanks, the missionary knew he needed to establish good relations with Mandara. Where could he find the mangi, he inquired, and was surprised to have pointed out to him "a fine young fellow" sitting upon a nearby log and "lolling upon the shoulders of another young man." It was hard to believe that this was the infamous chief who terrorized the area for miles around. New strode forward to shake hands. "Jambo!" he said in greeting. "Jambo, jambo, sana," replied the chief, rising to circle his guest, yet keeping him at arm's length. At last, satisfied that the Englishman presented no threat, Mandara laughed and joined New in his tent, anxious to see what treasures the missionary had brought for him. He watched with enormous interest as the white-skinned visitor washed and changed. New silently congratulated himself: Things seemed to be going well.

KILIMANJARO:
THE MISSIONARY EFFECT

ROLAND OLIVER

EMERITUS PROFESSOR OF AFRICAN HISTORY, UNIVERSITY OF LONDON

KILIMANJARO, with its dense population of industrious and ingenious Chagga banana farmers who inhabited the southward-facing ridges of the mountain at heights between 4,000 and 6,000 feet, was a natural target for Christian missionary organizations seeking to enter the East African interior whenever political conditions permitted. Johannes Rebmann of the Anglican Church Missionary Society was the first European to visit the mountain in 1848-49, traveling in the company of Swahili Arab merchants who introduced him to the Chagga chieftains of Kilema and Machame. But it was not until 1886 that the Society felt confident enough to send in a regular mission to build stations at Machame and Moshi. However, it was soon forced to retreat northward into the Taita hills after an Anglo-German boundary agreement allotted the whole of Kilimanjaro to the German sphere of influence. Its place was taken in 1892 by the German Lutheran Missionary Society of Leipzig. These were joined in 1893 by the French Catholic missionary order of Spiritans or Holy Ghost Fathers, pushing inland from their long-established circle of freed slave settlements around Bagamoyo, who built their first stations at Kilema, Kibosho, and Rombo.

In defining their attitude to the newcomers the Chagga, for their part, looked for guidance to their chiefs, some 30 in number, each of whom ruled over a mountain ridge that was normally separated from its neighbors by ravines too steep for easy communication. The chiefs had grown powerful by controlling the remarkably effective system of irrigation channels by which the perennial water flowing down from the snow-fields of Kibo was distributed to every family plantation. The chiefs were also the war leaders and as such controlled relations with foreigners of every kind, be they Swahili traders, German officials, or German settlers seeking land for plantations of their own, or French and German missionaries. The chiefs naturally looked at the missions primarily from the political angle and quickly identified them as the foreigners who could

best teach them about the outside world that was breaking in upon them and who could, when necessary, mediate between them and the other whites. They therefore competed with each other in offering them building sites and ensuring that they had servants and other employees for their buildings and gardens and, in due course, pupils for their schools. While mostly preserving their own personal neutrality in matters of religion, chiefs frequently designated some of their own children to attend the nearest mission and encouraged their court circles to do the same. Chagga-land thus became a classic case of conversion from the top down.

As in the rest of tropical Africa, it was through the mission schools that Christianity came to the ordinary people of Kilimanjaro. This necessarily involved several preliminary years of language study; the translation of Bibles, catechisms, and other school materials; and the recruitment and training of African teacher-catechists at the residential schools established at the main mission stations, whose successful graduates would later spread out to found bush schools in the *mitaa,* or parish subdivisions, of each chiefdom. But it was a process that happened faster on Kilimanjaro than in most other places, partly at least because of the keen competition between Catholics and Lutherans.

The Spiritans arrived with a formed policy to work as far as possible through Kiswahili, the language of the coast, which was being pushed by the German authorities as a lingua franca for the territory as a whole. This enabled them to use as their first catechists the converts from their earlier missions nearer the coast. It likewise opened to their Chagga pupils the whole range of elite jobs as teachers, clerks, and overseers in every part of the German colony. The Spiritans had also learned from their former freed slave settlements that the idea of forming special Christian villages for their converts merely cut them off from the rest of the community. They were therefore determined that their bush schools would be day schools, attended by pupils living in their own homes. By 1913, some 60,000 Chagga had been baptized into the

Catholic Church. The Lutherans, arriving with no previous experience, held strong pietistic prejudices about working only in the local mother tongue and were inclined to favor Christian villages in which their converts would be removed from the temptations of tribal life. But within a decade, largely through the advocacy of an exceptionally gifted and forceful colleague, Bruno Gutmann, who joined the mission in 1902, they had altered their position on both counts. By 1913, they had added some 20,000 baptized adherents to the Lutheran faith. Such figures suggest that in the course of only 20 years around half of the entire Chagga population had become Christians of one denomination or the other.

For all their impressive numbers, however, the Christians of Chagga-land, whether Catholic or Lutheran, belonged to churches that were still very flimsily constructed, served at the parish level exclusively by elementary school teachers who did duty as prayer leaders and lay preachers on Sundays. At monthly intervals, maybe, these would convene at the nearest mission station to receive guidance for their sermons during the following weeks. The only ordained ministers were the missionaries, who paid pastoral visits to the parishes at infrequent intervals to inspect the schools and dispense the sacraments. There would be some halting discussions in Swahili or one of the Chagga dialects about the interplay of Christian doctrine and inherited Chagga beliefs and customs. But the missionaries did not live close enough to the ordinary parishioners to know much about them, and the key people in the whole system were the handful of outstanding catechists who helped to staff the teacher training schools at the main mission stations. Such, for example, was Filipo Njau, the close confidant and colleague of Bruno Gutmann at the teacher training school at Moshi, who collected Chagga proverbs and folklore and worked the best of them into Christian hymns and biblical commentaries.

A handful of people of the caliber of Njau carried the Lutheran Church of Kilimanjaro through the testing

As in the rest of tropical Africa, it was through the mission schools that Christianity came to the ordinary people of Kilimanjaro.

time, that began with the First World War, when the Germans were driven from their East African colony, cutting the links between the German missions and their home bases. It culminated, however, during the years from 1920 to 1926, when the incoming British government of Tanganyika ordered the deportation of all German missionaries from the territory. Throughout this period the Lutheran mission houses on Kilimanjaro stood empty and their Chagga adherents were left to fend for themselves, which they did with amazing success. The parochial schools remained open. The teacher-catechists stayed at their posts, supporting themselves on the contributions of the local people. The training of new teachers went on, and so successfully that Chagga evangelists were able to help the less enterprising adherents of other Lutheran mission fields in the Usambara highlands to the southeast. The natural consequence of all their efforts was that, when the German missionaries returned to them in 1926, the Chagga leaders were less inclined than formerly to accept them in the paternalistic relationship that had existed in earlier days. In particular, they pressed for a proper training in theology, leading to the ordination of their own people as pastors of the Church. They achieved this in 1934, when 12 of their number were selected for a crash course in theology and subsequently ordained. In 1960 one of them, Stefano Moshi, was consecrated as the first African Lutheran bishop and three years later was elected President of the Evangelical Lutheran Church of a now politically independent Tanzania.

It could be said that in a delectable corner of East Africa, which might all too easily have been seized for German plantations, its population conscripted to provide labor, two companies of missionaries offered the Chagga people an introduction to the modern world, by which they might otherwise have been overwhelmed and enslaved. But it was the Chagga who responded to the offer and modified it to suit their own aspirations who deserve most of the credit. Missionaries are needed to light the spark, but it is the recipients fan it into flame.

**JACARANDA TREES MAKE A STRIKING DISPLAY WHEN
THEY BLOOM IN DECEMBER.**

Mandara recognized Sadi and began plying him with questions about the baron, or "Baroni," as he was remembered here. News of Baroni's death had saddened him for days, he said, had anything been done to avenge the murder? Then, quite suddenly, Mandara veered off on a different tack as he recalled that Baroni, although generous during his visit, had presented him with nothing upon leaving. Fixing the guide with a severe stare, he said, "Sadi, you deceived me," with which he whipped Sadi's cloak from his back and draped it around his own shoulders. "Just what I've been looking for!" he smiled, patting its texture and swaggering out. New resolved to be warier in the future: The man was "clearly something of a tyrant." At the same time he was indisputably fascinating. New devotes many pages in his book to Mandara, whom he reckoned to be not above 26 years of age, and certainly below 30, five-feet-nine in height, perfectly proportioned, sinewy and lithe. Mandara lost the sight of his right eye as a young warrior when retreating from a raid at night through thorn scrub. It was, New tells us, "nearly closed and as dark as pitch," but the good eye remained "full of light, and he uses it like a hawk."

That first evening New held a gospel meeting for the villagers, and afterward answered Mandara's many questions about Christianity and Islam. They also discussed slave raiding. "We never sold our people till the Wasuahili came with tempting offers of fine clothes, etc.," Mandara told the missionary. "And it is a bad business."

Later, just before sunset, when the villagers had retreated to their huts, New and Tofiki got their first good view of Kilimanjaro's "beautiful dome of stupendous proportions." Mawenzi remained hidden in clouds that night, but revealed itself in full rugged majesty many times later. Over hills upon hills of luxuriant tropical vegetation above Moshi rose "mountains upon mountains of dark forest; loftier still, heights upon heights of grassy hills." Beyond all these were what appeared to be "barren, rocky steeps," and then the region of perpetual snow. With its two culminating elevations, there could be no other such sight in this wide world, New concluded.

When summoned next morning to the mangi's stockade, New found Mandara sitting on a four-legged stool, "his only dress being his soft, brown, well-fitting skin." He was rather the worse for drink, and the ceremony of present-giving was put off until the following day. Laid out for inspection, New's items failed to impress the chief, who demanded instead his guest's rifle, thermometer, watch, binoculars, and accordian, which the missionary had no intention of handing over. Things might have gotten very ugly had not negotiations been interrupted by the warning of an attack. Letting out a war cry, the mangi quickly donned his waistband and feathered headdress and led his men, whooping and bellowing, into battle. The mountainsides soon streamed with armed men, bearing such weapons as bows and arrows, Masai spears and shields, muskets, clubs, swords, daggers, knives, hatchets, and billhooks.

The uproar and excitement were tremendous. It was clear that if Mandara's men lost, New and his party were lost too. "Missionary though I was, I prepared for defence," he wrote. With his guns loaded, he and others of his party joined Mandara at the head of his men. But the danger was already past. A Masai raiding party had been thwarted by the arrival of a company of Swahili traders, who paid them to go elsewhere. Even so, New's readiness to stand by Mandara clearly impressed the chief. The supposed niggardliness of New's gifts was more or less forgotten. The Swahilis were another matter. They were slave traders, New soon realized, and were suspicious of any influence he might gain with Mandara that might affect their lucrative business. They wanted him out of the country without delay, and to this end Sadi seemed to be in cahoots with them.

New watched and waited. He resumed his information gleaning, wandering around to get the measure of these luxuriant foothills. "Chaga is a garden," he wrote. "'Upon every high mountain, and upon every high hill, are rivers and streams of water.' The sun pours down its sevenfold brightness, warming into existence myriads of plants and trees, and these agents being ever at work, create a landscape as rich as it is charming, and as perpetual as the agents themselves—the result being a never-ending spring." The mangi spent the greater part of the next three days with New, chatting on all manner of subjects, and it soon became clear to the missionary that his host

was a man of considerable intelligence and learning. He even had a form of writing that he could read back afterward; he wanted, he said, to send a deputation to the Queen of England. By August 11, with things progressing so swimmingly, New felt emboldened to broach the subject of Kilimanjaro. Would the mangi permit him to attempt a climb? Would he lend him guides and porters for the purpose? Mandara agreed.

New had no better luck on his first sally up the mountain than had von der Decken before him. Rain, fog, and the reluctance of his party foiled the attempt before the forest was cleared. A week later he tried again with a

IN 1871, NEWSPAPERMAN HENRY MORTON STANLEY TRACKED DOWN MISSING EXPLORER DAVID LIVINGSTONE AT UJIJI, LAKE TANGANYIKA. HERE, THEY ARE PADDLED BY NATIVES ALONG THE RUSIGI RIVER.

stronger team, and this time the weather was kinder. Following elephant tracks where they could, and otherwise hacking through the thick vegetation, they came—he says, on the second morning—out of a wood of high broom into more open country with the clouds below them. Later in the day mists rolled up the slopes. It grew so cold they retired into a kind of cave and built huge fires to keep themselves from freezing. The sun rose next morning in a "flood of glory." East, west, and south, the country stretched out below them with nothing to bound the view beside their own "weak powers of vision."

They were away by 8:00 a.m., Kibo shining in the morning sun to their left and Mawenzi brooding to the right. New was reminded of the Jungfrau and the Aiguille du Dru in the Alps. Half an hour's steep scrambling up rocky ground with "frosty-looking" little plants left the barefoot locals with benumbed toes and hands. Another hour and they dared go no farther, but New's favorite, Tofiki, was still game. Together these two struggled on. Tofiki kept up the pace for an hour and a half more, though it was plainly a great effort, and finally he sank breathless to the ground. "You go alone," he begged New, vowing to wait where he was. "When you don't come back," he said, "I die here." The missionary was touched,

but, though he would never have sacrificed Tofiki for all the "eternal snows in the world," New was not ready yet to relinquish his quest. If he could just touch the snow he'd be content—and it looked now to be within reach.

By this time, the altitude was getting to him too, and as he plodded on he had to pause every few steps to regain strength. Luckily, he didn't need to go far. In a concealed hollow at his feet there was snow, "lying on the ledges of rock in masses, like large sleeping sheep."

Excitedly, New hurried back to Tofiki and coaxed him up to the spot. The snow was hard and frozen to the rock and they broke off several large chunks to take down and show their companions waiting below. "Tofiki put them into his blanket, slung them over his shoulders, and away we went down hill in triumph!" New wrote. "I made the more haste as my head was so giddy that I was

thwarted, when on reaching Zanzibar he was entreated to join an expedition sent out by the Royal Geographical Society in search of Doctor Livingstone who was missing in the interior. Reluctantly, he agreed to accompany the four men of the party, one of whom was Livingstone's eldest surviving son, Oswell. New's book would have to wait. However, while enlisting men and outfitting what could prove a three-year expedition, runners brought news to the mainland coast that Henry Morton Stanley had located Livingstone at Ujiji. All that was required now was to resupply him. At first, New agreed to lead this Relief Expedition, for which several thousand pounds had been raised by public subscription, but the impetus was lost. As the other members dropped out one by one, and nobody seemed clear what ought to happen next, Stanley's bombastic arrival clarified the issue. He took

MONDAY I knew that one of the small retreating ice fields on Kilimanjaro, to the south of Kibo's summit, was named after Rebmann, and I had expected this to be all we'd find commemorating this long-dead European visitor. So I was astonished, as we swung around one tight bend on the steep road up into Machame, to catch sight of a worn wooden sign to the left of the road. In Gothic script, it read: "Johannes Rebmann Memorial Library ....1.5 km." The sign pointed down a narrow unmade track that disappeared into a wall of vegetation. There was no time to investigate, as we were about to trek into the rain forest, but I hoped after the climb to be able to come back and find out more.

afraid of swooning; Tofiki, too, looked wild and strange." It was almost noon and welling mists could be expected at any moment. They needed to hurry while they could still find the way.

At the sight of the white "rocks" in the blanket, their companions were amazed, especially when chippings from them were found to melt in their mouths. By the time they had descended the mountain, there was only a gourd of water to show for the whole adventure. Still, it had to be accepted now, however ruefully, that it was not silver up there on the mountain top.

Within days of his climb New took leave of the mangi and turned for home, pondering the book he intended to write of his East African experiences.

His intention of returning directly to England was

control amid some acrimony, eventually dispatching a caravan of 57 men and bearers to Ujiji. It only remained for New, his fellows, and the triumphant Stanley to head for the Seychelles to pick up the monthly mail boat home.

Relations between the men deteriorated further by the time they arrived in England on August 1, 1872, to find themselves embroiled in public argument and accusation. New learned that in his absence the *Times* newspaper had vilified his efforts, and although subsequently exonerated of any blame by the Council of the RGS, he came out of this sorry episode bruised and humiliated. The one steadfast and shining light was the memory of Kilimanjaro. How he yearned to recapture the excitement and friendships that adventure had yielded him.

SKETCHED IN MOSHI BY EXPLORER AND EMPIRE BUILDER HARRY JOHNSTON, KIBO RISES ABOVE THE MISTS IN EARLY MORNING.

CHAPTER FOUR

INTO THE FOREST

These plants are the powerful life force here, and they
appear to grow before my eyes. I sense that if one stopped
and remained still too long in this place,
he would be entwined and overpowered, claimed as one of their own.

ROB TAYLOR, "THE BREACH," 1981

A BELT OF THICK FOREST encircles Kilimanjaro roughly between the heights of 6,000 and 9,500 feet. It varies in width from a few miles to around 15, according to aspect, the steepness of slope, and how much human interference it has suffered. It took the early explorers two to three days to get through virgin forest to the alpine zone above. But as the years passed and the demand for farmland, fuel, and animal grazing increased, tree clearance nibbled away at the lower boundaries of this lush growth. Most of what remains enjoys protection within Kilimanjaro National Park and Forest Reserve; even so, there remains justifiable concern for its future. More than 20,000 visitors trek into the park every year, causing inevitable disturbance to its ecology and putting some species of flora and fauna at risk, including, or perhaps especially, the larger mammals. ❧ The mountain's wetter southern slopes developed a denser and richer forest. To the west and east, substantial areas of original woodland have been cleared for softwood plantations, and these have been economically productive. Against that, however, they have compressed the range and disrupted migratory routes of animals such as the elephant and Cape buffalo, which, although still found in the

park, are rarely seen. Greater disturbance has both curtailed their numbers and made them more wary.

By approaching from Machame, as we were doing, we'd be climbing through the forest at one of its widest points and I was beside myself with anticipation at the wealth of indigenous plants and trees we were likely to see. I had little experience of tropical rain forests beyond strolling along a nature trail in Zanzibar and some short sections of popular trekking routes in Nepal. Without knowing how I'd perform at higher altitudes, it was pos-

sible that the forest might be all I'd see of this mountain. Yet, even if that proved the case, I was comforted that still it would be a lifetime's ambition achieved. I couldn't wait to get started. I'd been priming myself on what to expect. My brand-new East African flower book was stuffed into my brand-new rucksack: I was ready to be impressed. It came as a surprise therefore that the most obvious trees here, at the start of the trek, were not African at all, but white-barked eucalypts from Australia, whose alien, gummy scent filled the damp air.

Nicole Wineland-Thomson leads Hansi and me through Kilimanjaro's mossy forest. Following pages: Tree ferns rise above the undergrowth to occupy a vacant space below the forest canopy.

ern walkers, but there is no future in that. We were told that youths come here looking for work from all the surrounding regions—from Tanga, Dodoma, Singida, Tabora, Shinyanga, and Mara. As can be expected, this causes considerable ill-feeling among the local Chagga, who feel they should be given priority by park officials when it comes to allocating porters to the big tourist companies. Every so often factional resentment ignites into brawls and boycotts at the park gates.

With this rain, we could expect paths to be extremely slippery in the forest; we'd certainly need our staffs or ski poles—umbrellas, too, if we wanted to stay even marginally dry. And the light would be dim under the trees. It's hard to imagine any more challenging conditions for filmmaking. Nevertheless, we were enthusiastic to get started. The camera team's plan was to forge ahead of the rest and rig up vantage platforms from which to shoot the trekkers at different stages of the journey. At last the bureaucratic formalities were through and we trooped off with our porters into the half-mile forestry strip that girdles the southern and eastern fringes of the forest, separating the cultivated land from the forest proper.

This buffer strip was instituted in the early 1940s to provide local people with wood and wood products. Responsibility for its management has been passed around over the years between various local and central government departments, and now rests with the district council whose role is to encourage responsible husbandry. However, the trees here are young and spindly for the most part, and ominous sounds of chopping were to be heard off the trail as we passed. You couldn't help thinking that the long-term future of this zone, too, remains in jeopardy unless replanting can be made to keep pace with tree-felling.

"Just like Banstead Woods!" Roger Bilham jokes as we scramble up the broad, skiddy track. Though he lives now in Colorado and I in the north of England, our early lives, we had discovered, were spent within a few miles of each other in a leafy Surrey suburb. But he was wrong. Of course, it wasn't like Banstead Woods, not one bit; already we were seeing exciting endemic species. The exquisite jewel-like *Impatiens kilimanjari*, its spur curled like a

We'd arrived at the trailhead above Machame in steady rain to be greeted by huddles of disconsolate porters, waiting under their raincapes in the hope of being hired. Having booked our men in advance, it was easy to see that most of these fellows were going to be disappointed today, unless by lucky chance a flux of independent trekkers braved the rain. With little other employment on offer, these poor men and boys had to face rejection (and hunger) every single day. Some enterprising lads earn a few Tanzanian shillings by selling hand-cut staffs to west-

Continued on page 90

THE ELUSIVE ELEPHANTS
OF KILIMANJARO

Charles Foley and John Grimshaw, D. Phil.

Elephant conservation biologist, Princeton and Botanist

JOHANNES REBMANN saw elephants on the day he first sighted Kilimanjaro in May 1848 and they are featured in the accounts of most early visitors to the mountain. They were recorded on all slopes, inhabiting the forest and sometimes moving to the plains, using well-defined trails. One of these was to become the Marangu Route, adopted by climbers as the best-graded way up the mountain. Such trails were targeted by Wachagga hunters, who dug pit-traps to catch elephants using them. Hans Meyer himself fell into one such pit.

On the northern and western slopes, in Masai territory, elephants were not hunted, and by the 1880s, when they were rare elsewhere, Kilimanjaro was recognized as an elephant stronghold, probably because outsiders dared not hunt in Masailand. This changed with the weakening of Masai power following the cattle-killing rinderpest epidemic of the 1890s and the advance of European settlement. Groups of Arab-sponsored African hunters sought out elephants and killed herds indiscriminately. Among their victims was the great bull, shot as he came to drink at a waterhole, whose record tusks (weighing 226.5 and 214 lbs.) are now in London's Natural History Museum. The German conservationist G. C. Schillings recorded that, despite the proclamation of East Africa's first game reserve around Kilimanjaro by the German authorities, the elephant population fell from thousands in the early 1890s to 250–300 in 1906.

Elephants disappeared from the forests above the densely populated southern and eastern slopes by the mid-20th century. The last record from the Marangu area comes from the 1930s. Elsewhere, the Kilimanjaro elephant population benefited from increased protection and reduced demand for ivory. Numbers rose until the late 1970s or early 1980s. Estimates at this time suggest that there was a healthy population of many hundreds in the forests of the western and northern slopes.

The poaching frenzy of the 1980s hit the Kilimanjaro elephants as it did populations across the continent. The migratory elephants visiting Amboseli were noted by researcher Cynthia Moss to be nervous and bad tempered, and their relatively young ages suggested the loss of many adults. By the late 1980s the conservation community was taking stock of the elephant population, and that of Kilimanjaro was estimated to be about 1,000 strong. In 1988 elephant biologist Iain Douglas-Hamilton suggested that we, then undergraduates at Oxford, should undertake the task of surveying the Kilimanjaro elephants. The Kilimanjaro Elephant Project was the result; supported by funding from Friends of Conservation, we spent 1990 on the mountain.

We soon found out why nobody else had volunteered for the task. The Kilimanjaro elephants inhabit the forest of the western and northern slopes, between the tree line and farmland. The forest is often thick and nearly impenetrable, so all surveys had to be carried out on foot. The elephants, as we quickly learned, were hard to see in the forest undergrowth and impossible to count. Only when they emerged into clearings to browse or drink could we get a clear view. Most of those we saw were relatively young, but the existence of stable family units suggested that poaching had stopped and that the population was recovering. Monitoring the population from afar in succeeding years, we have been heartened to hear that the Kilimanjaro elephants are apparently still increasing, although this brings its own problems.

To census them we used a dung-counting technique, in which the number of dung piles in the forest can be statistically related to elephant densities. The method demanded straight-line transects, so up the mountain we went, following a compass and going straight through the obstacles of thorn thickets and steep ravines that got in the way. By the end of the year we had seen more of the forest than any other scientists, and were able to calculate that there were about 220 elephants on Kilimanjaro.

The elephants use the whole forest ecosystem, ranging widely in their search for food and water. Few forest trees are eaten by elephants, and their preferred food of soft browse and grass is most often found where logging has opened the forest canopy. By feeding in such disturbed areas the elephants perpetuate the cycle and

KILIMANJARO ELEPHANTS SPEND MOST OF THEIR TIME IN DENSE FOREST WHERE THEY ARE DIFFICULT TO OBSERVE, THOUGH THEY HAVE BEEN KNOWN TO CLIMB ABOVE THE FOREST. HERE, THEY HAVE VENTURED OUT TO DRINK.

prevent their reclamation by trees—a relationship in which plant diversity is actually increased.

Minerals are scarce in the forest, and the necessity of finding them may be the reason why the Kilimanjaro elephants have always migrated to the plains, where there are soda deposits. Today the only regular migration route links the mountain with Amboseli National Park. When we investigated this in 1990, we found that the elephants traveled on well-defined paths leading from the forest edge to the Amboseli plains, passing through a narrow strip of uncultivated dry bushland. Now known as the North Kilimanjaro Migration Corridor, this area has been protected since 1973 by the mutual agreement of the Masai people of Lerang'wa and Kamwanga villages. They enacted a village decree prohibiting agriculture in the corridor area, a move that protected natural vegetation.

By 1990 agriculture was again encroaching on the corridor; the village elders asked us to help them to achieve official protection. It was to be a unique arrangement: the traditional grazing and firewood collection was permitted, but agriculture and settlement prohibited. In addition, local herders were allowed access to the lower parts of the Forest Reserve during dry years when grazing was scarce elsewhere. The debate passed to the District Council, and thence to the Tanzanian Parliament, where the plan was ratified. Through their Community Conservation program, Tanzania National Parks (TANAPA) started providing assistance to villages adjacent to the corridor in 1995, funding several projects, including a new maternity ward at the Lerang'wa dispensary and improvement of the water supply to cattle troughs in the corridor area. In 1999, the elders told us that the corridor was being seen as an asset to the community, but recent news suggests that agriculture is spreading into the corridor; the farmers there complain of elephant damage.

Elephants and humans coexist uneasily. The human population of the arid western and northern slopes of Kilimanjaro is increasing rapidly and land use has shifted from pastoralism to subsistence agriculture. Unpredictable rainfall often causes crops to fail; shortages are not helped by elephant damage. A night's visit to a maize field by an elephant herd may mean hunger for the family for the rest of the year. The meager water supplies are often disrupted by elephants. Conflict ensues, and both humans and elephants can be victims. There are no easy answers: to balance the requirements of wildlife and humans is the greatest challenge to conservationists in the 21st century.

ABOVE: *IMPATIENS WALLERIANA* GROWS IN OPEN PLACES IN THE WETTER FOREST ON THE SOUTHERN AND EASTERN SLOPES OF KILIMANJARO. RIGHT: DAVID BREASHEARS PREPARES *IMPATIENS KILIMANJARI* FOR ITS SCREEN TEST.

chameleon's tail, occurs naturally nowhere else in the world than the wooded slopes of this mountain. It puts in an appearance the minute you step in among the first trees and stays with you, as we would discover, till you leave the forest. Flowers of this little balsam range from yellow through orange to scarlet. Alongside it grows its flashier cousin *Impatiens pseudoviola*, with long-spurred, shocking pink blooms that, as the name suggests, resemble violets or pansies in shape. I hugged myself: This was going to be every bit as good as I expected.

Soon we were on a steeper, narrower path as we moved into the National Park area. Sometimes the rain would ease off for a while, but the forest continued to drip and ooze. Mud sucked at our feet and plastered our clothes. We could keep nothing dry, nor stay upright on our feet. Even the gentlest slopes had us skating about ignobly, yet the green light filtering through the dense tree cover was magic. Tendrils of mist rose and tangled among the branches. Our new-issue brightly colored clothing, bought with the film in mind, glowed out of the gloom. Exotic birds and monkeys advertised their presence with raucous cries, though were hard to spot in

the foliage. Various plants flowered on the forest floor, but the real wonders were the flowerless plants. Wherever you stopped, you could count at least a dozen different kinds of fern—filmy ferns, polypodies, ostrich plume ferns, holly ferns, delicate maidenhairs. Botanists have identified more than 130 varieties living in this forest and cannot be sure all have been discovered yet. Mosses festoon the trees, along with creepers, lichens, and scrambling begonias. I was thrilled to see several varieties of small orchid, perhaps the most beautiful a pinkish-mauve *Polystachya* with broad, glistening leaves. We crowded round it to take photographs, our flashes firing off like fireworks. Other plants were related to those I grow on my windowsill back home, or in my garden. Some mossy tree trunks supported colonies of delicate *Streptocarpus*, miniature versions of ones in my kitchen. And the creeping club-moss, *Lycopodium*, scaly as an armadillo, looked identical, apart from its vigor, to specimens that grow on the British mountains of Snowdonia and Lakeland.

I was in paradise and for the moment completely insensible to the water trickling in at my collar and running down my skin. In this high humidity, we quickly heated up under our heavy waterproofs, which, as "stars" of the film, we could not take off for fear of upsetting the "continuity." We were getting wet from the inside and out-side, and began gently poaching as we worked up a steam.

And how is it that from a column of safari ants determinedly crossing the path, and over which you are extremely careful to step, always there are two or three outriders who manage to crawl into your boot and make their way under your gaiters and the layers of trouser to nibble at private and tender patches of flesh? No mat-ter how you slap and pummel at your knees and thighs, it is hours before you have slaughtered all the invaders, and days before you stop itching.

Filming and setting up the different shots involved a good deal of waiting around, and then it didn't take long to get chilled. Still, we remained high-spirited with the excitement of it all and chattered wildly. It provided an

opportunity to get to know others in the group who had come together only a day or two before. Similarly, it gave us the chance of getting to know our Chagga companions. Our head guide, Jacob, a slim dignified figure, came from Machame and was 50 years old, he told us, though he cer-tainly didn't look it apart from a touch of gray at the tem-ples. He was gentle and soft-spoken and had been climbing Kilimanjaro all his life. When he gets to the top this time, it will be his 241st ascent, he reckons—that is, since he's been counting. There will have been other times as a young porter, but he didn't think to keep a tally back then. Jacob knows the names and stories of all the plants and flowers. The palm we're standing under, with the ribbon-like leaves, a *Dracaena*, is specially signifi-cant to the Chagga, he says. Not only is it used to make a living fence marking the boundary of a person's home-stead, but also it is the plant that says "sorry." If you want to apologize to your father or your grandfather, say, you

pick young *Dracaena* leaves and plait them together with a special grass, then you dip the bundle in home-brewed beer and give it to the individual concerned. This alerts that person to the urgency and seriousness of what you want to say and binds him to give you a sympathetic hearing. The same is done if a young man—or an older woman—feels the time has come to leave the family home. By giving such a token, you are indicating to your parents that they should think about setting you up with a house and a banana patch of your own.

"Did you know that?" I asked Hansi, our 13-year-old fellow trekker, whose great-great-grandfather had been a Chagga chief.

"Oh yes, we all know this old custom," he said,

the extent that it is being over-harvested. Over centuries, almost every plant in this forest has been investigated to establish which is edible and which poisonous—and the number of purgatives identified must reflect those that fall between the two. Timber, food, and medicine are the most obvious benefits, but other properties are important too. Some fibrous barks yield good string, some twigs make good toothbrushes.

It looked as if the rain would persist on and off all afternoon. It's funny how you agonize over the simplest decisions. Should I, shouldn't I put on my overtrousers? Clearly I'd missed the right moment—better to have worn them from the word go. Belatedly now, I tried to redress the error, but it wasn't easy. I soon wished I'd

MONDAY We're at about 6,000 feet here, which means only another 13,000 to go. The beginning of an expedition is always an exciting time. But there's apprehension, too. You worry a bit about how you'll manage; I know there'll be times when I'll need to scramble to keep up with the younger ones. Well, to keep up with everyone. I read somewhere that to be fit to climb this mountain you should be able to run for half an hour without any appreciable change in your breathing rate. There is no way I could do that, no way I could ever have done that. But the main thing is I want to get as high as I can. People say the first step of any adventure is as important as the last. I'll just go on putting one foot in front of the other for as long as my legs carry me. And however high I get will be exciting.

adding with a smile that he hadn't had cause to try it out himself yet. But one day....

Other plants were pointed out to us. There was a fig (*mtini* in Swahili, *ngisi* in Chagga) whose long aerial roots are collected and boiled in water to give a mixture, which when drunk cold, treats skin diseases and stomach disorders. And the leaves of a mimosa relative *Albizia schimperiana*, one of the tallest trees in the forest, have medicinal properties when burned: You smell the smoke to cool headaches and reduce fever. Another common forest tree, *Macaranga kilimandscharica*, in the spurge family, has leaves from which traditionally a hot infusion has been made that checks diarrhea. The bark of *Prunus africana*, I was told, a tree related to the apple, is greatly in demand for European medicine, to

had a dress rehearsal before setting out. Hopping around on one leg, trying not to put my bootless foot down in the mud, I wriggled and zipped, unzipped, rezipped, many times, trying to construct trouser legs out of the huge, shapeless, and confusing flaps. Something for the porters to watch, at least this was amusing them. Roger was having a similar struggle, I noticed. But would it be worth the effort, or just another garment to get irredeemably muddy?

Opening my rucksack had revealed, to my dismay, that it was filling with water and the prized flower book lay totally immersed at the bottom. With conscious effort, I clung to my euphoria. However damp I and my belongings became, the surroundings were still stunningly beautiful. We passed through a grove of mature tree ferns, some as high as 30 feet or more, with the taller tree canopy arching overhead. Among them, in places, were giant forest trees that looked to be centuries old, massive roots buttressing their trunks and providing a network of hidey-holes for small animals and birds. Here and there, aged specimens had fallen across the path; others had toppled against their neighbors, providing mossy slopes for ferns and orchids that flourished in profusion. Some trunks hosted so many epiphytes they were like well-stocked gardens. There were trees that had been completely engulfed by the aerial roots of strangler figs, their life squeezed out of them. The ground, where it was visible beneath the undergrowth, was deep in decaying wood, leaf litter, and liquid clay. As a geologist, Roger was frustrated. Rarely did rock protrude anywhere through the mulch. On steeper sections, sometimes you thought you saw embedded stone, but more often than not this would prove to be ancient root-wood, hard, dark, and extremely slippery if you were incautious enough to step onto it.

In places, tree fern trunks had been positioned across the trail to afford footing in the mud, or to make steps up steeper sections. Though we made use of these gratefully enough, it was sad to think they had been cut down for the purpose. A growing tree fern is one of the most splendid and graceful sights with its filigree umbrella of fronds splitting the thin sunlight. I was even more upset to learn that tree fern stalks were highly prized also as poles for houses and verandas because they are so strong.

In the mist we sensed we were often walking along the crests of ridges, with the ground dropping away to one, other, or both sides. Radiating ridges, relics of old lava flows or mudslides, are characteristic of this old volcano, anchoring it like the buttressed tree roots to the surrounding plain. In former days and somewhat lower on the mountain, different chiefdoms would be based on the different ridges, separated from their neighbors by densely thicketed gullies. Above their territorial ridge, the inhabitants ranged in the forest in search of game, honey, and medicinal plants, doing their best to keep out of each other's way. In the middle years of the 19th century, when intertribal raids for slaves and plunder were at their height, the larger of these mountain villages became fortresses, protected by stout stone walls and perimeter trenches, each with its own professional army raised by the chief.

Although we were finding it strenuous scrambling over the fallen logs across our trail, we did have a trail. In those days people relied mostly on finding elephant tracks going in the direction they wanted and, when these ran out, they had to laboriously hack their way through dense vegetation. This is how it was when the pioneer climbers came with their guides. Charles New describes one well-beaten path, running laterally east to west of Chagga, above the limit of habitation. His party needed to cross it to climb higher, but the prospect clearly terrified his Wachagga guides. Signaling for him to duck down, they crouched a long while in silence, studying the track in both directions for any sign of movement. At last, satisfied the coast was clear, they scurried for cover on the other side. This was a public path, New was told afterward, but at that time the men from Mandara's Moshi were at war with almost any other villager they were likely to meet, and any encounter could mean war to the death. Although locals would always have used and needed the forest, and sometimes even ventured above it, New found they were none keen to spend a cold night on the forest floor. It's easy to see why not. With scarcely a stitch of clothing and a reasonable distrust of leopard and other wild beasts, they knew that any bivouac would be an ordeal, not to mention the risk of being surprised by their foes. However, to explore the upper mountain camps was necessary, and the early climbers needed to persuade their African companions to overcome their unwillingness. Huge fires would be built that hissed and spat under the dripping trees—fires large enough to roast an ox, New wrote, and in whose ghastly glare the surrounding undergrowth was transformed into "gaunt and goblin forms." But neither these, nor any amount of "jumping about and doing vigorous hand and arm exercises" could keep out the night cold. From the early hours New's Wachagga, and more especially the Wanika who accompanied him from the coast, had all but given up hope of seeing the dawn of another day. It was hard to stir them in the morning for anything but retreat, and by the second such night well-nigh impossible.

It is not easy from their writings to work out exactly which ways the different pioneers approached the mountain. Those who climbed from the territory of Chief Mareale, farther east, were presumably attempting a line more or less akin to what we now regard as the Marangu Route. This is the most popular of the seven routes available today, and in consequence is often referred to as the Coca-Cola Route. Those like Baron von der Decken and New, who climbed with Mangi Mandara's permission and with some of his men to

ROGER CHECKS HIS GPS POSITION NEAR MACHAME CAMP, AT 10,400 FEET. THE FOREST BEHIND HIM IS OBSCURED BY CLOUD THAT ONLY MERU PENETRATES.

guide them into the forest, must have tracked diagonally in a northeasterly direction from Moshi, as their descriptions talk of coming out of the rain forest onto a high plateau, or saddle, with Kibo away to their left and the jagged crest of Mawenzi on the right. It seems probable that they went far enough east to join the Marangu Route, though it's hard to see why they did not head directly uphill, for instance, where today's Mweka Route runs. Admittedly this is steep, too steep perhaps for elephants to have opened trails through it, or there may have been other practical or political reasons why it was not feasible at that time. Rebmann had wanted to launch his attempt from Machame, the line we were now attempting. Today, this is regarded as the most aesthetically pleasing approach and in consequence is known as the Whisky Route, the conoisseur's route, the finest distillation of Kilimanjaro's heady delights.

During the afternoon of our climb, the rain eased off, and an occasional shaft of sunlight penetrated the trees. There were more open patches here, probably as the result of earlier burning. Thickets of brambles grew in these glades and through them twined the sweetly scented climber *Begonia meyeri-johannis* with its delicate white and pink flowers. Butterflies danced in the sunshafts. We were now, I suppose, at an altitude of some 7,500 feet, about halfway through the forest. From here, the ground steepened and different types of trees began to appear with broad, glossy leaves. The tree ferns gave way to *Podocarpus* species, or yellowwood (another whose bark is recognized by Chagga and Masai to be good for stomachache), *Pittosporum*, and *Hagenia*. This must be where the upper tropical rain forest gives way to temperate mountain rain forest. It was difficult keeping track of trees that were so unfamiliar, and few of which have English names, even though all along Jacob had been doing his best to educate us. "This is the wild coffee," he would say, plucking a leaf and handing it to us in the vain hope that we would recognize it henceforward. "And this is a wild olive. Oh, look! And this is camphor; you won't see many large camphor trees any more." Unfortunately, he's right. East African camphorwood (*Ocotea usambarensis*) is one of the most valuable timbers found here, and it grows only where the soil is rich and moist but well drained. Its numbers were first decimated by a tremendous demand for quality timber in the Second World War, when it was mainly used for railway sleepers. One source says production rose from 5,000 cubic feet in 1941 to 583,000 cubic feet in 1942. Now, although it is illegal to fell these trees, they are poached regularly from the lower reaches of the forest for furniture making.

For much of this day, the national park's ecology officer walked with us, a young woman scientist who had trained at Aberdeen University in Scotland. Conservation comes high on her agenda, she assured us, and here one of the biggest problems faced is the illegal felling of trees by the locals—mostly for fuel. Once a tree is down, anyone can pick at it for firewood over a long period, claiming they are merely collecting deadwood. Of course, the people here need fuel and have traditionally

expect to see a belt of mountain bamboo toward the upper limit of trees. Here on Kili you don't, although such stands are well developed on nearby Meru. A small patch has been reported on the drier northern slopes by the British botanist John Grimshaw and others. Grimshaw can see that meteorologically and geologically the existing patch is occupying a site that is probably marginal for the species (*Yushania* or *Arundinaria alpina*). But it remains a mystery why this normally invasive species experiences apparent difficulty in getting established on wetter slopes of the forest.

By mid-afternoon my curiosity was beginning to wane as tiredness and the insidious dampness began to override all the more delightful sensations. Roger was keeping up the spirits of the children, feeding their curiosity with stories. In one place a massive tree had fallen and blocked the trail, its great roots tilted side-

MONDAY By the time we stopped for lunch, everyone looked as if we had been rolling in mud. A tarpaulin was rigged up to give the trekkers and crew some shelter as we tucked into pastries, samosas, cheese, salads, and fruit, which had been laid out appetizingly on a small table. But we felt uncomfortable to be so well cared for as our army of porters stood outside in the dripping forest, eyeing our feast while munching their modest rations. No one had brought tarpaulins or a special lunch for them.

taken it from the forest. They must resent the many foreigners tramping through their forest, bringing so little benefit to themselves, and resent, too, bureaucratic decrees about what they should and shouldn't do in their own backyard. This is the main reason why, increasingly, Tanzanian policy is to devolve responsibility for natural resources, woodlands, and wildlife to local groups. But local demand exceeds what it is sustainable to supply. Kilimanjaro has been designated a World Heritage Site; it is reasonable therefore to take it that the world beyond Kilimanjaro places a value on it and bears some responsibility to see it protected. Ideally, part of the income brought into the area by tourists should be directed toward supplying and subsidizing fuel for those who live in or on the fringes of the national park. Otherwise they have no option but to take wood from the forest.

In any other East African montane forest, you would

ways into the air. Where it had been was a deep hole, embedded in which was some charcoal.

"My goodness, Hansi, Nicole, look at this," he handed them each a piece of the charcoal. "Where did this come from?"

"From a fire, of course," Hansi replied.

"And how could you have a fire underneath a great tree?" Roger prodded.

Nicole thought a moment before venturing, "Was it before the tree was here?"

"That's it, you're right! And look at the size of the tree. How long do you think that took to grow? Hundreds of years, perhaps, but before that there were some people here, some hunters or a family, who built a fire to cook their dinner and to keep warm by. And after they'd gone, perhaps a long time after they'd gone, this tree grew up and lived its long, long life till it fell over. And here's the

CLIMBING OUT OF THE FOREST, WE PASS GIANT HEATHER
DRAPED IN OLD MAN'S BEARD, THE LICHEN *USNEA BARBATA*.

charcoal again underneath. So it's really, really old. What
do you think about that?" They were impressed, clearly.
And they stuck close to Roger during most of our walks,
not to miss any of his observations.

It had been a long day after a very short night. We'd
been faced with a lot of high stepping over fallen logs and
up steep, rocky inclines, which I'd found particularly
strenuous. I was ready to flop when thermoses of warm
sweet tea were sent down to us from our first camp,
which had been set up already ahead. That encouraged us
to press on up the last lap. One of the porters offered to
add my slopping daybag to his already impressive load.
We strode off with more purpose. The trees were definitely thinning out now and nothing like as high. Under
them, the ground was covered by thick, spongy mosses.
Runners of *Lycopodeum* (clubmoss) rampaged over
everything in its path and even clambered into the trees
where long trailing veils of gray lichen draped every twig.
This Old Man's Beard (*Usnea barbata*), which resembles
Spanish moss, is the orchilla weed, once commercially
valuable as a source for purple or deep red dye.

Quite suddenly, tall new herbs and shrubs bordered
the path, and there were many more flowers. Robert
Schauer grabbed my hand and scooted me along until, in
a short while, we had cleared the forest, emerging into
the evening light. The sky was clear of clouds and the
mountainside bathed in a golden glow. Ahead was
Machame Camp with our tents pitched under a grove of
tree heather and *Hagenia*. Soon I was sitting in the door-
way to my own tent, easing off my mud-encrusted boots,
gaiters, and overtrousers. Within minutes a bowl of warm
water arrived—at least we could wash off some of the mire.
One mess tent had been set up for the camera crew,
another for the "talent"—the seven trekkers appearing in
the film. And the porters had their shelters. It was a temporary village, which we'd pull up in the morning and
transfer to the next campsite. We fell upon our food rav-
enously, but did not linger afterward. Everyone was tired,
and we had another early start to make next morning.

As we switched on our headlamps and picked our way
back to our tents, tripping over the guylines of our
neighbors, the moon came up, and ahead of us, looking
impossibly distant, was the pale gleam of Kibo's cone,
ghostly against a navy-blue sky.

CHAPTER FIVE

SCRAMBLING

My map of Africa lies in Europe.

OTTO VON BISMARCK, GERMAN CHANCELLOR

WE WERE WOKEN

before sunrise with a cup of sweet tea. At least trekkers were allowed bed-tea to keep up their spirits. I doubt the camera crew was spoiled in the same way; but if this was unequal treatment, you'd hear no complaints from me. "Pack your bags before coming in to breakfast," we were told. It sounded easy enough, but what had come out of my duffel the night before, all neatly folded, seemed impossible to stuff back after a night's crumpling. Nor could I expel all the air from my Thermarest without a great deal of breathless jumping up and down on it in the small tent. No matter how I squeezed and squashed, struggling with different packing permutations, in the end I had to settle for two pieces of baggage instead of one. This wasn't going to make me popular with my porter. ∾ I was last into breakfast, as would become the pattern throughout the trip. Whenever we moved camp, although I got niftier at repacking, only rarely could I get from sleeping bag to scrambling outside the tent, kit assembled, in anything less than three-quarters of an hour. It was amazing how time slid away in those last cold minutes before the sun came up. ∾ Once we had eaten, we set out across the grassy shelf on which this camp lies and began climbing steeply

PRECEDING PAGES: HELICHRYSUMS, IN FRENCH *IMORTELLES*, SURVIVE THE HARSH SOLAR RADIATION OF THE ALPINE GRASSLANDS.

LEFT: JOSEPH THOMSON SET OUT IN 1883 TO RECONNOITER A SHORT ROUTE TO THE NORTHERN END OF LAKE VICTORIA.

through a bank of tree heather. It was easy to see from the blackened soil and tree trunks that this whole hillside had burned not so long ago, but fresh new growth was being pushed out. Under the small trees tufts of different grasses were growing with, among them, some astonishing splashes of color. The showiest blooms were the flame red spikes of a delicate gladiolus (*G. watsonioides*) and the red-hot pokers (*Kniphofia thomsonii*), sometimes scarlet, sometimes primrose, and often a spectrum of reds and yellows on the same spike. But these were isolated blooms: What were really conspicuous, and could be considered most typical of this

heathland region, were the mounds of everlastings, the helichrysums. They came in an almost endless variety of color—sun yellow, frosty white, deep rose, tawny brown. Their blooms, like double daisies, are dry, papery, and shiny and their leaves mainly silverish in color—adaptations to protect them against solar radiation. In the daytime, where up here even the rocks cook in the sun, and where we were being urged frequently by our African companions to protect our exposed skin as we could burn severely in no time at all, these helichrysums have come up with a means to reflect most of the incident radiation, and they flourish. So successful are

they, helichrysums of one sort or another can be found almost to the summit of the mountain.

Before long the giant heathers began thinning out. To me the word *heather* conjours images of low-growing ground cover on sea cliffs, mountains, or grouse moors, cover that in late summer flushes into misty purple bloom. It's true that in gardens we're accustomed to more varieties, some of which may grow to a few feet in height, but *Erica arborea*, the largest of the heath species found here, has been known to reach a preposterous 50 feet. Long slender trunks bear sparse crowns of feathery foliage stippling patterns against the sky. Leaves are tiny,

---

as are the heather's white flowers. The plants are highly mobile in wind and spectral in mist. A bushier variety, *Erica rossii* (formerly *Philippia excelsa*) is also abundant here, intermingling with gorse or broom-like shrubs, such as *Adenocarpus mannii*. I would have loved to spend more time exploring at this level, where a whole range of plants has been recorded, most of which I'd never seen nor would be likely to encounter anywhere again. There was an anemone I missed, and an orchid, a couple of swertias, and the gently arching, pendulous pink iris, *Dierama pendulum*, but my biggest regret was not having spotted the indigenous protea, *Protea kilimandscharica*, a stiff-leaved shrub with large creamy flowerheads. Proteas belonged to flower shops in my experience, to where they're flown in daily from South Africa. I'd never seen one in the wild.

As we reached the top of this first steep hill, the landscape opened out to reveal a series of lava ridges crisscrossing each other over the vast mountainside. We began following one of these dark lava ribs, which curved upward. Sometimes behind us, sometimes to one side, across a sea of cloud rose the perfectly shaped pyramid of Kili's sister peak, Meru. In the course of this climb we would see almost as much of Meru as we did of our own summit, and nearly always as an ethereal island afloat on this cloud that during the day swaddled the forest and plains below.

Before long we were thrilled to encounter our first giant groundsel, one of the iconic plants of tropical East African mountains. Three different giant groundsels are found on Kilimanjaro. These arborescent *Senecios* (or more properly *Dendrosenecios*) are closely related, and sorting them into species and subspecies has exercised botanists for decades. The one here could have been *Senecio kilimanjari*, which, textbooks say, "is largely confined to the ericaceous belt and lowermost part of the alpine belt in favourable localities"—and presumably found nowhere else at all. It certainly would be the right altitude for it. Even so, I think, it is more likely to have been *S. Cottonii*, by far the commonest and most widespread variety, which we'd be seeing frequently from now on. It was a battered specimen, its trunk stripped and blackened by fire, a trauma which it had nonetheless survived. You would have thought we'd discovered a new species ourselves the way we danced around it, patted it, took its portrait, and took our portraits standing proudly beside it. This was one of the things we had come to see. We might get blasé later when we met them in greater numbers, but for the moment we were stirred. It is the weirdest looking plant, prehistoric and gaunt. The fat cylindrical trunk forks into two after several feet of growth, each branch then forking again some distance higher. Lax rosettes of cabbagy leaves crown the branches, and these leaves, we could see, were shiny above and felted below with a thick white down. They do not drop off when they die, but form a thick, insulating mantle around trunk and branches, which in normal circumstances clings to the plant throughout its long life. This particular senecio, whose dry leaves had been burned away, was left particularly vulnerable to radiation and temperature change.

There was a steep bluff to climb before lunch, in reality the blocky edge to one of the lava flows. This section was being filmed by two IMAX cameras perched in exposed positions on the cliff top. A series of shots was taken before we were allowed, finally, to clamber over the rocky crest to a picnic spot with spectacular views. A tent had been set up and food laid out inside. With no great rush and plenty of large boulders supplying seats and a little shade, we allowed ourselves a leisurely lounge in the sunshine. Afterward, we retraced our steps down the cliff so that the film crew could get one last take of us clambering over it before we set out along an undulating traverse up another escarpment.

The scenery was subtly changing. We still had all the marvelous helichrysums—if anything, more than ever— and all sorts of lowly senecios and daisies and pungent little herbs. But as the afternoon wore on we began to see our first giant lobelias and these caused as much excitement as the arborescent senecios. At first we found them tucked into the rockwall on small ledges, two or three together, but as we climbed higher up the Machame escarpment they became more frequent, with some conveniently positioned alongside the track for us to investigate. This was where the film breaks were ideal—I treasured them.

We pulled up the last steep stretch into Shira Camp at around 5 o'clock, a little breathless but not too tired. After another hearty meal, we turned in early with the prospect of a wonderfully long night ahead. Tomorrow was designated as an acclimatization day to get us used to being at almost 12,500 feet. What bliss the thought of not having to get up before dawn and move on.

In 1871, missionary New made a collection of plants from this moorland region on Kilimanjaro, which was forwarded on his behalf to Dr. Hooker at Kew. The Herbarium was delighted to receive its first specimens from the "previously unknown Alpine zone of Africa," and cataloged them eagerly. Two new species were named for the explorer: *Conyza newii*, a shrubby plant in the daisy family with yellow tansy-like flowers, which New probably found close to the forest edge, and *Helichrysum newii*, a silver-white everlasting, one of those plants New describes in his book as having "frosty-looking leaves and exceedingly pretty flowers." This, it would turn out, is the hardiest plant to grow on the mountain; stunted specimens have been collected at 18,900 feet near one of the fumaroles in the crater. Here at Shira, where conditions are testing but not abominable, we can see it's an exceedingly pretty plant. I was glad there was some memorial to New on the mountain, for there is no glacier or point named after him as there are for other early climbers. We can't even know exactly how high he went without knowing where the snow level was in those days. One supposes it to have been around 14,500 feet.

Back in England after his trip, New was faced with having to clear his name following his aborted endeavor to locate Doctor Livingstone. Coming hard on the heels of eight grueling years in the mission field and his expedition to Kilimanjaro, it's easy to picture him utterly exhausted in body and spirit and taking solace in preparing his book. *Life Wanderings and Labours in Eastern Africa* made its appearance the following year, 1873, and quickly ran into a second edition. It was a stirring tale of exploration and endeavor, although its popularity owed much to its serendipitous timing. New included a report on the horrors and "frightful magnitude" of East African slavery, which coincided with Livingstone's graphic dispatches from central Africa brought home by Stanley. Emphasis was given to both testaments by the dramatic news of Livingstone's death in Ilala at the beginning of May 1874. He had succumbed at last to fever, dysentery, and the rigors of African travel.

The endemic brutality of slave trading was beyond question, but it was so profitable that it had proved hard to eradicate. Until the Atlantic slave trade was outlawed by Britain and America in the first decade of the 19th century, West Africa had been the main source for this iniquitous cargo. The East African trade, based on the Indian Ocean, had existed in some measure in ancient times, but really only developed significantly in the first half of the 18th century, reaching its terrible peak in the 1860s and 1870s when as many as 70,000 men, women, and children were being sold annually through Zanzibar. For half a century British diplomats and others made unsuccessful efforts to stifle the trade, even running a blockade off Zanzibar. When Livingstone's account reached Britain of the massacre he'd witnessed at Nyangwe, when hundreds of Africans were slaughtered by Swahili merchants, it was seized upon by the abolitionist lobby and used to goad Gladstone's government into speedy action. The banning of African slave dealing, whether for domestic use or for export, finally began

New's speculation that the slopes of Kilimanjaro offered potential for colonial development, being possessed of that rare commodity in Africa, a "delicious climate suitable for Europeans," was a matter of great moment.

New's writings give the impression of a man of impulse, easily swayed by his emotions—as when he spontaneously volunteered as a missionary after the railway accident. By setting off for Africa following his brother's death there, he cannot be said to have gone into the business with his eyes shut; he certainly didn't lack courage. He'd nurtured his dream of climbing Kilimanjaro for eight years; constancy, then, was another of his attributes. And in Chagga, he'd demonstrated boldness in leaping to the side of Mandara with his gun loaded. If sometimes New betrays himself as opinionated and self-righteous, with too great a sense

> **TUESDAY** Today we are to climb to the Shira Plateau at almost 12,600 feet, a rise of more than two and a half thousand feet from here. It doesn't sound too daunting since yesterday we gained almost four thousand. And it's a glorious morning, crisp and sunny, with the porters singing as they break camp and assemble their heavy loads. Looking up toward the bright summit, the tree heather foliage and blond tussocky grasses are beautifully backlit in the low early light.

to take hold with the closure of the slave market in Zanzibar on June 5, 1873. New's book, appearing as it did within weeks of this momentous event, therefore had great topicality. Equally, all the publicity surrounding the opening of central Africa and the search for the source of the Nile had served to stimulate a growing appetite for news of discovery and developments. Momentous changes now faced the continent.

Livingstone had written that the liberation of Africa depended on the "three Cs": commerce, Christianity, and civilization. His words proved a clarion call to speculators and missionaries alike, who began surging inland along the established trade routes. At the time of Livingstone's death, the diamond rush was well under way in southern Africa, and various parts of the African continent had already fallen to European imperialists, but the mid-1870s are usually deemed the start of what has become known as the Scramble for Africa. Thus,

of his own importance and a tendency toward intrigue, at the same time we see a man, nervy, transparent when it comes to emotions, and easily crushed. Stanley easily outwitted him over the Livingstone rescue business—and New could not conceal his hurt over Stanley's accusation that he'd abandoned the quest, nor his subsequent jubilation at being exonerated by the Royal Geographical Society. What New fails to mention, strangely, is that the RGS presented him with a gold watch in honor of his efforts on Kilimanjaro.

Ah, Kilimanjaro! It's easy to see from the ten years of his African labors, it was his Kilimanjaro adventure that he'd found most thrilling and gave him the greatest sense of identity. With warmth he remembered loyal Tofiki and wished they could be back on the mountain.

FOLLOWING PAGES: PORTERS CARRY LOADS FROM SHIRA CAMP INTO THE VALLEY OF THE GREAT BARRANCO.

Buoyed up by these memories and his new-found literary acclaim, in May of the following year, 1874, Charles New returned to East Africa, bound once more for Chagga. He wanted another crack at Kilimanjaro.

WHAT EFFECT the closure of the Zanzibar slave market had made on Mandara and his fortunes does not seem to have entered New's mind. Slave raiding had dominated the monarch's whole life. Going on the offensive—or at very least putting up a strong defense—offered a chiefdom the only possible escape from bloodshed and pillage. When Mandara first came to power around 1860, he strengthened his army by hiring

the slave trade an important source of wealth and security for Mandara. Before long, a small Swahili settlement grew up within his capital, by which time he was at war with practically every other clan.

Mandara was open to the idea of more contact with the outside world. He'd made a point of learning Swahili and he employed Arab and Swahili secretaries in order to be able to exchange letters with dignitaries on the coast. He was in contact with Sir John Kirk, British Consul General in Zanzibar, and with the Sultan; later he even wrote to "Queeny" of England. He was hungry to learn and frustrated by his failure to induce any of his European visitors to stay on as teachers. Their obses-

> **TUESDAY** Maybe it had been a bit tiresome hanging about in the wet jungle, but here in the sunshine with so much to look at, the children provided a delightful opportunity for a breather and a chat. They were great stimulators of conversation, keeping themselves going all day by telling each other stories and begging everyone else to tell them, too. One stop stays in my mind. We were sitting among the crisp everlastings while a shot was prepared when Nicole's father, Rick, told how years ago, on safari in the Ngorongoro Crater, his group's tents were pitched under an enormous fig tree. This had been a popular site for a camp over many years. But on this particular afternoon a sudden storm with heavy rain drenched the tree, weighing down its dense foliage. Then a wind blew up and, in one gust, the giant tree fell without warning. Rick had been running toward it for shelter. One girl in their party was already in camp, and she was crushed to death in her tent. In the silence that followed the telling of this terrible story, Rick was not alone in brushing away a tear.

Masai and Arush warriors from the plains to assist in storming the fortresses of enemy chieftains. Yet he had little hope of success against the most powerful chief in the district, Sina of Kibosho. Recognizing this, Mandara resorted to political intrigue, striking up alliances with other clans, with a view to isolating Sina, and taking as wives the daughters of neighboring royal houses. His major coup was to forge a bond with the Swahili merchant-adventurers who were responsible for most of the slave-raiding havoc. They offered him military backup in return for the captives taken in battle and the ivory looted from the huts of his enemies. Thus, Moshi had become an important base in the slave trade, and

sion with the great domed mountain mystified him. Mandara's own weakness for the acquisition of fine goods—fabrics, metal, tools, trinkets, arms, and instruments—which in time became insatiable, dominated his dealings with anyone who made it as far as Moshi. "Rapacious and greedy" are the words most frequently used to describe him in all the old travelers' accounts.

When New arrived in Mandara's realm for the second time, he expected to be welcomed on the same footing as before. He had convinced himself that he had the measure (and thus the upper hand) of the mangi in all his moods, and he never gave a thought to how political events may have changed things. From the start Mandara let it be known that he was disgusted at the paltry gifts New had brought with him and then proceeded to fleece New of almost everything he owned, including his silver aneroid and the precious gold chronometer presented to him by the Royal Geographical Society. There were no concessions and never any possibility of the Englishman being given leave to attempt Kilimanjaro again. "Broken-hearted, and sick with anxiety and fatigue" (as we are told by one of the next incomers to the region, H. H. Johnston), New "turned his steps toward the coast, and died ere he reached Mombasa."

From Harry Johnston's conversations with Mandara, it was clear that New had unwittingly contributed to his fate. By inveighing against slavery at every opportunity, and with such Wesleyan fervor, New led Mandara to the conviction that the missionary was openly inciting his serfs and subjects to rebel against him.

AT THE TIME of his death, Charles New had just turned 35. He was the only European to have visited Kilimanjaro throughout the 1870s, as Baron von der Decken had been in the 1860s. But the 1880s proved a different story. In the spring of 1883, two separate exploratory missions set off for Kilimanjaro and the interior. First away was a German outfit under Gustave Fischer, who prophetically observed that the Kilimanjaro region "seemed well adapted to European settlement." Hard on his heels came a young Scottish geologist, Joseph Thomson, only 25 years old but with two expeditions to Africa already under his belt. This time, he was being financed by the Royal Geographical Society to investigate a shorter route to the northern end of Lake Victoria Nyanza by crossing Masai country. He left Rabai on March 13 and followed the known route to Mandara's kingdom. Possessed of more native diplomacy than New, he managed to strike the right note with the wily monarch. Even so, he found himself parting with rather more than he intended: Mandara was equipped with the tweed suit, boots, and double-barreled gun of a country gentleman. At the same time, Thomson was able to trade a battery for the gold watch extorted from Charles New almost a decade before. On Kilimanjaro, Thomson climbed in the forest to a height of about 8,850 feet, making a small collection of plants before passing around to the north side of the mountain and across Masai land toward Mount Kenya and, from there, to Lake Victoria. The German, Fischer, came no closer to the mountain than 30 miles, but he

passed Meru and was able to introduce the world to a new bird of the region, *Touracus hartlaubi.*

Sir John Kirk, a keen botanist, had long been urging Kew to investigate the flora and fauna of Kilimanjaro with a view to ascertaining their relationship with that of other African highland regions. He probably pressed the RGS similarly, because that society had hoped Thomson could undertake a study along these lines. However, even during the planning stages of that expedition it was clear that things were becoming overambitious. A Kilima-njaro Committee was thus set up to organize a separate venture for the purpose in the year following. Financial backing was promised from the Royal Geographical Society and the British Association for the Advancement of Science, and this is where Harry Johnston enters the picture. A colorful 26-year-old, whom history has recorded as "bumptious," "unmistakably middle-class," and possessed of "an ebullient, aggrandizing nature," he was recommended for leadership of the Kilimanjaro Expedition by the Zoological Society of London. Johnston was a multitalented individual with a sponge-like capacity for absorbing facts and a facile pen. A trained artist of considerable skill (he'd exhibited at the Royal Academy), he was also a keen amateur naturalist and interested in ethnology and language. If that were not enough, he had a nose for world affairs, and was lively, witty, and outgoing in temperament.

From childhood, Johnston had longed to be famous, and he instinctively knew the best way to go about it. Before he was 20 he'd traveled in Tunisia, then went on to explore in Angola and the Congo, where he met and struck up a friendship with Stanley. On his return, he wrote the first of his 40 books, *The River Congo,* and was invited to give "a full-dress evening lecture" at the Royal Geographical Society. There he shared the platform with Viscount Ferdinand de Lesseps, builder of the Suez Canal, who was heard to remark, "What a country, where even little children are explorers!"—a reference, not just to Johnston's youth and precocity, but also to his baby-faced appearance and diminutive stature.

Johnston was allocated £1,000 to meet the expenses of his Kilimanjaro trip. Unfortunately, it wasn't enough to allow him to take along any seasoned European collectors and, although the Calcutta Botanical Gardens offered to send two assistants at their expense, no Indian collectors could be induced to join an expedition to the African interior. Kirk secured instead the services of two men who had traveled with Dr. Fischer—but no sooner was the mountain reached than these rogues defected to a neighboring chief—to organize his slave-trading caravans, Johnston was convinced. From this, we gather that, despite the closure of the Zanzibar market and other slave markets under the control of the Zanzibari sultan, the business was far from stamped out. Paradoxically, the suffocation of the export trade at the coast led to greater brutality inland where slaves were still rounded up for domestic use, or as hostages to be used in exchange for ivory, or to carry the ivory to the coast. This continued throughout most of the century, to the extent that the final quarter of the 19th century is looked upon as the bloodiest of all. Stanley said of eastern Congo in 1889 that "Slave-raiding becomes innocence when compared to ivory raid-ing." A freed slave who eventu-ally became an Anglican priest remembered that "in those days all over Africa there was terrible trouble for all black men; war everywhere and raid-ing, and no peace at all." To give some sense of scale to these events, it has been worked out from trading and auction records that, by 1880, 60,000 to 70,000 elephants a year were killed in East Africa, generally taken by gangs of black hunters armed by Arab traders. A lot of slaves would be needed to transport 140,000 elephant tusks.

Johnston's instructions were to spend six months in the vicinity of Kilimanjaro, collecting as many animal and plant specimens as possible, particularly from near the snow line. First, he passed a month in Zanzibar as Kirk's guest. He secured his first sight of Kilimanjaro from 40 miles away, after a restless night around a fire: "Kibo and Kimawenzi and the parent mass of mountain rose high above a level line of cloud." Seen thus, as if it were severed from the Earth, Kilimanjaro put Johnston in mind of the suspended island in Gulliver's Travels, Laputa. "Kilima-njaro," he wrote, "was weird in the early flush of dawn, with its snowy crater faintly pink against a sky of deep blue-grey, wherein the pale and faded moon was sinking, and the stars were just dis-cernible, but as the stronger light of perfect day pre-vailed, and the clouds which concealed the base of the mountain disappeared, its appearance was disappoint-ing." The ethereal quality was lost in the harsh light, leaving Johnston with the uncomfortable impression of a "cheap Italian water-color drawing of Vesuvius."

Disappointment didn't curb his descriptive powers; they remained as exuberant as the "herbage." He tells us he plunges through "umbrageous" trees, "rampant" euphorbias, and various vicious acacias with thorns like grappling hooks. "Other plants of the lily tribe (debased and wicked members of a beautiful family) grew like swords stuck in the ground point upwards, and woe betide any careless person who put his hand on the apex of their rigid, blade-like leaves—their rapier points would pierce his palm as readily as a sword of steel."

Throughout his lively narra-tive, Johnston is sparing with dates, but he reaches Moshi, we gather, in early June and pres-ents to Mandara his letter of introduction from Sir John Kirk. The two men hit it off well enough, though Johnston is not to be hoodwinked and refers to Mandara as "our variable friend." Among the benefac-tors he later acknowledges in his book, Johnston writes, "...and with all his faults, Mandara, Chief of Mosi; who, though he once threatened to cut off my head, neverthe-less in his brighter moods supplied me with valuable information." Kirk had been under the misapprehen-sion that Mandara was the paramount chief on Kiliman-jaro—an image carefully nurtured by Mandara himself—but Johnston soon learns differently:

I had formed an exaggerated estimate of his power for good and evil, and fancied that the fate of my expedi-tion lay in his sable hands. Nor was I alone in this impression, for the men of my caravan held Mandara in excessive awe and dread, and the rabble of Rabai, who were already grovelling before him, would have cut my throat cheerfully if that had been pleasing to the great chieftain, in whose power they were....

At first glance, Mandara appeared to Johnston as a grand old dame. "The full, rounded, beardless face, the somewhat graceful column-like neck, and full bosom, with above all the head-dress—a red handkerchief, worn as women wear it in Zanzibar—and the sweeping folds of the long faded cloth wound loosely round his body, gave one the impression of a superb virago rather than of an African chief in the prime of life." This towering sibyl of five feet ten inches, Johnston continues, plunged his spear in the ground with an emphasis that sent the blade quivering, fixed him a very sharp look out of his serviceable eye, then affected to ignore him. At length, curiosity got the better of the chief, who began plying Johnston with questions, rarely waiting for an answer in his impatience:

"What is the braid on your coat made of?" "Silver?" "Is silver the same as that white stuff on the top of Kilimanjaro?" "And have you come all this way from Ulaya (Europe) to gather the glittering thing that makes Kibo shine in the sun?" "Why is your sultan called Queeny?" "The Arabs tell me Queeny is a woman; is that true?" "Did Queeny send you here?"

Eventually Johnston strikes a deal to purchase a patch of land on the slopes of Kilimanjaro, about two miles to the northeast of Moshi, where he sets up a permanent settlement, his "central collecting station." More than 20 huts are built on the plot, plus his own "spacious residence," comprising kitchen, cow-stable, and fowl-house. The soil is tilled, seeds sown, and the whole surrounded by a sturdy palisade or boma. So fertile is the volcanic earth and so benign the climate that within a week, Johnston boasts, he is eating his first home-grown salad. This delightful spot, perched on a spur at just under 5,000 feet,

LEFT: HARRY JOHNSTON BROUGHT HOME HUNDREDS OF NEW OR RARE SPECIMENS AND MADE A SPIRITED CLIMBING ATTEMPT IN 1884. ABOVE: MASAI WARRIORS WERE ILLUSTRATED BY JOSEPH THOMSON IN HIS *THROUGH MASAILAND*, 1887.

ALTITUDE PHYSIOLOGY
AND ACUTE MOUNTAIN SICKNESS

JAMES S. MILLEDGE

RESPIRATORY PHYSICIAN, MEMBER OF THE "SILVER HUT" EXPEDITION IN THE EVEREST REGION

KILIMANJARO. By the normal route, it is not a difficult mountain, yet many fail to reach the summit. The most common reasons for failure are lack of altitude acclimatization and mountain sickness.

ACCLIMATIZATION

Altitude acclimatization is a series of physiological changes that enable the body to adapt to reduced availability of oxygen at high altitude. The barometric pressure at the summit of Kilimanjaro is half that at sea level and so is the partial pressure of oxygen. Oxygen is, of course, a vital fuel for all animal life, and the amazing thing is that we can adapt as well as we do to the supply pressure being halved. Imagine running a 12-volt motor on a 6-volt battery!

However, acclimatization does take time. How long depends upon the altitude we are talking about and the individual. The process is rapid over the first few days but continues for weeks. There are aspects of the acclimatization that are still unknown, but the most important change that we do know about is the increase in breathing that takes place over the first few days at altitude. This occurs because of changes in the control of breathing—without thinking about it, we breathe deeper and faster at rest, during exercise, and while asleep. This raises the oxygen level in the lungs and blood, counteracting the lower pressure in the air breathed. The best known effect of altitude acclimatization (though not the most important) is the increase in the concentration of red blood cells, which enables the blood to carry more oxygen. This increase starts by a reduction in plasma volume in the first few days after arrival at altitude. Later, over weeks and months, there is an increase in the mass of red cells due to increased production from the bone marrow stimulated by the hormone erythropoietin. The result of these and other changes is that, after a week or two, a person functions much better than on first arrival at altitude. He climbs faster and with less fatigue, his appetite improves, and he feels more normal. The risk of mountain sickness recedes as acclimatization takes place.

ACUTE MOUNTAIN SICKNESS

Acute mountain sickness (AMS) is a condition affecting previously healthy individuals who ascend rapidly to high altitude. There is a delay of a few hours to two days before symptoms develop. The symptoms are headache (usually frontal), nausea, vomiting, irritability, malaise, insomnia, and poor climbing performance. In simple AMS the condition is self-limiting, lasting three to five days. After this time it does not recur at that altitude, though it may do so if the person goes higher. In a small proportion of individuals there may be progression to the malignant forms of AMS, that is, high-altitude pulmonary edema (HAPE) or cerebral edema (HACE) or a mixed form of these two. If not treated, these conditions are frequently fatal in a matter of hours.

In the old days, mountaineers gained altitude gradually with long approach marches, and thus largely avoided altitude problems. Now it is possible to fly and drive to considerable altitude in a few hours. This is certainly true of East Africa. Therefore, AMS is much more common nowadays and is common on Mounts Kenya and Kilimanjaro. Anyone can get AMS; there is great individual variation in susceptibility, which does not depend upon age, gender, or even fitness. The important thing is to recognize and to admit to symptoms when they occur.

Prevention is better than cure, and is achieved by a slow enough ascent to avoid AMS. A rule of thumb is, "Above 3,000 m, each night should be spent not more than 300 m higher than the previous night." However, though many can manage a faster ascent, even this modest rate will be too fast for the susceptible individual. Therefore we must add the rule, "If there are symptoms of AMS, go no higher. If they persist, go down." Enough fluid to avoid dehydration should be taken (keep the urine flowing).

There are drugs that have been shown to reduce AMS. Their use is an individual matter. Natural acclimatization is best, but circumstances may make this impossible. The best researched drug is acetazolamide (Diamox®). It works by increasing the breathing, thus giving a sort of artificial acclimatization. It does not mask the symptoms of AMS and, having been used for many years for glaucoma, seems to be very safe. However, most people taking it have the side effect of tingling in the fingers and toes and a few complain of stomach upset. Some find these side effects intolerable. It's a good idea to try the drug at sea level. Previously, a dose of one tablet (250 mg) two or three times a day was used but most now recommend half that dosage as being adequate to relieve, if not abolish, symptoms, with fewer side effects.

HIGH-ALTITUDE CEREBRAL AND PULMONARY EDEMA

Although simple AMS is only a short, rather miserable experience, a few unfortunate people go on to get a much more serious illness, with increased fluid in the brain, lungs, or both. High-altitude cerebral edema (HACE) seems to be a further development of simple AMS. The symptoms are the same, but there are added signs of brain disfunction. The first of these is often unsteadiness (ataxia) on walking, progressing to difficulty in sitting up straight and steady. There may be other signs such as paralysis of certain eye muscles, then mood changes, irrational behavior, hallucinations, coma, and eventually death in a few hours or days if untreated. High-altitude pulmonary edema (HAPE) is due to fluid leaking into the air spaces in the lungs. The patient first becomes more short of breath than is normal for that altitude. He lags behind his climbing companions and is very fatigued. Then a cough develops, dry at first, later becoming productive of frothy white sputum that becomes blood-tinged as the condition develops. With a stethoscope, crackles can be heard in the bases

AT ARROW CAMP I FOUND A PLAQUE COMMEMORATING A YOUNG AMERICAN CLIMBER WHO SUCCUMBED TO ALTITUDE SICKNESS THERE IN THE 1970S.

of the lungs and, later, bubbly breathing can be heard by the unaided ear as the patient literally drowns in his own lung fluid.

Prevention of HACE and HAPE is the same as that for AMS: Ascend slowly and come down if symptoms persist. HAPE particularly seems to have an individual susceptibility, and a history of a previous HAPE makes subsequent attacks very likely upon going to altitude.

Treatment starts with recognition of the condition and prompt action if there is suspicion of the diagnosis. The most important action is to GET THE PATIENT DOWN. A reduction in altitude of even as little as 300 m often results in significant improvement. If evacuation is impossible or delayed, the following can be used:

1. Oxygen can be given with benefit, but it is seldom available
2. Drugs for HACE: dexamethasone, a steroid, has been shown to be beneficial in relieving the brain edema; 4–8 mg is recommended. For HAPE: nifedipine, 20 mg, should be given.
3. Portable, blow-up, one-man pressure bags are available that allow a patient to be pressurized to 2 psi. This, in effect, brings the patient down in altitude by almost 2,000 m. Treatment is usually for about one hour and is effective, but unless the patient is then brought down, the good effect does not last.

CONCLUSION

The altitude of Kilimanjaro, though not great by Himalayan standards, is serious, especially compared with the European Alps and North America (south of the 49th parallel). Due to the ease of access, most people plan to climb it in too short a time to allow for adequate acclimatization. Hence the incidence of AMS is high. The golden rules for avoiding AMS are:

1. Ascend slowly.
2. If symptoms of AMS are felt, go no higher.
3. If symptoms persist, go down.

and looking out across the plain to the perfect pyramid of Meru, is known locally as Kitimbiriu. It is Johnston's "African Switzerland," and for several months he lives there with a number of the men he's brought from Zanzibar. Mandara surely believed he'd managed at last to entice a European to stay and become his mentor.

The first weeks in his paradise garden pass idyllically, Johnston dividing his time between collecting, painting, hoeing his crops, and gathering as much information as he can on the life and language of his neighbors. He would describe this as the most enjoyable period he ever spent in Africa. Thus settled, he sends back to Taita for more supplies, and gets his first inkling that Mandara is not kingpin of all Kilimanjaro. To be a friend of Mandara made you the foe of almost every other potentate on the mountain. Johnston's returning caravan is hotly pursued into camp by angry warriors, who soon engage in a bloody battle with Mandara's men. With presence of mind Johnston speedily erects a rough platform on the battleground from which that evening he reveals his secret weapon: "I blazed out on the astonished natives with Bengal lights, red fire, Roman candles, serpent squibs, and lastly, a magnificent flight of rockets." As the first rocket rose with a shrieking rush and a flaming shower then broke into a mass of stars, "friends and foes alike fled in dismay," he tells us, "and we found ourselves alone on the field, whence we journeyed peacefully home by the light of a late rising moon."

IN TIME, the explorer is given permission by Mandara to climb as high as he chooses on Kilimanjaro, even to the white "salt" covering the top. Guides are procured for a price of four yards of cloth each, but the attempt founders when, at a height of little more than 9,000 feet, Johnston's party is alarmed to see a force of Kibosho warriors approaching at full trot. Luckily the sight of the theodolite halts the aggressors, who retire in the belief that it must be some new weapon or instrument of sorcery, but none of Johnston's men can be persuaded to continue farther across hostile country.

Johnston decides his only hope, so far as Kilimanjaro is concerned, is to quit Mandara's territory, which is clearly blockaded by his enemies and in any case does not appear to extend beyond a height of about 6,000 feet. He would do better, he reckons, to approach the mountain's slopes through the state of Marangu, and accordingly dispatches an emissary to Chief Mareale, seeking his permission.

Mareale, Johnston soon discovers, is every bit as avaricious as Mandara, perhaps more so, but the explorer at last receives grudging sanction to head off up the mountain. At 10,000 feet, in the moorland region, Johnston camps a week collecting specimens, assisted—to his surprise and delight—by his former enemies the Kibosho. Now he is under Mareale's protection; they can be firm friends. On October 16, he launches his grand attempt.

By afternoon he is on the Saddle at 15,150 feet, though mist prevents any comprehensive views. Mawenzi rises impressively "with its jagged peaks and smooth glissades of golden sand"; Kibo remains obstinately hidden in piled cloud and Johnston finds it impossible to tell how close he is to the snowcap. And then, fleetingly, the clouds part to reveal "a blaze of snow so blinding white under the brief flicker of sunlight that I could see little detail":

But before I could get out my sketch-book and sharpen my chalk-pencil the clouds had once more hidden everything, indeed had enclosed me in a kind of London fog, very depressing in character, for the decrease in light was rather alarming to one who felt himself alone and cut off at a point nearly as high as the summit of Mont Blanc.

With what he describes as "stupid persistency," Johnston struggles on toward the site of his vision, all the while hoping to burst through the clouds and find himself "gazing down into the crater of Kilimanjaro from its snowy rim." But it is not to be. Snow appears under his feet, but almost at once he is overwhelmed by what he supposes to be mountain sickness. Some people might laugh at the puny difficulties Kilima-njaro presents, he afterward tells the Royal Geographical Society,

...a mountain that can be climbed without even the aid of a walking-stick, and where the most serious obstacles arise from mist and cold which would scarcely deter a cockney from ascending Snowdon. But the feeling that overcame me when I sat and gasped for breath on the wet and slippery rocks at this great height was one of overwhelming isolation. I felt as if I should nevermore regain the force to move, and must remain and die amid this horrid solitude of stones and snow.

A sip of brandy and water from his flask restores a modicum of courage. By boiling his thermometer, he ascertains he has reached a height of 16,315 feet. But it is almost half past four and he is soaked from the mist and chilled. With the thought that he can try again the next day, he hastens down to where, at lunchtime, he'd left his three companions in an improvised shelter. They have disappeared. Johnston stumbles on until, finally, he regains his 10,000-foot encampment by moonlight, where his men are sitting around glimmering watchfires. They take him for his own ghost as he steps through the palisade.

Johnston tells us he made one further and futile attempt to climb Kibo before retreating. By now his provisions were finished, and his time almost up. The decision to turn for home is taken reluctantly, but at least he will explore a new route on the way back. After a rest, he heads out through the forests of Kimawenzi to Lake Jipe and on to Gonja—and thence back to the coast.

He'd dreamed of conquest, and in that he was disap-

eign Office extolling the country and its climate and recommending it for colonization by English settlers. By that time, of course, he'd procured his own stretch of land in Moshi. In addition, a few months later, he negotiated absolute rights over six square miles of forest near Taveta. It cost him "300 yards of assorted cloth and thirty-five pounds of beads." Here, too, he had buildings constructed and began cultivation. He was staking a claim in the colony he so ardently advocated.

Until then the British government had dragged its feet over further investment in Africa, but events were changing fast. Increased industrialization in Europe was intensifying competition for raw materials and cheap labor, and all the major powers were seeking profitable and exclusive sources of both. It had not gone unnoticed in Whitehall that German explorers were sniffing around Kilimanjaro. Johnston's letter to Fitz-

> **WEDNESDAY** I'm sitting on the Shira plateau looking out of the door of my tent at Meru, rising from a sea of cloud. The sky is a pale, clear blue. We had a bit of a sleep in this morning, but we've breakfasted now. It's 9 o'clock and the camera team is out working. I feel a bit stiff, and walking makes me very breathless, so I'm enjoying the view—and calling it research!

pointed. Nonetheless, he claimed to have added 1,000 or maybe 2,000 feet to New's record. Later climbers were skeptical that he'd been anything like as high as he said, or even higher than New, but his collecting had been a great success. He brought home masses of botanical, zoological, and other information, and all his specimens arrived intact. The Herbarium at Kew was enriched by nearly 600 species of new or rare plants. His plentiful animal collection included six new species of birds, a new colobus monkey, butterflies, beetles, a river crab, and a hitherto unknown worm.

Ultimately, perhaps the most historically significant consequence of Johnston's Kilimanjaro expedition was political. He liked to imply afterward that he'd been a secret agent for the British government in Chagga—and well he may have been. The young explorer had come to the notice of the Foreign Office. From Moshi, he wrote a long letter to Lord Edmond Fitzmaurice of the For-

maurice hammered the point home. Within a few years, he declared, the area around Kilimanjaro must be either English, French, or German. "I am on the spot, the first in the field, and able to make Kilimanjaro as completely English as Ceylon." The cost of doing so, he promised, would not exceed £5,000. Invite a certain number of chosen colonists to occupy the beautiful sites allotted to them, he advised. They'd find they could cultivate vines, coffee, sugar, rice, wheat—and indeed "every vegetable production of the tropical and temperate zones."

By the autumn of 1884 the Foreign Office was convinced of the need to act swiftly to forestall a foreign power—in the words of historian Thomas Pakenham—"from grabbing this juicy plum below the snows of Kilimanjaro. It was now or never." If the region fell to the Germans, Zanzibar's monopoly of the caravan trade would be broken, and with it would go Britain's presence and influence in the area. Were the French to gain

Kilimanjaro, the prospects for British enterprise could be even worse. Sir John Kirk did not share the FO's desire to make Kilimanjaro a British protectorate, served by a port on the mainland; he was strongly against action that could weaken the authority of the sultan—something he'd been long cultivating. His solution would have been to bring Kilimanjaro into the sultan's empire, but that British Prime Minister Gladstone refused to countenance. In fact, Gladstone could see no rational or urgent reason for doing anything about that "mountain country behind Zanzibar with the unrememberable name." And thus the moment passed.

Even before Johnston made his last climbing attempt on Kilimanjaro, the fervent German empire-builder Carl Peters had come on a hush-hush mission to secure territories in East Africa. Peters deplored the way the newly united Germany had fallen behind in "the partition of the World" and sought to provoke his government into expansion by direct action. He's been described as an "adventurer, thruster, dreamer, orator, liar and imperialist," though Africans came to know him as Mkono wa damu, the man with the bloodstained hands. Having founded the "Society for German Colonisation," he and three friends landed in Zanzibar on November 4, 1884, disguised as mechanics. They kept out of Kirk's way and quickly crossed to the mainland, heading west into Usagara and signing fraudulant "treaties" with chiefs as they went. These offered Peters, as the representative of his society, all that chief's "territory with all its civil appurtenances...for the exclusive and universal utilization for German colonization." It is highly doubtful that the chiefs understood the implications of these contracts that were written in German and amounted to surrender of their authority and land, but they were induced to put their marks upon them. Once in possession of a dozen such documents, Peters hastened home to Berlin where the Imperial Chancellor, Bismarck, was prompt to assert their validity. He made them the basis of a new German protectorate, the administration of which was to be entrusted to Peters's society.

There was a flurry of international consternation, although nobody thought to tell the Sultan of Zanzibar that he had lost territories he believed to be under his control. When he woke up to what was happening, and to forestall further annexations, Sultan Bargash dispatched parties of armed men up the coast to Witu, and northwest to Kilimanjaro. At Moshi on May 30, 25

chiefs from the mountain and its surroundings, and including Mandara and Mareale, pledged their allegiance to Zanzibar by signing what has become known as the "Declaration of the Sultans of Chagga and Kilimanjaro." Within three weeks one of Peters's henchmen, Carl Jühlke, was in Chagga waving fresh treaties at the bewildered chiefs. Mandara is said to have declared, "The Sultan of Zanzibar wants my country, the Germans want my country, the British want my country. Whoever wants my country must pay for it," whereupon Mandara concluded a further deal with Jühlke.

Peters, still in Germany, was delighted in July to learn that his delegates had extended his frontiers by several hundred miles. By August, German warships were standing off Zanzibar. The sultan was obliged to duck out of the picture. Over the course of the next year, diplomatic maneuverings between Britain and Germany resulted in the partitioning of East Africa between themselves under the Berlin Agreement of November 1886. Only Zanzibar, its islands, and a ten-mile coastal strip on the mainland remained under the sultan's jurisdiction. The southern area became German East Africa, and the northern part, the East Africa Protectorate administered by a chartered company, the British East Africa Association under William Mackinnon. A further Anglo-German agreement in 1890 finalized these borders and deprived the sultan of all influence.

Kilimanjaro lay just inside the German sphere—the boundary line, elsewhere straight, making a curious kink to encompass it. Taveta, to the east of the mountain, remained on the British side of the line in recognition of Johnston's negotiated claim there.

You will often hear it said that Queen Victoria gave Kilimanjaro as a birthday present to her grandson Wilhelm, the German Kaiser, because he was peeved that she had two great East African mountains in her share, and he none. So far as records show, this is metaphorical history, although the truth is scarcely less bizarre. Britain, in this particular episode in the Scramble for Africa, conceded the mountain and its fertile slopes to Germany along with Heligoland, a windswept island in the North Sea of strategic interest to Bismarck and the Kaiser. In exchange, she obtained as additional protectorates Uganda, Equatoria, and Zanzibar—in other words, in return for one mountain and a three-square-mile rocky island in Europe, she secured control of 100,000 square miles of Africa.

JOHNSTON SETTLED IN HIS "AFRICAN SWITZERLAND" ON THE SLOPES OF KILIMANJARO ABOVE MOSHI.

CHAPTER SIX

PERSISTENCE REWARDED

The only thing about which Purtscheller and I ever quarrelled was the washing of the dishes; not that we were so overwhelmingly anxious to save each other trouble, but because each hungered for the luxury of a pair of clean hands.

HANS MEYER, OF HIS SUCCESSFUL 1889 EXPEDITION, RELATED IN *ACROSS EAST AFRICAN GLACIERS*, 1891

BY THE MID-1880S THE road to Kilimanjaro was becoming more frequently trodden by travelers. In 1885, the Church Missionary Society sent in its first East African Bishop, the ill-fated James Hannington, to set up permanent mission posts in Taveta and Moshi. Mandara was at last to have his resident mzungu. Hannington stayed in Chagga just long enough to get things moving, and to collect 38 species of moss from the slopes of Kilimanjaro, before delegating the day-to-day missionwork to other workers and embarking on a pastoral visit to Uganda. It proved an ill-judged trip at a time when the regions around Lake Victoria were extremely jittery over Carl Peters's annexations farther south. The Bishop followed the northern route from Kilimanjaro reconnoitered by Joseph Thomson. He passed safely around the lake's northern shores, only to be speared to death at Mumias on the outskirts of Uganda along with 30 or 40 of his porters—a massacre undertaken on the direct orders of the Kabaka of Buganda. ❧ When it came to the occupation of Kilimanjaro, Mandara hoodwinked Carl Peters (as he had done Kirk before him) into believing that his was the most powerful chiefdom on the mountain, and he—not Sina—was the paramount ruler. Thus, Moshi became

PRECEDING PAGES: ELEPHANTS IN AMBOSELI NATIONAL PARK REGULARLY MAKE THE TRIP TO KILIMANJARO'S NORTHERN AND WESTERN SLOPES. LEFT: IN THE EARLY 20TH CENTURY, MUSEUMS WERE BUILDING UP THEIR ANIMAL COLLECTIONS.

Germany's regional headquarters, and in time developed into an important economic and political center. German scholar-explorer Hans Meyer, who paid his first visit to Chagga in the summer of 1887, some months before the German station was established in Moshi, observed one of the first visible effects of a permanent European presence—the "sudden irruption of English and American sporting caravans." Meyer traveled to Kilimanjaro with the new Kommissar, Baron von Eberstein. In Taveta the two men met Count Samuel Teleki von Szek and Lieutenant von Höhnel, who'd been exploring in the area and now intended pressing northward on a journey that would take them past Mount Kenya, ultimately to discover Lakes Rudolf and Stefanie. They'd ranged as far as Meru and the count had made a spirited attempt on Kilimanjaro. From Marangu, he'd crossed the saddle plateau, climbing to a height of 15,800 feet before exhaustion, bleeding lips, and a "rushing noise" in his head checked progress. This places him some 500 feet lower than Johnston's supposed high point, but Meyer—who never had much time for Johnston—held that Teleki was "the first seriously to attempt the ascent of Kibo."

Teleki was a big game hunter as well as an explorer. Still, it was not him to whom Meyer refers when inveighing against the irruption of sporting parties. Meyer's condemnations are reserved for Willoughby and Harvey, two Britons who made several excusions to Kilimanjaro between 1886 and 1887. Perhaps they added their quota to scientific knowledge, Meyer is prepared to allow, but their wholesale slaughter of all species of game was repugnant. So far as he could see, they killed for no better reason than to swell their reputations as big-baggers, and he feared they would inspire others. "The rich preserves of East Africa will share the fate of the vast hunting grounds of South Africa and North America, and in the not far distant future will utterly cease to exist," he predicted. The Chagga had always dug pits in the forest and moorland for trapping elephants and other game, as he knew, but this profligate destruction was on an altogether different scale. He didn't put Teleki in this class, for the man was a geographer like himself.

Enthralled by Teleki's colorful tales, Meyer couldn't wait to make his own attempt on Kilimanjaro. Von Eberstein, who was supposed to be scouting out a site for the new German district headquarters, insisted on joining him. On Teleki's advice, the pair headed straight for Marangu, where they arranged to leave the main body of their caravan under the care of Mareale. With a few well-chosen companions, they then quickly passed through the forest to the wide "pastureland" above. In five days they'd reached the Saddle between Kibo and Mawenzi at around 14,000 feet, where they rested one day, sending their men to wait at a lower camp. When it started snowing the next day, after they'd climbed to 16,400 feet, von Eberstein's enthusiasm began to wane. Meyer pressed on alone for another 1,500 feet until a solid wall of ice, which he recognized as the lower edge

of Kibo's ice cap barred his way. Alpine experience warned him that crampons and an ice axe were essential to go higher and, possessed of neither, with the snow thickening he hastened back to von Eberstein. Together they descended to Marangu and soon afterward parted, Meyer to proceed to Arusha before heading back to the coast, von Eberstein to attend to his government business. Meyer took home formidable collections of scientific specimens, photographs, and measurements—plus a burning desire to return and finish the job.

Ironically, in view of his outspoken jibes at the exaggerated claims of others, Meyer's own climb was at first misreported. Even the normally scrupulous *Alpine Journal* declared in its November 1887 issue that the great volcano, the highest mountain in Africa, had been "ascended for the first time by Dr. Hans Meyer of Leipzig." Meyer quickly published a more accurate and

detailed narrative in which he gave his estimated high point as 17,880 feet.

As he made preparations for a return, others were busy in Chagga. An American naturalist, Dr. Abbot, spent 18 months in the area, during which time he attempted Kilimanjaro with Otto Ehlers of the German East Africa Company. Ehlers claimed to have climbed alone to 16,400 feet on Mawenzi, then proceeded to the "north-western side of the summit" of Kibo, achieving a height that "could not have been less than 19,680 feet"; he had seen no crater. Ehlers's "preposterous narrative" was demolished by Meyer, among others, and Ehler conceded he must have been "mistaken" in supposing he'd reached the summit.

Meyer, meanwhile, was experiencing difficulty getting to the mountain. A few miles from the coast, he and his traveling companion, the Austrian geographer Dr. Oscar Baumann, were seized by armed men and thrown in chains into a dark hut. Swahili Arabs, incensed at the blatant seizure of lands by Germans, had launched a major revolt. Some days later the leader of this insurrection, the aristocratic Sheik Bushiri bin Salim, arrived in Usambara and agreed to release the two men upon payment of a heavy ransom—everything, in fact, that Meyer possessed. The two were thankful to escape with their lives; the expedition was scuttled. With their equipment and trading goods for two years' travel lost, Meyer's dream of Kilimanjaro and his planned journey to the great inland lakes had to be abandoned. Amazingly, he was not put off. If anything, his resolution to survey and climb Africa's highest mountain was stronger than ever. And 1889 found him bound for Chagga once more, this time with the acclaimed Austrian mountaineer Ludwig Purtscheller.

What do we know of Meyer, whose portraits show a solemn, thin-lipped individual sporting a wing collar, pince-nez, and a neatly clipped moustache? He was born in March 1858 in Hildburghausen (Thüringen)

ABOVE: MEYER'S CAMP IN MARANGU IN 1889 FLIES WHAT THE CHIEF CALLED THE "OBJECTIONABLE BLOOD-AND-POWDER FLAG." RIGHT: AUSTRIAN LUDWIG PURTSCHELLER WAS CONSIDERED THE BEST ICE CLIMBER OF HIS DAY. FOLLOWING PAGES: MORNING MISTS BISECT KILIMANJARO: FOREST BELOW, ICE-WRAPPED SUMMIT ABOVE.

into a well-to-do publishing family. Early access to books fostered his innate interest in geography, which he went on to study, along with history and political science, at the universities of Berlin, Leipzig, and Strasbourg. His travels in Europe as well as high tours in the Alps sharpened his curiosity for the natural world and confirmed him as a walker and climber. In 1881, at the age of 23 and soon after his graduation, he set off around the world. The journey that kept him from home for two years took in the Middle and Far East as well as the United States, Mexico, Cuba, and several months' walking through the Philippines. Once home, he worked for a couple of years in the Bibliographical Institute in Leipzig, the family business, before heading off once more, this time for the gold fields of South Africa. And from there he made his first excursion to Chagga.

By 1889, to Meyer's reckoning, no less than 49 Europeans had visited the mountain. If he wanted to be first up Kilimanjaro, he couldn't afford to leave anything to chance; it could be only a matter of time before the prize would fall. Instead of a fellow geographer as in the previous year, he chose to partner with a man whose alpine reputation was built on guideless first ascents. Companion of the talented

Zsigmondy brothers, Ludwig Purtscheller had a deserved reputation for planning and carrying out difficult expeditions, and for superior ice craft. Fellow climbers used to say that Purtscheller's experience and skill had hardly, if ever, been equaled and never excelled—by guide or amateur. He was retiring and modest, a frugal Tyrolean, teacher of gymnastics, and a lover of beauty who strove to live honorably. For him, mountains were the noblest and fairest tests of a man's spirit and endeavor, and he sacrificed career advancement to gain more time in the mountains and closer bonds with his students.

Meyer financed his own expeditions. This time, with Purtscheller to advise him, he furnished a comprehen-

sive outfit: a large tent for their "half-way camp" at the upper edge of the forest; a small, well-made tent for camping on the plateau between the two peaks, large enough to accommodate both men and an African attendant if necessary; waterproof india-rubber groundsheet; plentiful camel's hair blankets; sheepskin sleeping bags, which he tells "enveloped the entire person all but the face"; warm woolen clothing and gloves; strong Alpine boots; knapsacks; ice axes; manila rope; snow spectacles; veils; and lanterns of "Muscovy glass" (mica).

"Herr Purtscheller was also the happy possessor of a pair of climbing irons," Meyer says, adding ruefully that his own had mistakenly gone on to Ceylon with another tent. They were well supplied with survey instruments, including a theodolite; they had a boiling-point thermometer, photographic apparatus, and "everything needed for preserving geological and botanical specimens."

Food was to be sent up from base every third day to the camp above the forest at 9,480 feet, from where the climbers' share would be ferried higher by the men in this halfway camp. Mareale promised two guides, one of whom failed to appear on the morning of departure but joined them later.

The halfway camp, comprising the large tent and a couple of grass and brushwood huts, would remain in place for the next few weeks. Meanwhile, the two men struck out for the Saddle. They found a more or less sheltered spot for their forward camp, with a sleeping crevice nearby for Mwini Amani, a trusted 28-year-old from Pangani, veteran of one of Meyer's earlier expeditions and the one who "always marches at the head of the caravan carrying the flag." Their five porters retreated and very early on the following morning (2:30 a.m.) the two climbers shouted good-bye to Mwini in his cleft and stumbled into the darkness.

An hour was lost taking a line too far to the north. But

by 10:30 they were on ice, roped together, Purtscheller in the lead wearing his climbing irons and cutting steps. The ice, as they got higher, became more corroded, in places honeycombed to a depth of more than a few feet, and with a treacherous crust. Sometimes, they'd sink in up to their armpits; it was exhausting work. At around 2:00 in the afternoon they stood on Kibo's crater rim, too weary to continue. They'd been climbing for 11 hours and were the first to peer into the gigantic hollow that occupied the entire mountaintop. The long-suspected crater "burst upon us with such unexpected suddenness that, for a moment, it quite took away our breath," Meyer said. Several hundred feet of climbing separated them from the loftiest pinnacle on the southern edge of the crater's rim, the true summit of Kibo. As close as they were, there was nothing for it but to retreat for now to Mwini's welcome bonfire, which they reached just before 7:00.

Next morning they slept in, then in the afternoon took their scientific readings and photographs. On the morrow they decided to move their top camp higher—establishing it at nightfall in a convenient hollow at 15,260 feet. At 3:00 a.m. on October 6, 1889—Purtscheller's 40th birthday—the climbing pair set off again "in capital trim," reaching their previous high point by 8:45. Another couple of hours and Meyer was unfurling a small German flag on the summit, planting it in the weather-beaten lava to "three ringing cheers":

In virtue of my right as its first discoverer [I] christened this hitherto unknown and unnamed mountain peak— the loftiest spot in Africa and in the German Empire— Kaiser Wilhelm's Peak. Then we gave three cheers more for the Emperor, and shook hands in mutual congratulation.

Meyer's narrative, always full and thorough, is for the most part soberly matter-of-fact. But at the point where his long-desired goal is finally achieved, he allows himself a poetic moment. "Njaro," he says, "the guardian spirit of the mountain, seemed to take his conquest with a good grace, for neither snow nor tempest marred our triumphal invasion of his sanctuary":

The icefields flashed and glittered in the dazzling sunlight, the wind sighed whisperingly in the crannies and crevices, and in the depths of the yawning cauldron at

our feet light wreaths of vapour curled softly and ceaselessly.

The two climbers had earned themselves a hearty meal, after which there were more sketches and observations to make before the descent, when a cold, clammy mist wrapped round them like a winding sheet. Their hands grew so numb it was hard to grip their ice axes, but at one o'clock they reached the lower limit of the ice "without breaking our bones, though as much could scarce be said of our skin":

Here we divested ourselves of our veils and spectacles and, to Purtscheller's intense astonishment, I drew from my pocket a handful of cigarettes and a couple of cakes of chocolate, which I had been hoarding up as a little surprise for him ever since we left the coast. We sat down and demolished our treasures on the spot, enjoying ourselves like schoolboys in a pastry-cook's.

Then, "merry as crickets," they raced down, with "many an echoing shout" to warn Mwini of their coming. He, as instructed, had everything packed up and ready for them to continue down to their camp on the Saddle. From here, they had hoped to climb Mawenzi the following day, but news came up from Marangu of trouble in the village below over their flying of the German flag. Meyer felt obliged to go down and sort out the matter with Mareale. He explained that hoisting his national colors over his tent was "a matter of no importance" to either of them, because the ownership of Kilimanjaro was a matter settled and sealed between the English and the Germans at headquarters long ago. Nevertheless, he assured the chief, he'd be more than happy to fly Mareale's family colors—a white star on a red ground—alongside the red and black German ensign—or, as Mareale was pleased to call it, the "objectionable blood-and-powder flag." This appeased the chief. To show him there was no ill feeling, Meyer put on a fireworks show for the locals that evening.

Though he managed to set fire to the roof of a grass hut with one of his rockets, no one was too bothered. Bits of straw and white ants rained from the sky, sticking to the zinc ointment that Meyer had thickly smeared on his sunburned face. His appearance, it seems, caused more consternation among the villagers than the lost hut.

There was time next morning to prepare bulletins for the post runner before climbing up again to rejoin Purtscheller. (Thanks to the missionary presence, and regular mail runners, letters between Moshi and Europe now took only a month or so in either direction.) The climbers spent more than a week exploring, surveying and observing, and visiting the crater rim once more. They reconnoitered Mawenzi and climbed one of the lesser pinnacles along its rugged ridge. Excluding those days lost when Meyer came down to parley with Mareale, he and Purtscheller spent no less than 16 days between the altitudes of 15,000 and 20,000 feet. They named a good many of the mountain's features and came home with material for a comprehensive map of Kilimanjaro and Lake Jipe. It was a

British East Africa Company operating in what is today Kenya and Uganda. He gathered more treaties with chiefs, but as Professor Oliver has remarked, "most Africans lost their independence without signing any treaties at all." Within 18 months some 30 sub-companies had been established and exports of goods such as tobacco had already begun. The Sultan of Zanzibar conceded to Germany for 50 years his ten-mile coastal strip on the mainland.

It should not be thought from this, however, that everything went swimmingly for the new overlords. Insensitive occupation of the Swahili Coast sparked a fierce uprising in 1888 that could have wrecked the new German colony and threatened both British interests in Africa and her links with India. This was the incident

THURSDAY Kazimoto, who is 47 years old and married with six children, turns out to be quite a philosopher, with strong views on the way Africa's progress has been held back by a persistent belief in sorcery, and by greed. Selfishness and greed are still evident today, he says, in the way power and wealth are amassed by self-centered big shots in the government and big business, leaving the masses poor and at their mercy. The areas around Kilimanjaro where the Germans settled are the best developed, and produce more ministers and big shots, he says. In other regions, such as Shinyanga, the scourge of witchcraft is so rampant that old women are murdered very cruelly. The government has to protect them in separate housing schemes.

superlative performance and brought the initial exploratory period on Kilimanjaro to an end.

HAVING SEIZED their East African colony, the Germans were quick to consolidate power. Industrial growth at home had created urgent need for both raw materials and markets abroad for their products. At the same time, a wave of nationalism was strengthening the call for expansion overseas. There were plenty of young adventurers like Carl Peters waiting in the wings to exploit the situation. No sooner had Bismarck and the Berlin Conference recognized Peters's treaties and established principles for occupation than settlers began pouring into the new territory and infrastructure built up. Peters reorganized his society into the German East Africa Company, modeled on the

in which Meyer and Baumann found themselves unwittingly caught up on their way to Kilimanjaro that year. Though Bismarck had been slow to warm to the idea of a colony in East Africa, now that it existed the prize was deemed worth fighting for. German and British gunships blockaded Zanzibar, troops mustered, and Maxim Machine-Guns were brought in to mow down the rebels. Ultimately, might prevailed and Germany regained control of the vital seaboard. Rebel leaders were publicly executed—including Bushiri, who'd taken Meyer and his companion captive. In 1890, the Imperial German government assumed direct control of the colony's administration; Peters's company continued to hold a monopoly of trade, though he himself was later indicted for abuse of power and unwarranted cruelty to natives.

KILMANJARO AS BATTLEFIELD

AUDREY SALKELD
AUTHOR, MOUNTAINEERING HISTORIAN

IT'S PROBABLY TRUE to say that the outbreak of World War I caught East Africa by surprise. With an undefended border running from Lake Victoria to the Indian Ocean, the settlers in the British and German spheres suddenly realized their vulnerability. At special risk were the two fine new railways, the British Uganda Railway from Mombasa through Tsavo and Nairobi to Nakuru, and Germany's Northern Railway, the Kilimanjaro line from Tanga via the Usambara and Pare Mountains to New Moshi (Neu Moschi). The countries' two governors favored declaring neutrality in Africa, regardless of what was happening in Europe, but such a truce would have been virtually unworkable and increasingly so as war progressed.

In the wake of the damaging Maji Maji rebellion (1905-1906), Germany had been reforming its colonial policies. If widespread unrest was to be avoided in the future, abuses of forced labor and excessive punishments had to be eradicated, and economic development conducted in a way that offered incentives to Africans as well as the European settlers. Its commitment to the colony intensified and, coupled with considerable investment, this meant that by the start of the war in August 1914, German East Africa could be considered a success, colonially speaking. In fact, a well-advertised grand trade exhibition was due to be held that very month to advertise its potential—and to attract more settlers.

At more than 384,000 square miles, German East was twice the size of Germany itself and the acknowledged jewel of her foreign possessions. It has been said that, to the Fatherland, it was "like a darling son, for whom nothing was too good," in contrast to which the Germans felt the British treated her protectorates to the north "as if they were unwanted and unwelcome stepchildren." Nevertheless, the European presence in German East was still small—said to be under 6,000 in 1913—so that when the war began reservists had to be drafted to boost its military strength. Their commander was the experienced campaigner General P. Von Lettow-Vorbeck, who had mastered bush-fighting tactics during the Herero and Hottentot rebellion in German South West Africa.

Historians agree that Von Lettow-Vorbeck must have realized from the start that he was unlikely to defeat the British; they had better access to stores and reinforcements and would surely blockade his coastline. Yet that did not have to mean they could defeat him. By playing a determined cat-and-mouse game he could tie up men and resources over a lengthy period, keeping them out of the major theaters of the war.

In the first 15 months of the conflict, Von Lettow-Vorbeck and his Schutztruppe held the initiative, launching a number of raids across the border into British East Africa and occupying the slope of Kilimanjaro in the southeastern corner of that country, around Taveta. He'd benefited from the windfall of the masses of European products stockpiled in Dar es Salaam for the anticipated influx of visitors to the trade exhibition. With these, he had provisioned dumps all over the country for the skirmishes ahead. His recruiting campaign enabled him to start the war with 260 European troops and 2,470 African askaris, which outweighed the British resources. At no time in the war, however, did his army number more than 3,000 Germans and 11,000 African soldiers.

At the outset, patriotic British settlers and Boers flocked to volunteer themselves and their mounts for duty, to boost the few available professional soldiers of the King's African Rifles, a native corps that had never seen action beyond peacekeeping duties on the border. Within days—as one contemporary reporter testified—Nairobi was reduced to "khaki-clad chaos."

What occurred in Nairobi took place on a smaller scale in Mombasa and some Uganda towns. In September their numbers were reinforced by the first contingent of Indian troops, bringing some Maxim guns and a mountain battery. In November 1914, European and Indian troops were landed at the German port of Tanga in an attempt to capture the railhead there. It was a fiasco. They were repulsed disastrously, though details were kept quiet at the time. Von Lettow-Vorbeck continued to harry the Allies and keep them on the defensive, but when another year of desultory fighting failed to yield much of an advantage to either side, British headquarters decided more forces were needed if Von Lettow-Vorbeck was to be pushed into retreat. The start of 1916 saw a large expeditionary army assembling in Kenya, drawn from around the British Empire and under the command of South African general Jan Smuts. The plan was to invade German East from the north, first seizing "the Kilimanjaro Gap," which meant encircling the mountain simultaneously from east and west, retaking Taveta and capturing Moshi before forcing Von Lettow-Vorbeck southward through the difficult interior. There they would be joined by Belgian forces, advancing eastward from Lake Tanganyika.

The kink in the border between the two East African colonies played into British hands here by lessening the amount of mountain to be encircled. To assist operations, a military rail line had been laid from Voi as far as Njoro—within striking distance of Taveta— and a pipeline brought in water from the Bura Hills to Serengeti, though this still fell short of requirements. More water and fuel were supplied by the new railway, several thousand trucks, and other vehicles.

PAUL VON LETTOW-VORBECK (SECOND FROM RIGHT) WAS COMMANDER-IN-CHIEF IN GERMAN EAST AFRICA DURING WWI. THE FIRST BATTLE WAS ON KILIMANJARO'S SLOPES.

The first pincer arm, the 1st Division, set out on March 5 and advanced from Mount Longido, northwest of Kilimanjaro, moving across rough steppe to approach Moshi over the western flanks of the mountain. The going was slow and exhausting, but they met little resistance on the way. Two days later, South African forces under Benera Van Deventer marched out from Mbuyuni and Serengeti in the evening, bound for Lake Chala, north of Taveta. They met greater opposition, but fought through, the enemy pulling back ahead of them. Meanwhile, the 2nd Division had been bombarding Salaita, northeast of Taveta, to be able to advance and dig themselves in there, ready for the major assault. Van Deventer took Taveta on the morning of March 10, forestalling German plans to regroup there. The Germans then withdrew into the wooded Kitovo Hills and the difficult battle for the Latema Ridge ensued. Morning revealed that the ridge was in Allied possession and the enemy in full retreat—not to Moshi, but south down the line of the railway to Kahe. Moshi was occupied by General Smut's forces on March 13, 1916, after a bombardment of some four to five hours.

Though Von Lettow-Vorbeck had been ousted from the northern highlands, there was to be no definitive engagement or swift victory in German East. He continued an astute guerrilla campaign, blowing up almost every road, railway line, bridge, and river crossing in his retreat and outwitting all attempts to capture him. Finally he slipped into Mozambique, and was still at large and fighting by the time the war ended in Europe in November 1918.

The brunt of the losses on both sides was borne by native Africans. Winston Churchill, who was British Secretary for War, was asked when hostilities ended how many natives had enrolled in the Carrier Corps during the East African campaign and how many had died. The total figure was unavailable at that time, Churchill replied, but the largest number on strength at any one time was about 137,000. And from beginning of operations up to the end of October 1917, deaths from "disease or accident amongst 'Followers' were: Indian, 243; East African, 28,830; South African, 1,214; West African, 793; Seychelles, 246."

Writers today put the numbers in East Africa alone at more than a million carriers, and 50,000 troops, of whom more than 100,000 sacrificed their lives. Nor was that the end of it. Famine and disease followed in the wake.

The major political impact was the end of German rule in East Africa. German East was divided between Belgium, who took possession of Rwanda and Burundi, and Britain, who gained administration of the bulk of the country as a League of Nations mandate—and renamed it Tanganyika.

With the coast subdued, the Germans moved inland along the major trade routes. They met some resistance, and this would be the pattern. Where the occupiers met passive resistance, they exerted weaker influence, always "careful not to employ their guns and powder in distant areas unless it became absolutely unavoidable" (G. C. K. Gwassa). When it came to dealing with the many petty chiefdoms of Chagga, the twists and turns of the story,

the maneuverings and outbursts are not easy to interpret.

The Chagga chiefs were masters of the politics of intrigue with a habit of authority:

They liked flattery and disliked opposition; they utilized every new thing and every new kind of human being coming into Kilimanjaro to suit their own ends; they showed extraordinarily versatile political skill.... They

before the Germans arrived had been his ongoing rivalry with neighboring warlord Sina of Kibosho and his heavy reliance on the coastal caravan trade. That did not change.

Never had Mandara been able to relax his guard with the Kibosho. In the 1860s Chief Sina's predecessor had ousted Mandara from his throne for a number of years. There was always the possibility that Sina, with his superior military strength, could do the same. Mandara hoped an alliance with the Germans could be manipulated to bring down his rival. And it worked. In 1891 the Germans marched on Sina's fortress with their Maxim gun. The Kibosho chief fought long and bravely, but finally had to conclude a truce, after which he was allowed to continue as a peaceful divisional chief until his sudden death six years later—which was widely attributed to poisoning.

If Mandara's guile contributed to the downfall of Sina, similar intrigue by Mareale of Marangu ultimately brought down other chiefs. Mandara did not live to see that. He died in 1892, leaving Moshi to expand rapidly under German rule. Mandara's successor, his son Meli, was an impetuous young man with none of the statecraft of his father. This gave Mareale the chance to promote himself as the natural leader of all Chagga. The more one learns of Mareale, the more contradictory his character appears. Johnston and Meyer were wary in their dealings with him; historians today usually write him as an arch schemer of great ruthlessness. Yet he enjoyed the complete trust of the German colonial authorities, initially at least. And a genteel Christian lady—resident in Marangu at the end of the 1920s, just after Mareale's death—devoted 40 pages in her memoirs to painting him as a saintly, wise, and inspirational leader.

There is consensus that Mareale's early life was one of precarious struggle, and that part of his youth was spent in exile at Mandara's court. Doubtless, he picked up a wrinkle or two from the older chief. For the first years of his reign, Mareale made no particular mark on history, but in 1892, after Mandara's death, his stature suddenly changed. He hatched a stratagem to discredit

used hired informers to provide political intelligence service, other agents skillfully to spread rumour and foretellers to make timely and calculated political prophecies. (Kathleen M. Stahl)

Mandara, as we have seen, avoided friction by persuading the colonists that he was the supreme chief of the area and happy to cooperate. His pressing concerns

fellow chiefs and improve his standing. This Machiavellian ploy resulted in the deaths of the German officer in charge of Kilimanjaro, plus another European and several Africans. Meli of Moshi found himself framed for these murders, along with the chief of the adjacent kingdom of Kirua.

A lawless period followed when the Germans pulled back from Kilimanjaro altogether, but Mareale persuaded them to return with sufficient force to quell the "Chagga revolt." Meli was discredited, the Moshi Chagga crushed, and Mareale entered upon the most glorious period of his reign. Having become a very close friend of the local commander, Captain Johannes, he willingly provided auxiliary warriors for campaigns to extend German authority. Under Johannes's influence the chief picked up a taste for life's luxuries. He learned to ride a horse, accepted a gold braided uniform and cocked hat from the Kaiser, and "now lived in open state with his wives and retainers, playing cards, sipping vermouth, laughing over his exploits" (Stahl). In the nine years of Johannes's term of office on the mountain, Mareale enriched Marangu with plunder and enhanced his own prestige with his diplomatic triumphs. He drained the wealth of Rombo to the east, carrying off cattle and goats and drafting men, women, and children to work in Marangu. In 1900 Mareale pulled his biggest stunt of all. A plot to discredit his old enemies, the chiefs of Kibosho and Moshi, by linking them with unrest among the Arusha and Masai resulted in the execution of 19 chiefs of the Kilimanjaro area.

One of those 19 chiefs apprehended and hanged by the Germans at Kitimbiliu in Old Moshi was Mangi Ngalami of Kibongoto, the great-great-grandfather of our team member on this Kilimanjaro climb, 13-year-old Hansi Mmari. Hansi mentioned this fact only briefly to western members of the expedition, but was

THE ENIGMATIC CHIEF MAREALE OF MARANGU
PROSPERED UNDER GERMAN RULE.

far more forthcoming with fellow Chagga in the porters' tent. One of our porters, Moses Kazimoto, a writer on Chagga history and other matters, has filled in some of the details we missed.

Chief Ngalami, he told us, probably came to the throne of Kibongoto (to the west of Machame) in the 1880s when the Germans were already signing treaties with the local chiefs. He was one of those who refused to accept German rule, but by the end of that decade the Germans, having won over or subdued most of the chiefdoms on the mountain's slopes, were anxious to force their authority on those who remained uncooperative. Ngalami continued to resist, and thus was his fate sealed.

At his death, he left five children. Word circulated that the Germans would also be coming for his eldest son, Barnabas, then 12 years old and the rightful heir to the throne of Kobongoto. The boy was taken by his family to the missionaries where he was hidden in church buildings. There he attended school, was baptized, and eventually introduced to a young lady, Lydia Kileo, whom he married. When the British came to power after the First World War, Barnabas expected to be reinstated as the rightful chief of Kobongota, but it was not to be. Dissent within the chiefdom was resolved by the Chief of Machame Central appointing his own son, Gideon, to the post. From then on Barnabas, who was Hansi's great-grandfather, kept on the move for the sake of his own life and the safety of his family, until in 1933 he settled at the foot of Meru in Arusha. In all, Barnabas had ten children. He became a successful timber merchant and, when he realized he had an incurable illness, he made his own coffin from the best and hardest wood available. He died in 1944.

Hansi was able to recite the names of all Ngalami's children, and those of Barnabas, their wives, and their children. There is a lot to be said for a tradition of oral history, although one can see that for some details it would be difficult to know where fact and myth mesh. Kazimoto tells me that, according to their tradition, the Germans hanged these Chagga chiefs from a baobab tree, and that the skulls of the hanged men were taken back to Germany.

Well, the Germans may have used a handy baobab tree for their grisly retribution, but it would not have been, as Kazimoto supposed, the traditional German way of hanging witches and miscreants; there are not many baobabs in the Fatherland. Also, I have seen other photographs of massed hangings in German East Africa where temporary scaffolds were employed. So we are justified in suspecting an element of embellishment here. But what about the skulls? Certainly, that sounds far-fetched. Why would the Germans have

chief's attitude changes: He humiliates his guests, extorts their goods, and sends them packing. The missionaries and other travelers go on deciding how many beads and yards of cloth they can offer, based on what they want to part with, failing to appreciate that this is not merely a matter of trade, or even tribute. For a chief to maintain his standing with his people, and his guests, he should not be belittled. If the visitor has a rifle, it stands to reason if they are to discourse as equals that the king will want one too. Beads may have worked on the first visit, but times were changing fast and the chiefs were aware of this change and the value of commodities. The missionaries never understood this, seeing chiefs merely as grasping. For decades they made the same mistakes, went on bringing the same mundane goods from the coast that other trading car-

THURSDAY Always, when you start going high, you have to expect to snatch sleep in short bursts. And your night is further interrupted by one or two urgent trips outside. The best protection against altitude sickness—apart from gaining height as gradually as possible—is to be sure to stay well hydrated. Some experts recommend that you drink up to four quarts of water a day, which is almost impossible to achieve. Diamox tablets (acetazolomide) are often prescribed to aid acclimatization, but they are themselves diuretic and only exacerbate the situation. There's no point being shy about it; up here, we are all in the same boat.

taken them away? But the turn of the century was a period when museums and scientific establishments around the world were avidly collecting specimens of man and beast and formulating theories of ethnicity. Perhaps the idea of retaining these skulls is not so outlandish after all.

WHAT WE KNOW of the Chagga chiefs who ruled when the first Europeans came to Kilimanjaro has largely been gleaned from the writings and perspective of those visitors. Coming in with their various prejudices and private agendas, they frequently mishandled their dealings with native leaders, and failed utterly to learn from the experience of others. There is a dispiriting repetitiveness in the way relationships start well between host and traveler, and then we are told that the

avans supplied regularly, without for a minute realizing that it was the latest knowledge, weapons, and medicine that the chiefs were after.

Also, with so much of this history written by Europeans, I wanted to know how men like Mandara are remembered among today's Chagga. Was he a cruel despot, as he's usually depicted, or a wise leader? Freddie Munna undertook to find out for me, going out to talk with some old men of Old Moshi village. Without exception they told him what a great and intelligent leader Mandara had been, "My dear son," one said, "you can ask anybody in this village, the answer will come back that Makinara (Mandara) was a Hero Man. He was Msoro (Powerful Man), a man without fear, a complete male human being."

We shouldn't forget that African education now

teaches that missionaries were the pump-primers of colonialism. There is a famous saying of Jomo Kenyatta: "When the missionaries came, the Africans had the land and the Christians had the Bible. They taught us to pray with our eyes closed. When we opened them, they had the land and we had the Bible." Mandara and other chiefs are seen to have done right in giving the likes of Rebmann, New, and the other early explorers a hard time.

THE IRRUPTION of sporting parties that had so appalled Meyer in the 1880s became more pronounced as time went by. Expeditions swarmed to East Africa in the first years of the 20th century under the banner of science, though this science usually took the form of indiscriminate animal slaughter. Part of the impetus came from the desire of different scientific establishments around the world to build up their natural history collections and outdo their rivals. In 1909 Carl Akeley was collecting for the American Museum of Natural History in New York, at the same time as another caravan of monstrous proportions was following "African Game Trails" collecting specimens for the Smithsonian in Washington, D.C. This latter enterprise was headed by former president Theodore Roosevelt, who spent ten months marching from Mombasa to the upper Nile with 500 bearers and askaris, during which (to quote Charles Miller, author of *The Lunatic Express*):

...the barrels of his three rifles practically never stopped smoking. He personally shot no fewer than 296 animals, including nine lions, eight elephants, thirteen rhino (of which nine were the rare white type) and six buffalo. The expedition's total bag came to upward of a thousand specimens of 164 different specie, ranging from bull elephant to Naivasha pygmy mouse. The four tons of fine salt which the porters carried for curing skins could have been only barely adequate to their task.

The toll was shocking by today's standards, but the explorers did not have everything their own way. Akeley, whose expedition secured the specimens that form the popular elephant family tableau in the entrance to the New York museum, was almost killed when a bull elephant gored him on Mount Kenya, and his assistant cameraman, Arthur Newman, had a lung punctured in a similar incident. A Boston-based hunting and exploration trip incorporated an attempt to climb Kilimanjaro, hoping for the prize of "first English-speaking venturers to the summit." For them, too, things didn't go entirely according to plan.

Peter MacQueen and Peter Dutkewich spent a "delightful" week with German colonists in Moshi, where Chief Sulima (another of Mandara's sons) assisted them in finding 16 strong young Chagga porters and a chief guide, Souho, recommended as the most experienced man for the job. The fact that Souho's previous attempt a few months earlier with a Dr. Ahlbory lost several men on the upper slopes from extreme cold appears to have rung no warning bells for MacQueen and Dutkewich, the two New Englanders. They'd provided each of their porters with a blanket, and had four

each themselves, and saw no reason to make any adjustments to this.

Jauntily, they set out on July 6, 1908, and the onset of weeping rain in the afternoon merely serves to remind them of their native Adirondack Mountains. Stopping early, they get three great fires burning and settle down to a "lordly lunch of hot tea and hard biscuits." The team's adventures come to us through the diary of Mac-Queen, who we soon detect is a man with a poetic flourish and a tendency to reach for a jewel when he needs a metaphor. Jasper, amber, chrysoprase, are all called

into play to describe cloud cities at sunset seen amid their walls of "refulgent" gold. Kilimanjaro's glorious crown flashes back the ruby and the diamond of the sun; in her diadem of snow are the purple of the jacinth, amethystine fire, the brilliance of the emerald, and the soft shining of opal. Nevertheless, he is a keen observer, with a light and amusing touch.

The nights prove colder than they'd bargained for, even donning all their warm clothes, which in MacQueen's case includes his khaki coat, mackintosh, and a skating cap. The freezing porters have to be brought into the shelter of their tent. Dutkewich falls into a few animal traps while out boar-hunting; they face a mutiny when their men run out of posho, or corn cobs. It transpires that the Wachagga kept back some of the posho-money allocated to them at the beginning in order to buy wives.

On the third day, MacQueen sets off with Souho toward the snow line:

He did not seem to mind the rarefied air; but when we had risen a thousand feet I got dizzy; from that time onward for two thousand feet the diziness continued, till up at the snow line, sixteen thousand feet, I became fearfully nauseated. My guide was as polite as Lord Chesterfield and kindly as the finest gentleman of the world could be. So I owe much to the bare-footed natives of this country, who patiently for eight cents a day bear the white man's burden. On the wild desolate uplands I thought of what the Scotchman said of the Kyles of Bute: "The works o' God is hellish." For athwart the landscape are rocks, hills and mountains thrown in dreadful confusion, the wreckage of a former world.

ON THE AFTERNOON of July 12, they climb to Meyer's cave under Kibo, close by which they pass two corpses from the previous expedition. "The vultures had pecked out their eyes, the leopards had taken a leg from each." It is a subdued party that shivers in the cave that night in the spooky light of a campfire. Fortified by a cup of cocoa, a potato, and some cold goat's meat, they are away at 6:30 next morning, but it quickly becomes clear that the porters have never been on this mountain before, nor are they well informed about it. On reaching the edge of the ice at 16,000 feet, they pick up a few handfuls and exclaim, "Oh, masters, this is magic; this is water turned to burning wood," and scoot off downhill in a fright (with all the food). A storm in the afternoon drives the white men back also, telling themselves they'll go to the top the next day. A small American flag is left standing at 19,200 feet to mark the highest any of their kind have been in Africa.

Before reaching the cave, Dutkewich, carrying his camera and plates, slips on an icy slab, fracturing several ribs. Assisting him down, MacQueen and Souho get lost in the rain and mist, and only rediscover their way to the cave when they come upon the dead bodies they'd seen earlier. Their porters are inside and, after a day or two's rest here—the diary becomes a little confused at this point—they start bringing Dutkewich down. He's been getting steadily worse, with an irregular pulse and high temperature; it isn't possible to fashion a stretcher until someone has been down to the woodland and cut some poles. The 15th finds them carrying Dutkewich on his litter through the tall grass above the woods. Everyone is sodden, cold to the bone, and some of the porters are running fevers. MacQueen helps carry the man worst affected, but on reaching the trees leaves him in the care of two companions as he doesn't want to lose sight of Dutkewich.

MRS. AKELEY POSES WITH TUSKS BAGGED WHILE COLLECTING FOR THE NEW YORK MUSEUM OF NATURAL HISTORY.

KILIMANJARO IN FILM AND LITERATURE

RICK RIDGEWAY

FILMMAKER AND ADVENTURE WRITER, AUTHOR OF *THE SHADOW OF KILIMANJARO*

IN BOTH THE FILM and the literature of East Africa, there is no image more emblematic than Kilimanjaro: the equatorial snow shimmering in the blue distance, the foreground umbrella acacias framing an elephant or a giraffe. In film, the position of Kilimanjaro as icon began early in the 20th century when adventure promoters such as Martin and Osa Johnson offered the public some of the first views in moving pictures of Africa's wildlife. Their perspective was through the lens of big game hunting, and this continued through the 1950s with the popularity of adventure and hunting shows on television, especially ABC's series *The American Sportsman*, which frequently featured hunting expeditions to East Africa. Nearly all these shows included the requisite shot of Kilimanjaro, making the mountain, in the public's eye, the continent's overlord not only in fact but also in symbol.

In literature, the position of Kilimanjaro as the continent's icon reached its symbolic peak with its placement as background in Hemingway's fictional short story "The Snows of Kilimanjaro." The story begins with an epigraph, archetypical in its evocative power: "Kilimanjaro is a snow covered mountain 19,710 feet high, and it is said to be the highest mountain in Africa. Its western summit is called the Masai 'Ngaje Ngai,' the House of God. Close to the western summit there is the dried and frozen carcass of a leopard. No one has explained what the leopard was seeking at that altitude."

With the brevity that was Hemingway's signature, the epigraph sets the tone of death and decay, as well as evokes the mystery that accompanies any being's path toward self-destruction. The story that follows then becomes a meditation on mortality. As the main charac-

...there is no image more emblematic than Kilimanjaro: the equatorial snow shimmering ...the foreground umbrella acacias framing an elephant...

ter, Harry, lies in a cot, dying of a wound in his leg that has turned gangrenous, attended by the woman he abuses, he considers the life he failed to lead. As a writer, he reviews the things he has saved to write "until he knew enough to write them well. Well, he would not have to fail at trying to write them either. Maybe you could never write them, and that was why you put them off and delayed the starting. Well, he would never know, now."

As he drifts into what will be his final sleep, he dreams that the plane that would rescue him arrives and carries him aloft, high above the acacia-studded plains, through a rain squall and out again until all Harry can see ahead is "wide as all the world, great, high, and unbelievably white in the sun... the square top of Kilimanjaro."

The leopard in Hemingway's epigram did, in fact, exist. Ascending the mountain in July, 1926, Dr. Latham of the Government Agricultural Department of Tanganyika reported finding the frozen carcass of a leopard near the rim of the summit crater at a position that later became known as Leopard Point. Eva Stuart, ascending the mountain two months later, photographed the leopard, and her porter cut off a piece of its tail. The missionary Richard Reusch saw it three weeks later, and returning the next year cut off an ear, and reportedly would have liked to have had the head as a souvenir but was unable to detach it from the frozen carcass. In 1933, the inimitable British climber and adventurer H. W. Tilman, climbing solo, found the desiccated remains still there. Perhaps giving inspiration to Hemingway, Tilman, in his own book *Snow on the Equator*, wrote "I have never heard any explanation of how it came to be there."

When the two porters catch up, their sick companion isn't with them, and the full horror of the situation catches up with MacQueen: He can neither go back for the stricken man himself, nor has he anyone strong enough to send. Though probably no more than half a mile away, the man will surely die. Souho is sent down to raise the alarm at a German fort, and he returns that evening with a hammock, a tent, some fresh porters to help with the carry—and two bottles of champagne. Immediately he's sent farther into the forest to find the abandoned man, whom he brings in on his back next day.

Dutkewich meanwhile remains in great pain, made the worse for the stretcher being set on sloping ground, pitching him constantly into the mud. He is given one of the bottles of champagne, which, we are told, revives

Met a boy carrying hammock. Offered him three rupees to get me to Lutheran mission. On I went; fell in the stream fainting. Took a little champagne from the second bottle. Got out of the stream; dragged myself onto my feet and began to repeat in German the words: "I will give any man five hundred marks who will bring my friend down from the hill today."

After a couple of hours he meets Dr. Ahlbory and another man, and these two climb immediately to Dutkewich, finding him deserted now, except for one *askari* (trained-man) and another dead Wachagga.

WHEN HE WAS brought down, Dutkewich was found to have three ribs "crushed in over the heart" and had to remain in the German hospital in Moshi,

---

THURSDAY I shouldn't have been surprised, I suppose, to learn that high on Kilimanjaro there's one of those legendary elephant graveyards. A deep pit, so the Chagga say, contains an enormous quantity of ivory, because every old elephant who feels death approaching is compelled to climb up to this pit and cast itself in. If a greedy man comes up to steal the ivory, he will be struck blind and die horribly, but anyone who happens upon the pit innocently may carry away without penalty the first tusk his hand encounters. That alone. He must never come back.

---

him greatly. It rains torrentially for the full 15 hours they lie on the forest floor. One porter, who has been shivering with fever for the past two days, abandons hope. He stiffens, grows cold, and dies during the night. By morning, it is seen that another poor wretch has died also, and Dutkewich is so still and quiet that MacQueen fears at first he's lost him, too. They have now been wet through for 27 hours and without food or fire. Everyone is demoralized.

MacQueen divides up the last of his chocolate and passes it around—which gives one man strength enough to run away. It's clear now to the leader that their only hope is for him to get down to the Germans and beg for additional help. Leaving Dutkewich a bottle of whisky and taking the second champagne bottle for himself, MacQueen heads downhill:

under the care of Dr. Ahlbory for ten weeks. MacQueen continued his journey alone—not, it seems, unduly daunted by the experience. As he explained to his readers, "Mr Dutkewich and I were the first Americans to try the ascent and the only men who ever tried it in rainy weather...we would have climbed to the summit but for the accident to Mr. Dutkewich. We did the best we could." Indirectly he has revealed that in the years when climbing Kilimanjaro was first becoming popular it was not unusual for the lives of strong local men to be squandered on this mountain. MacQueen indicates that at least five, and possibly more, died during six months of 1908 alone, and that these lives might have been saved with better preparation and a little extra clothing. It is an appalling revelation.

HERE AT 19,200 FEET ON KIBO IN 1908, PETER MACQUEEN'S AMBITION WAS TO BE THE FIRST ENGLISH SPEAKER TO THE SUMMIT.

CHAPTER SEVEN

SUMMER EVERY DAY, WINTER EVERY NIGHT

This, then, is the tragic paradox of the white man's encroachment.
The deeper he went into Africa, the faster life flowed out of it,
off the plains and out of the bush and into the cities,
vanishing in acres of trophies and hides and carcasses.

PETER BEARD, FROM "THE END OF THE GAME," 1977

O UR REST DAY AT SHIRA Camp worked wonders. Headaches were reduced to a niggle with painkillers, and Rick was back on his feet and cheerful after half a Diamox tablet. Of course, the richest benefit for most of us came from a relaxed day around camp and the opportunity to consume more liquids than was possible on the trail. We are camped on an open brow above the Machame Escarpment. It appeared somewhat bleak on first impression, and is very exposed, but in truth it is an exciting place, with fine views in all directions. On one side we look out over the escarpment to Moshi and the endless Masai Steppes. The jagged Shira Ridge snakes down to the west of us. This is the ruined rim of the old Shira crater and, by projecting its circle around in your mind, you gain a startling realization of the extent of this almost vanished mountain. Out on the horizon, 40 or 50 miles away, is that other volcano, Meru. This, too, though it appears a near-perfect cone in silhouette, is but a relic of its former self. A great hole has been gouged from one side of it. ∼ The prospect that draws our closest attention is that toward the summit of Kibo, to the east of us. It still looks dauntingly far away and unreal. More than 7,000 feet higher than here,

PRECEDING PAGES: KIBO GLOWS IN MOONLIGHT, FROM SHIRA CAMP. LEFT: THIRTEEN-YEAR-OLD HANSI AND TWELVE-YEAR-OLD NICOLE, THE TEAM'S YOUNGSTERS, TREK ON THE SHIRA PLATEAU.

it's hard to imagine what it would be like to be up there. And, from this angle, it looks very steep. We are gazing head-on at its western glaciers: the Credner, Drygalski, and Penck, which, although far less extensive than they used to be, still shine blindingly in the tropical sun. The Western Breach, which is to be our approach, can be plainly seen, but it's difficult from here to make out exactly the line we'll take up.

The literature talks of this Shira Plateau as "grassy" but that's an extravagant description just now. There

has been no rain for months and although we see size-able tussocks of grass, they are all dried out, bleached, and widely spaced with plenty of stony ground between. In places you still find a few clumps of heather, though nothing really arboreal beyond one gaunt specimen on the ridge edge, which has managed some six windswept feet, its scrawny branches streaming horizontally to the leeward. Looking more closely, things are not as arid as they seem, however. Various plants that get lost in the bigger picture introduce themselves as little splashes

HEIDI AND THE REST OF THE TEAM PACK UP AFTER A
LUNCH BREAK ON THE WAY TO THE GREAT BARRANCO
AS EARLY AFTERNOON MIST ROLLS IN.

vived its dunking in the rain forest. It's still sodden two days afterward (as is my rucksack), and I keep riffling the once-shiny pages to prevent them from sticking together as they dry out. It's a losing battle: Several are already tightly fused and all are crinkled. In any case, a plant book will be a luxury as we climb higher, not worth its weight. We've all been told to send excess baggage down the hill. I think it will have to go. It's not such a wrench for me as that facing Roger, who has to decide what of his scientific equipment to let go down.

He has this trunk of gadgets, which I'm not alone in calling his "toys." The children like to tease him about his toy box, too. But it's a treasure chest, and provides the answer for almost any scientific query. He continues to turn most of the questions the youngsters ask him into practical games, which keeps them amused without realizing how much they are learning along the way: How far is the horizon? How far will we be able to see when we reach the top? What are these rocks made of? He has instruments for every eventuality—microscopes and magnifying lenses, calculators, cameras, computers, GPS receivers, a geological hammer. Also, he's brought some small electronic probes—thermal data loggers—with which he's been recording the night temperatures within some of the giant rosette plants. He compares these to the temperature outside, where it routinely drops below 32°F at night, sometimes dipping as low as 14°F. They take a reading every minute.

Faced with extremes of temperature between day and night, yet no marked seasons, plants have to get their growing done when it's warm and devise ways of battening down to protect their delicate new growth at night. They cannot remain dormant through a cold season like other plants. The giant groundsels (*Dendrosenecios*) and the lobelias have evolved various strategies to cope. Both close their leaf rosettes at night to protect the core growth from frost; the lobelias, we had heard, also exude a slimy liquid within their rosettes that stops plant cells freezing. Was this—as was sometimes said—some sort of natural antifreeze? Up here at Shira we got our first good opportunity to examine the endemic giant rosette plants (*pachycauls*). The campsite itself is a little too exposed for them, but if we drop

of color. The most common is a silvery clump-forming helichrysum with small white flowers, probably *citrispinum* or *newii*. A wild "carrot," growing from a rosette of emerald leaves, is so astonishingly fresh against the dusty ground that, once your eyes are attuned to it, you can pick out the plants like scattered jewels across the hillside. There are several smaller flowers that I don't identify very well—little yellow helichrysums and daisies. I wish I'd learned more of the names before I came. My flower book has not really sur-

back over the escarpment or into an adjacent side valley good specimens of lobelias and groundsels abound. Roger tramps down the escarpment night and morning to monitor them. I also wandered into this valley to find specimens to photograph, and hopefully to spot the malachite sunbirds who plunder the lobelia flowers for honey. Unfortunately, the birds were busy somewhere else this afternoon, which was a disappointment, particularly since Roger and some of the others had been watching them there in the morning and have been raving about them ever since. I tried not to feel envious—I'd surely see plenty later in the trek. Meanwhile, I made do with the chubby little hill chats, which also have a taste for lobelia nectar and were far less elusive.

FROM THE LITTLE RIDGE above camp where we've been filming—the blocky edge of a volcanic dike, I suspect—you get an even better view of the Shira Plateau. This large eroded crater extends roughly five miles across in each direction. Today, with a 4-wheel-drive vehicle, you can approach to within half an hour of Shira Camp, following a track from the Londorossi Glades Park Gate. Our party is having some of its supplies sent up this way each day, and that's how we'll send down our unnecessary baggage. The main purpose of the road, however, is for fire fighting and to be able to get rescue vehicles into the moorland region quickly when sick tourists need to be evacuated from the higher slopes. In all cases of serious altitude sickness, a speedy response is vital; the only treatment for pulmonary or cerebral edema, which are both killers, is to get the patient to a lower altitude as soon as possible—either physically, or these days it could be virtually, in a "Gamov bag." Before the track was constructed, this western shoulder of Kilimanjaro was seldom visited and even more rarely written about.

The first Europeans to explore this plateau in the early years of German rule were the botanist Georg Volkens, geologist Carl Lent, and Kurt Johannes, commander of the German military post at Moshi, Mareale's friend, remembered now as the infamous Captain Johannes. In March 1894, these three climbed to the Saddle by the normal route from Marangu, then traversed around the northern side of Kibo. They kept to a level between 9,500 and 11,500 feet, somewhat lower than the Northern Circuit route adopts today. Entering the plateau on its northeastern edge, they spent the night in what became known as the Galuma Cave before briefly investigating

the crater floor. Volkens's botanical collection was one of the most thorough there has ever been.

Next came Hans Meyer again. After his successful climb with Purtscheller, Meyer had published a 1:250,000 map of Kilimanjaro, and was now keen to make a wide-ranging survey of the full mountain block. Geologists were rapidly learning how to read the rocks and work out the sequence of the lava flows and how they interleaved each other. This information was being correlated with the known ice ages of the Quaternary period. With the Chagga unified under German control, Meyer hoped it would be possible to explore more freely than when the territory was divided into rival chiefdoms. Having gathered information from the south and during his high-level hike from Mawenzi around Kibo's northern side, his main goal now was to extend the survey westward and see what could be learned of former volcanic activity and glaciation.

He made straight for the Galuma Cave, his companion this time the well-known alpine artist Ernst Platz, whose name would be borrowed for the most prominent feature in Shira's crater—the Platzkegel, a conical hill, which geologists say is the remnant of a vent infilled with lava and agglomerate. Meyer and Platz spent considerable time in the region, and their map appeared in 1900. Despite some misjudged features, such as the position of the Shira Ridge, Meyer demonstrated an adequate appreciation of the size of Shira's crater, which he called the "Galuma Plateau," a name that has since fallen into disuse. It's now known universally as the Shira Plateau. He reported his dismay at how much the mountain's icy cap had retreated since his climb nine years before. Meyer continued studying equatorial volcanoes after Kilimanjaro, going to the Virunga Mountains of Ruanda and to South America.

In 1906 the western side of Kibo was visited once more, this time by Fritz Jaeger and Eduard Oehler. They reconnoitered a route through from Machame, which involved cutting their way through the upper forest. They were interested primarily in Kibo's western glaciation, spending time on the Penck Glacier and in what is known today as the Western Breach. They also visited the Drygalski Glacier and the Lent Group, but they were unsuccessful in reaching the crater rim from the west or northwest. Shira itself was of little interest to them on this trip, although Oehler returned six years later with the geographer Fritz Klute and spent another five months on the mountain making a photogrammetric survey. He and Klute based themselves for half of this time on a camp above the Machame Escarpment at 13,645 feet—probably close to the site of our own camp. They were the first to descend from Kibo's crater rim by way of the Western Breach. They also spent several days on the western side of the Shira Plateau, close to the Shira Ridge. Their map, which appeared in a book published by Klute in 1921, was described by later Kilimanjaro geographers as "indispensable for the study of upper Kilimanjaro."

WHEN THE FILM CREW were reconnoitering the Shira Plateau a week before we came up here, they stumbled across the skeleton of a Cape buffalo, prompting the obvious questions: What was it doing at 12,000 feet?

Climbing to Shira, I picked up a skull about the size and shape of a cat's. Kazimoto thinks it could have been a genet, or more likely a serval, both of which are present all over the mountain though rarely seen.

In 1965, eyewitness reports of mammal sightings over the years were correlated with contemporary fieldwork to produce a checklist. The conclusion reached by G. S. Child of the College of African Wildlife Management in Mweka, who supervised the work, was that more than 80 different mammalian species were represented on the mountain, either in the forest or the alpine zone above, or in both. These ranged from little shrews and mice to antelope, bushpigs, porcupines, and the bigger fellows such as lions, leopards, elephants, black rhinoceros, and buffalo. Question marks hung over one or two more.

THURSDAY This morning I have to appear in a long shot for the film, walking along the skyline of a little ridge above camp. I'm wired up with a microphone, although scrambling around has left me so breathless I manage to produce little on tape except puffing and blowing. The sky is flawless, but for the tiniest wisp of cloud in front of the summit and a faded half moon. From before 9 o'clock the sun has been so hot it drills into your flesh. Looking down on camp I can see quite a bit of activity, and one or two solitary ravens are floating about on the scavenge. It really is a radiant morning.

Had it wandered up by accident? Become lost in the mist? Or do these animals regularly climb as high as this? They are hefty vegetarians; delightful as the vegetation is here, it is decidedly spare and scrubby when viewed as food. Only the giant lobelia rosettes have much substance and, I must say, frequently they do look chewed. Kazimoto told us of elephant bones he'd seen even higher, at 15,000 feet—a story that David had picked up also from local climbers.

We have seen disappointingly few animals up here. Part of the reason for rhapsodizing over the flora is that this is the most obvious wildlife the visitor sees. It's true we've been encountering more birds here in the open than in the forest, but animals are shy. It's almost impossible from casual observation to know what makes its home up here, or visits as a matter of routine.

A couple of decades later, the state of the larger mammals was reviewed again for a Kilimanjaro conservation symposium, by which time the habitat had seen many changes. The forest was further eroded and less of it comprised original growth. More significant was the increasing isolation of the mountain from nearby natural areas. Elephants and the other large animals known to migrate regularly between Kilimanjaro and Amboseli National Park, just across the border with Kenya, were having a tough time. As farming extended its range, only a narrow wildlife corridor to the northwest of the mountain remained to connect the two areas. Our porters told us that when their parents and grandparents were young, before the Second World War, large mammals could be found on all sides of the mountain and wildlife generally was more abundant. The Chagga have always been great

ABOVE: A GIANT LOBELIA ROSETTE CLOSES ITS LEAVES AT NIGHT TO PROTECT DELICATE NEW GROWTH FROM THE FIERCE NIGHT FROSTS. RIGHT: FORMING AT NIGHT AND SOMETIMES ATTAINING SEVERAL INCHES IN HEIGHT, NEEDLE ICE HOISTS LOOSE PEBBLES ALOFT UNTIL THE ICE MELTS THE NEXT MORNING—SOLIFLUCTION.

meat eaters, and very few animals remain now on the heavily populated southern slopes of the mountain. Elephants and buffalo coming from Amboseli and heading for the western forest sometimes cross the Shira Plateau as they probably always have done, though why they should go as high as the skeleton Kazimoto was telling us about is something of a mystery. Kazimoto is happy to put it down to a kind of hypnosis: He says that if human animals find mountains awesome and are attracted enough to climb to their highest points, how can we be sure animals don't feel a similar pull? More likely, it seemed to me, the elephant was chasing a special salt lick, or could smell moisture in the snow and ice.

Later, I did some reading and asking around to see how high animals have been seen on Africa's mountains. There is the famous leopard, of course, whose mummified remains were found up on the crater rim in the 1920s, and which inspired the opening lines of Ernest Hemingway's "The Snows of Kilimanjaro." The elephant record appears to be some bones found at 16,000 feet on Mawenzi in the first half of the 20th century. Another

elephant, Icy Mike, landed at a similar height on the Lewis Glacier of Mount Kenya, although climbers say that was a wounded animal, chased up there by hunters, which fell into a crevasse and died. There are scattered references to other remains, including one of a carcass found at 14,570 feet on the western slopes of Kibo by a park ranger in 1977. I wondered if this could be the same elephant Kazimoto was telling us about near the Moir Hut, and to which he later led our film crew and Heidi and Hansi. Elephant expert Charles Foley confirmed that these animals were probably attracted to mineral licks, which was why they also liked to migrate to Amboseli. He imagined they'd make such high climbs infrequently. Certainly, with so many corpses, it didn't appear to do them very much good, though of course we don't know over how long these bones have accrued, or if other elephants went up and down safely. Perhaps the most mysterious find was of buffalo bones on a narrow ledge on the East Face of Mawenzi, discovered by the first climbers to go there in 1964. The place was inaccessible except by hard climbing. Even to imagine the beast had fallen from above seemed unlikely as there are few places on either side of Mawenzi that can be easily scaled.

PLENTY OF LOBELIA PLANTS were in bloom on this hillside, their flower spikes erupting as stiff conical pillars several feet tall. Birds would flutter off them as we approached, then hop along in front as if leading us safely past. The higher we went, the better the view back over the Shira Plateau and its jagged rim. There was the Platzkegel Roger had trekked to see, there the Shira Tower. Before long we'd reached the crest of the lava ridge, one of several radiating from the cone of Kibo. The feature known as Lava Tower, a great shark's tooth of rock, was visible now at the foot of the track up to the Western Breach. We'd be coming back to that later, but meanwhile were traversing around Kibo in an easterly direction as an acclimatization exercise. We would cross a couple more of these arid ridges before reaching the deep Umbwe Valley, the Great Barranco. What vegetation remained at this height was mostly tucked under the many boulders spattered about this upland desert—volcanic bombs, presumably.

Between the rocks the ground looked raked, like a Japanese garden, and in places it bore polygonal patterning, a process known as solifluction. These are effects of the frequent freezing and thawing endured by the surface soil. It is reported from many places in the world, usually occurring as the result of seasonal temperature changes, but here on Kilimanjaro and other equatorial mountains it is especially pronounced because it is a diurnal phenomenon. Every night the ground freezes; every day it bakes. There was a thick frost when we'd left Shira Camp this morning, and we'd noticed in places how long needles of ice were lifting up the top inch or two of soil and pebbles, separating them from layers underneath. As the day warmed and these ice crystals melted, the hoisted material plopped back down again. Such reg-

ular heaving of the topsoil keeps its texture loose and open—creating what gardeners might call a fine tilth—but at the same time the restless motion makes it extraordinarily difficult for seedlings to establish themselves. They are uprooted as soon as they start to germinate.

Solifluction also induces sorting and grading of different size particles. The needle ice, which builds up as a result of capillary action, is very effective in bringing to the surface stones from deeper down. Pebbles become separated out from smaller material and laid down in geometrically regular rows on the finer-grained soil, hence its raked appearance. These sorted stripes are especially noticeable on gently sloping ground. The polygonal patterns, by contrast, are more commonly found on flatter sections where the ground is damp during the day, and thus also susceptible to needle ice formation. The larger particles get conveyed to the polygon edges, where they tend to build up and reinforce the striking effect.

A few plants have developed strategies to cope with this regular earth heaving. One moss, for instance, grows back on itself to adopt a spherical shape and lies loosely on the surface, rolling around as the ground freezes and thaws. We were anxious to photograph examples of such moss balls, but most of the loose moss we found had just slid from rocks onto the ground; I am not convinced we saw the real thing. Some lichens and algae don't require attachment either, and they survive here all right. Mat-forming plants and those with rhizomes or runners can often invade the mobile ground, but rarely establish themselves in it from seed. Seedlings of an umbellifer, *Haplosciadium abyssinicum*, are either remarkably accommodating or they germinate at times when the solifluction process is less pronounced. Once growth is underway, the plant quickly thrusts down an enormously long taproot into the unaffected subsurface soil. In old age this becomes

so thick and gnarly that it can provide a raft for tussock grass and other plants to colonize.

On this high, open ground, a few more old bones were visible among the rocks, including more buffalo skulls. We stopped for lunch as the mist slunk in and it grew chilly. We were glad, soon afterward, to start dropping into the beautiful Great Barranco. Jakob told us that he took part in the construction of the footpath into this valley. It was built as a rescue and evacuation route, but now plays its part in alleviating the pressure on more popular trails. Very quickly, it too has suffered from overuse. The ground is steep and covered with loose stones. People—particularly heavily laden porters—are apt to fan out in search of the safest way down, and the vegetation gets worn away. Great scars of scree have built up around the zigzagging track, and the groundsel groves were suffering there. Nevertheless, this is a most beautiful and verdant valley and it comes as a surprise to suddenly drop into it from the desert ridges.

It's like a tapestry, this valley. There are so many shades and textures together. The valley floor is littered with boulders, and even these are textured; they're full of crystals. It's a coarse porphyritic lava, rough to the touch, and encrusted with lichens. The predominant flowers are the marvelous, silvery helichrysums, or straw flowers; they grow in compact hummocks, mimicking the shape of the rocks, just adding a different tone and texture. There's surprising color variation in this billowing scene. Many greens and yellows, but it is silver that dominates and appears to ripple as the light changes, or a breeze ruffles the foliage.

There's so much contrast here. Mornings have been bright and clear, but in the afternoons this becomes a spooky sort of place with mist slipping in and among the knobbly groundsels.

Particularly, I like the birds here. We have been lucky to see lammergeyers, which are great vultures. Perhaps that doesn't sound at all attractive, but in reality they are most handsome—orange-breasted, with long narrow wings and a diamond-shaped tail, quite unmistakable. And they are said to be rare, but we have seen them repeatedly up here patrolling the slopes. A pair seem to be "working" this Great Barranco basin; in the morning when we were filming around camp, one spiraled round and around us, coming in quite low to get a good look at what we were about before wheeling off to soar on some thermals. We haven't noticed them bone breaking,

which is perhaps their most famous characteristic. They carry bones to a great height, then drop them on rocks to crack them open. Besides the buffalo skulls, we saw a number of smaller bones on the higher ground as we crossed over. I remembered wondering at the time why these were just bits of creatures and not full skeletons. My guess now is that it was the work of the lammergeyers—or wild dogs, perhaps.

There have been other raptors, too. One, hunched on a groundsel stump at sunset, was quite large, with dark wings and a white chest. I thought at first it was a Martial eagle—having seen one of these earlier in Arusha National Park—but it's more likely to have been an Augur buzzard, waiting for the hyraxes and rodents to come out and feed in the fading light.

White-necked ravens keep a close check on camp. They are common all over the mountain—"mountain cleaners" the porters call them, because they'll gobble up everything campers leave behind. They look solid and well fed. But when they fly, they can be so acrobatic—you can't believe such heavy, ungainly birds could achieve such elegance. Alpine swifts, we saw too, and sunbirds in the lobelias. I've seen and heard plenty of these glittering birds now, but I still can't keep up with Roger who has found a nest with a baby chick in it. He won't say where, of course, but they hope to film it at some stage. I guess I'm destined always to be jealous of Roger's discoveries.

I had hoped we'd see more wild animals here, and I've no doubt elands and duikers must often graze on the rich grassy vegetation at the head of the barranco although we've seen only small creatures such as the four-striped grass mouse. But, then, we're such a large party that, whether we mean to or not, our talk and clatter must warn most of the shyer species to keep their distance.

The first evening we were here we met two American ladies who'd come into the Great Barranco late in the afternoon and they claimed to have seen African hunting dogs. These dogs, which hunt in packs, are only distantly related to domestic dogs, or, apparently, to any other canid, their evolutionary twig having split off from the main wolf and jackal tree about three million years ago.

THE PINNACLES BORDERING THE SOUTHWEST RIM OF THE SHIRA PLATEAU HOVER ABOVE EVENING MISTS. FOLLOWING PAGES: MATTED WITH BLOOD, AN AFRICAN WILD DOG PAUSES FROM DEVOURING KILL TO WATCH FOR PACK MEMBERS.

THE BREACH WALL VISIBLE BEHIND, NICOLE AND I EXPLORE
A GIANT GROUNDSEL FOREST IN THE GREAT BARRANCO.
FOLLOWING PAGES (162-163): GIANT GROUNDSELS, *SENECIO
COTTONII*, CLUSTER ON THE SLOPES OF THE GREAT BARRANCO.

Several sightings of them were recorded on Kilimanjaro
in the 1950s and 1960s—one, famously, by the explorer
and traveler Wilfred Thesiger, who told how his party met
five wild dogs at 19,000 feet. They followed his party in
the snow around the crater rim, or sat and watched when
they stopped, always maintaining a distance of about 500
feet between themselves and the men. One of Thesiger's
companions photographed the dogs at the summit.

Since then, Africa's wild dogs have had a rough ride. A
NATIONAL GEOGRAPHIC article that appeared a year before
our trip claimed that no more than 5,000 exist anywhere
in sub-Saharan Africa—as that was their entire original
range, only these few thousand survive anywhere in the
world, hanging on in just a few isolated pockets. Kilimanjaro is one of those pockets. A National Park checklist suggests they can be found anywhere within the
reserve, but its own last accredited sighting was in 1989.

Wild dogs have always had a bad press. The magazine
article recalled a hunter in 1914 dreaming of "the excel-
lent day...when means can be devised... for this unnecessary creature's complete extermination." For many
years, even in national parks, packs were routinely wiped
out because they preyed on other wildlife. Game Scouts
are said to have shot more than 50 individuals in the Kilimanjaro vicinity. People simply didn't like them, and
deemed their method of hunting barbaric, though it's
scarcely different from other predators. They will con-
verge on a weak animal, run it down, and disembowel it.
The myth has grown up that they enjoy subjecting their
prey to a lingering death, that they kill for the sport of
the chase and wantonly rip ribbons of skin and lumps of
flesh from terrified victims. As if that weren't enough,
they are accused of being cannibals and man-eaters, too.
Here on Kilimanjaro the porters will tell you stories of
young boys who, new to the job of portering, have fallen
behind the main column and been killed by wild dogs.
Despite such stories, the two ladies were delighted to
have seen their pair of dogs, and there was no indication
that Thesiger and Webb felt threatened by the five that
trailed them around the crater rim. I was so eager to see
them for myself that I spent every spare moment scour-
ing the valley for movement. If the wanton reputation of

Lycaon pictus is overstated, that of being the most efficient killers of larger species is well deserved.

NICOLE AND I were filmed on our first day here in a
little groundsel "forest," tucked against the Barranco
Wall on the east side of this valley. We had to wait a long
time for just the right silvery light to play on the groundsel leaves. At least it gave us the chance to get acquainted
with these extraordinary plants. They were growing in a
gloppy, squelchy bog, which dragged at our boots and
threatened to root us alongside them. We had to keep
fidgeting to bring our feet back to the surface as the

minutes stretched to hours. The first time we got the magic atmosphere David was waiting for, I goofed the shot by walking across the line of sight and blocking Nicole from the camera's view. It was hours before it came right again, so that in the end we were there all morning and afternoon.

Around us were giant groundsels at all stages from germination through to old and fallen stumps. Some of the trees were so well branched they could be among the oldest on the mountain, but it was especially encouraging to see that plenty more were ready to follow on. This was really a *Dendrosenecio* nursery.

The guides had a rule of thumb for telling how old these giant groundsels were. They flowered, so they said, once every 25 years from the terminal rosette. After they'd done so, the parent branch would fork, grow another 25 years, flower again, branch again. Count the number of forks one branch makes, we were told, and multiply that by 25 to give the age of the tree. Somewhere else I heard you could tell these trees' age by their height: A mature plant puts on two centimeters of new growth each year, less than an inch, if no untoward factors have interrupted its progress. By either reckoning, the largest trees here could prove to be a couple of hundred years old.

Continued on page 164

KILIMANJARO HIGH-ALTITUDE PLANTS: TOUGH SURVIVORS

HENK BEENTJE, PH.D.

EDITOR OF *FLORA OF TROPICAL EAST AFRICA*, ROYAL BOTANIC GARDENS, KEW, ENGLAND

HIGH UP ON the mountain there is plant life, but it differs enormously from that in the forest. In the forest it is hot and steamy, and abundant life-forms teem in vast numbers and in dense competition with each other. Above the forest, from about 9,000 to 10,000 feet (2,700 to 3,000 meters) it is a different matter. Just above the forest stretch the moorlands and the heath zone, an area with wide views but tough going underfoot: grass tussocks, dense giant heath, and bogs. Even higher up, from 13,000 to 13,700 feet (3,900 to 4,100 meters) upward, the surroundings are austere and rocky, the sky, invisible in the forest below, dominates the scene, and here and there a few plants struggle to survive the blazing sun and icy nights. These plants may go up a long way: Individuals of *Senecio telekii* (a member of the sunflower family) have been found at 18,000 feet (5,400 meters).

…plants at high altitudes have to cope with extremes, have to protect themselves from radiation and cold, and have to get enough water to survive.

SURVIVORS

Life is harsh on the mountain, and plants at high altitudes have to cope with extremes, have to protect themselves from radiation and cold, and have to get enough water to survive. There is less competition for resources than in the forest below; In fact, at very high altitudes, there is cooperation and mutual help. And that is necessary, because it is tough at the top.

Temperature: Annual variation in temperature is slight—after all, Kilimanjaro is not too far from the Equator. But daily variation is high. Often there are strong frosts at night, with a rapid warming up in the morning and blazing sunlight by noon. Radiation can be intense, especially in the ultraviolet and infrared wavelengths. This has led Professor Hedberg, the acknowledged expert on Afro-alpine plant adaptations, to describe the weather at this altitude as "summer every day, winter every night." In addition to this daily rhythm, sudden changes in cloud cover and wind force can cause around a nearly 20°F drop in as little as 30 minutes. Even distance from the ground matters: Day to night temperature difference at valley bottoms may be as high as 35°F, while on the adjacent ridge, just over 15 feet higher up, this difference was measured as only about 20°F. This might be a reason why it helps to be a giant groundsel—grow yourself away from extremes in temperature.

Water: Rainfall is very low in the Afro-alpine belt, and the Saddle between Kibo and Mawenzi is almost a desert because of this. On the other hand, the cloud cover and the low mists, that can be so common, contain moisture, and where plants do survive, they can sieve out this moisture from the air so it drips down the leaf and can be absorbed by the roots. Normal plant breathing also takes in some water. I believe this might be a reason for the gigantism in the giant *senecios* and *lobelias*—big leaves with lots of surface to catch the moisture.

In early morning, the cold temperature of the soil causes slow water availability, as plant tissues do not work very well when cold, while the morning sun already causes leaf transpiration. The result can be a real drought in wet conditions. Plants certainly need to insulate themselves against all these extremes. Plants have developed different techniques:

BE DENSE: The denser a group of plants or plant community, the more it creates its own microclimate with a buffer zone protecting and insulating the core.

Grass tussocks work like this; air trapped in the middle layers protects the innermost core. This buffering is also much appreciated by local sunbirds, which nest in tussocks. The same technique, incidentally, works in subarctic islands.

TAKE A SHINE: A shiny leaf surface reflects sunlight. This protects the plant from extreme temperatures. Any sunshine that is reflected and not absorbed does not produce heat. And heat can be intense. Shiny leaves are quite common, and occur in *Haplocarpha*, several *Senecio*, and several *Lobelia* species.

GET FAT: Leathery leaves with thick skin and small stomata (breathing pores) are very common. This aids water retention in order to cope with great heat during the day. *Protea* and *Helichrysum* are examples.

GROW YOUR HAIR: A thick layer of hair reflects sunlight (see above), diminishes outward radiation at night and hence decreases cooling, and forms a buffer layer of trapped air to reduce transpiration by reducing air flow over leaf breathing pores. *Alchemilla* and *Helichrysum* species are examples of this technique. Giant groundsels can be densely hairy on their lower surface, which comes in useful at night when their rosette closes to form a so-called night bud.

STAY SMALL/COMPACT/LOW: Variations on a theme. Small plants or those with cushion growth have a smaller surface to absorb heat and stay cooler (*Haplocarpha*, *Swertia*, *Myosotis*). Some plants do not even develop aerial stems: *Ranunculus*, *Carduus*, and *Haplosciadium* have both leaves and flowers at ground level. If you're not small, you can still decrease your leaf surface, either by having small leaves (heath, *Helichrysum*), or rolled-up or folded leaves (heath, *Senecio*, *Helichrysum*).

A SENECIO CLINGS TO LIFE IN THE
HIGH-ALPINE DESERT.

HANG ON TO THOSE DEAD PARTS: Old dead leaves retained on the stem such as in giant groundsels really make a difference. The stem pith also is very watery, serving as an emergency water supply, like the camel's hump. Older stems, where dead leaves have disappeared, develop a corky layer for the same purpose. When campers remove dead leaves for making fires, chances are that plant will die, as they are unable to transport water in early morning—they die of thirst. A plant very similar to the giant groundsel, espeletia of the High Andes, has developed the same technique.

GO WITH THE FLOW: Frost works on soil containing moisture, making it expand when freezing (say, the top two inches), and contract when thawing. A daily rhythm of this makes the earth move, at least in small bits. The only plants living on such surfaces are floaters that follow these movements—Algae (*Nostoc*) and lichens (*Parmelia*) lay on top and move up and down with the soil; and moss balls (*Grimmia*) form, with a thin layer of moss surrounding a small core of earth. For higher plants, life is very difficult, as seedlings cannot establish themselves on a surface like that. Resulting patches of bare soil can be colonized only from the edges. Strategies include establishing yourself in the shelter of other vegatation or next to a rock, and thinking lateral— grow outward into the bare zone and colonize it bit by bit. In the higher zones it is very obvious that plants grow in patches, with bare soil in between. Mutual cooperation works, the plants giving each other shelter and their own microclimate. And so it goes. Plants cope by using techniques also found in subarctic islands, to cope with the cold; or with techniques found in hot deserts, to cope with drought and great heat. Or with combinations of the two, to cope with the strange climate of Kilimanjaro.

When Nicole first came into this groundsel forest of huge old trees with their dry, leafy skirts and stiff, long arms, her first words were that it must be "Doctor Seuss-land"; they were so unlike any trees she had encountered before. We used our day in the swamp to find out all we could about them. In the first place, we discovered they rocked gently when even slight pressure was applied. They resonated when tapped, so that when we saw a dead one on the ground, we were not surprised to find that the trunk was hollow. Sharing the groundsel's spongy habitat were mosses, grasses, and lichens mainly, but also several plants with small daisy-like flowers, such as *Euryops dacrydiodes* with its bract-like scales that are in fact the leaves. If not in the bog

munching creatures, and we saw when we folded back the leaf, that the insides of the rosettes were infested with little grubs and flies. It has been suggested that when the giant groundsel is visited by sunbirds, they may be after protein-rich insects as much as the nectar.

The other thing that took us by surprise was the smell of their leaves. It was by no means sweet, nor was it unpleasant either. It was more everyday than that, and hard to describe: something between wash days and fresh cabbages. One botanist has described the flower heads as having a "fetid 'groundsel' odor," attractive only to pollinating flies, but I cannot say we noticed anything rank or repellent in the smell of our groundsel grove.

FRIDAY Roger got up very early on our rest day here, and set off with his geological hammer to explore the Shira Crater for himself. He was anxious to visit the Platzkegel in the hope that he could find there rocks from deep in the Earth's mantle. Nor was he disappointed. When he trudged back later in the afternoon, damp and a bit done in after several hour's walking, he was euphorically brandishing lumps of limburgite from below the crust of Africa, containing large green crystals of olivine and some ferrous minerals. His digital pictures of the dike swarms, which he showed us over dinner that evening, were astonishing. They looked so archeological, like ruined stone walls, blocky and straight. We all rather wished we'd had the energy to go, too.

itself, certainly within a hundred yards of it, on the drier banks of a stream, there were modest little senecios—probably *S. schweinfurthii*, one of several groundsel varieties on Kilimanjaro that has evolved more conservatively and not adopted gigantism. It's hard to believe they shared a common ancestor. Other lowly senecios on this mountain are named after its first ascensionists: *Senecio meyer-johannis* and *S. purtschelleri*.

The undersides of the giant senecio leaves—white and mealy, like felt—give the plants their silvery look when the wind ruffles them. What I hadn't appreciated until we spent time with them was that, tough as these leaves are, they are relished by certain insects. The edges of some leaves were pinked or perforated by

A CHARACTERISTIC of all life is that it has to exist between the extremes of heat and cold. Most plants cannot thrive below 32°F, and very little can survive above the boiling point of water. So most plant life on the planet exists between these two extremes. On Kilimanjaro, where it falls below zero every night and bakes under the tropical sun by day, the plants have had to devise ways of dealing with extremes. All, like the senecios and lobelias, have adopted special mechanisms to prevent the interior heart of the plant from dying as the cells pass through the freezing point.

In the Great Barranco, we are surrounded by giant lobelias (*L. Deckenii*), which means Roger is in his element. The children are helping him to monitor their nighttime temperatures, but he has grown so infatuated with these plants that he visits them at all hours, observing and photographing them. The tall flower-spikes, once they appear, grow very rapidly from a few inches to four feet or so in a few weeks, and the flowers open in close succession. This means that birds are able to get fresh nectar from the one spike daily, which maximizes the plant's chances of pollination by these birds. You see the chats and sunbirds checking out the plants on a regular basis. The flowers themselves are protected within deep bracts, so the sunbirds' long bills are of great advantage in reaching the nectar at the base of each flower. The hill chats have to manage with shorter beaks, yet clearly get similar satisfaction even if they have to spend more time on the plants. The bracts of the older flowers are often seen to be heavily scratched by the visiting birds' feet.

The lobelia insulates itself, not only by closing its leaves into a tight ball at night to protect the delicate new growth in the center, but also by secreting a kind of slime that is often referred to as an antifreeze. In fact, it is quite the opposite. Within the fluid are modified pectins or polysaccharides that induce ice-nucleation at the highest possible subzero temperature.

Pure water has to supercool below 32°F before it allows ice-nucleation to occur. If this happens within a leaf, the plant sustains frost damage because of the formation of large ice crystals that disrupt the internal anatomy of the leaf. The giant lobelias, and indeed the giant senecios at high elevation, have a loose, open cell structure in their leaves instead of a more typical, densely packed layer of photosynthetic cells. The plant's modified pectins coat the outside of each cell. By inducing ice-nucleation at a temperature higher than the freezing point of water, these pectins ensure that a multitude of small ice crystals develop in the intercellular spaces rather than large disruptive crystals.

Some species have taken this a step further, secreting the polysaccharide fluid into the leaf rosette where it becomes trapped and provides a "water bath" around the growing point and young leaves. This heats and cools more slowly than air (or leaf tissue), and at night serves as a capacitor that stabilizes the fluid at 32°F even though the air temperature may reach 23°F to 14°F.

The mechanics behind the lobelia's anti-freeze strategy were not known to us the first time we were on Kilimanjaro. We discovered its slimy fluid, of course, and saw how a skin of ice would skim the "water bath" in the morning, underneath which the liquid appeared not to freeze, thus protecting the sensitive leaf bud from subzero temperatures. Roger had Nicole and Hansi help him apply his thermal data loggers: one tucked right inside a lobelia leaf rosette, one out on the open ground beside it to monitor fluctuations in air temperature. Synchronous readings were taken every minute to be fed into Roger's computer later. Usually Roger was the only one awake early enough to retrieve the loggers each day. One morning, he rushed into breakfast fizzing with excitement. "You'll never guess what!" he said. "That lobelia: It's not a plant, it's a machine! It's simply amazing." The readouts for the previous night had shown that while the outside temperature fell, the inside of the lobelia did not merely echo the fall a few degrees higher, but made a significant increase. The plant appeared to be manufacturing heat. It wasn't a result he was able to repeat in subsequent experiments on this trip, but that didn't necessarily mean it was a rogue reading.

Sufficient lobelia fluid in the rosette sustains the internal temperature at, or close to, the freezing point of water however low the air temperature drops outside—so much we were sure of. But the process could be affected one way or another by the concentration of the liquid, he supposed: "Evaporation during the day may concentrate the polysaccharide in the fluid, thereby reducing the freezing point. Rain, on the other hand, dilutes the fluid, which could raise its freezing point."

What was needed, Roger decided, was for more readings to be obtained over a longer period. He would leave the lobelia wired up after we left Great Barranco and commission one of our guides to come and retrieve it some time later. When he was finally reunited with his equipment, he had nine days' worth of readings that supported his theory, followed by six weeks when the temperature barely changed from 72°F. It was easy to see what had happened. The guide, worried about the safety of this expensive piece of equipment unattended up there on the mountain, had retrieved it early and kept it in a drawer indoors where no harm could befall it.

Several plants found on Kilimanjaro occur nowhere else in the world, although its flora bears a striking similarity to that of other isolated equatorial mountains, such as Mounts Meru, Kenya, and Elgon, and the Ruwenzori. It's easy to understand why botanists have

referred to these scattered peaks as the Afro-montane archipelago. Their floristic affinity is as evident as its dissimilarity from the plants growing on the plains that separate them. You see the resemblance at all altitudinal levels, suggesting that they share a gene pool, but that each has evolved somewhat differently.

These plant colonies are said to date back to the Tertiary period, coinciding with the onset of African volcanism. But although it used to be thought that at some time in the past these islands of montane vegetation must have been linked, or at least been closer than they are at present, as scientists learn more about ancient weather patterns and geophysical changes, this idea is being abandoned. The belief now is that plant seeds have been exchanged between the mountains by other agencies, such as wind or birds, but over a long enough period to allow subsequent speciation (that is, to generate new species). This appears to be substantiated by the absence of large-seeded plants on the mountains that would require large animals (or water) for disper-

◆ **Sherpa Wongchu, David Breashears, and Jack Tankard film in the alpine desert two hours above Shira Camp.**

giant lobelia in the northern forests, and can recognise different forms of the commonest species. Lobelias on the Shira Plateau, he says, are visibly distinguishable from those in the Great Barranco, for instance. Scientists may well find, on closer study, that many species need further subdivision.

I've always found it hard to grasp the scale and implications of evolution, and how geophysical events and other natural forces can prompt a living species of plant or animal suddenly to evolve. For thousands or millions of years a species may settle comfortably into a niche, its circumstances giving it little need for more than minor genetic tinkering to enable it to better exploit the facilities on offer within that niche, or to gain a measure of advantage over fellow settlers or invaders. It's the timescale and element of chance that boggles my mind: how unicellular blobs of vital jelly can have been transmuted into the immeasurable variety of living things that grace this planet, or have done so in past eons.

Even accounting for survival of the fittest, it can take many generations to acquire a beneficial genetic change, and hang on to it. It was no wonder to me that evolution is often referred to as the blind watchmaker. But I've been thinking on too large a scale, and should have concentrated on the niche. Adaptations in plants can be a rapid process. Grimshaw reminded me how plantsmen exploit this and in one or two generations can produce new varieties. In nature it may take a little longer, but it is a dynamic process. The impetus that speeds things up, when required, is disturbance. When a niche becomes intolerable to its occupants, or it disappears, then those creatures or plants that made it their home have to be able to move on or adapt, or they die.

In and out of the periods of glaciation, the East African forests will have contracted, then regenerated if relict patches of woodland remained. One can wonder idly how much richer the Afro-montane and Afro-alpine flora might have been if *Homo sapiens* had delayed his appearance on the global scene. If Kilimanjaro had been granted an extra half a million years, say, to speciate quietly in isolation, just think what we might see now. Even so, and notwithstanding its relative youth, the mountain's flowering plants outnumber the indigenous plants of the British Isles.

sal; along with the fact that many of the species are known as aggressive colonizers.

Because of its youth, Kilimanjaro has fewer endemic plant species than more ancient East African mountains, such as the Usambara, but some have diversified well. One thinks particularly of the lobelias and the senecios, where evolution can be seen as an ongoing process. The botanist John Grimshaw, who carried out exhaustive fieldwork on the slopes of Kilimanjaro in the first half of the 1990s, discovered a previously unknown

CHAPTER EIGHT

GOLDEN AGE OF CLIMBING

We were level with the upper tier of the Great Breach Wall itself...
draped with fantastic icicles; one, a slim pillar linking the snow band
to the tiny Diamond Glacier overhanging the Wall, was 500 feet long!
That was the line! But it would wait for the next generation.

JOHN CLEARE, FROM "MOUNTAINS," 1975

CLIMBING FROM THE southwest, as we were doing, gives no awareness of Kilimanjaro's second peak, Mawenzi, which remains hidden from this side until you reach the summit. Had we come up from Marangu by the standard route, its rugged outline would have been a dominating presence once the Saddle Plateau was reached. "Dark and threatening the shattered bulwarks of Mawenzi rose sternly into the upper air," Meyer had written in 1889. Not that he was intimidated by its defiant skyline: After success on Kibo, he was reluctant to go home without tucking an ascent of Mawenzi under his belt also. He and Purtscheller launched their first attempt on October 13. ~ A proliferation of vertical fissures and narrow, tilting ledges led them toward the bristling skyline, which in places tapered to only a few feet thick. The crumbling lava, Meyer said, offered the most breakneck bit of climbing he'd ever undertaken, and the constant falling fragments were unnerving. Although the pair gained the ridge, a chasm at their feet dashed all hopes of following it along to the higher summits. In a second attempt two days later, they managed to climb one of Mawenzi's tops by angling toward the central rock towers from lower down, but it was not the highest, and this time

PRECEDING PAGES: FRANK CANNINGS LEADS UP THE LOWER SECTION OF THE HEIM GLACIER ON KIBO'S SOUTHWEST FLANK.
LEFT: ROB TAYLOR READIES TO START CLIMBING THE UPPER BREACH WALL ON THE DAY OF HIS ACCIDENT IN 1978.

171

THE JAGGED RED SPIRES AND WHITE ICE STRANDS OF THE
BREACH WALL STAND DEFIANTLY AT SUNSET.

THE JAGGED RED SPIRES AND WHITE ICE STRANDS OF THE
BREACH WALL STAND DEFIANTLY AT SUNSET.

two jagged pinnacles barred their way along the serrated crest. Disappointment was mitigated by the stupendous view they were granted over the opposite side of the mountain. "We stood on the brink of an abysmal gulf, surrounded by an array of peaks, and spires, and craggy pinnacles," Meyer described:

On this, its eastern side, from an altitude of about 16,830 feet, the mountain sinks sheer downward into a gigantic cauldron, the sides of which are scarred with innumerable rugged ravines. As we gazed from our dizzy height upon the hills and valleys, the streams and bushes, the endless profusion of gullies and gorges 6000 or 7000 feet below, it seemed as if we had a bird's-eye view of earth from a balloon.

Were they looking into the original crater of Mawenzi? Meyer was not sure; as a geographer, he could not reconcile that interpretation with the prevailing dip in the beds of lava. Yet, next to Kibo's crater, this was the most wondrous sight they had been granted on Kilimanjaro. They saw it again a few days later from a different angle, when having one last try at Mawenzi by approaching from the north. Still, the highest point eluded them: "Sixteen hundred feet above towered the titanic rampart," Meyer bemoaned, "unapproachable here as elsewhere." But from a deep notch at the head of the northeastern ridge they once more gazed into the "yawning cauldron" of Mawenzi's Great and Lesser Barrancos. Though the line of their route is uncertain, Meyer and Purtscheller were credited as having made the first ascent of what today is known as Klute Peak, one of Mawenzi's lesser summit pinnacles at 16,716 feet (5,095 meters).

Meyer had wanted to name the summit they climbed after his doughty companion, but this did not stick. Two higher points now bear the names of these pioneers, peaks upon which they never set foot: Hans Meyer Peak, the tallest of all at 16,896 feet; and Purtscheller Peak, immediately south of it, at 16,798 feet. The peak they did climb, Klute Peak, commemorates the glaciologist F. Klute who, with E. Oehler, was the first to top Hans Meyer Peak in 1912. In time, all Mawenzi's summits were scaled, traversed, named, and renamed. But many years

would go by before anyone took a serious look at the peak's appalling East Face.

Meyer's "great cauldron" is in truth the conjoined heads of two deep and precipitous river gorges. The Great and Little (or Lesser) Barrancos, often described as Himalayan in scale, leave the mountain in a northeasterly direction and extend for several miles before coming together above Tarakea. You can't see right into them—not from the crest of Mawenzi, nor from the air—for the sides are several thousand feet deep, and

their beetling cliffs are deeply eroded and masked in vegetation. In places, the valley sides even overlap one another. Separating the two barrancos is the slender Downie Ridge, known also and more prosaically as Middle Buttress.

The first tentative exploration of the Great Barranco took place in 1949 when three members of the Mountain Club of Kenya (MCK) approached Mawenzi's South Peak with a view to traversing around the mountain's east side, thus to approach Kilimanjaro's Saddle from the opposite direction to normal. They were keen to see the fabled East Face, which they knew as "Crater Wall," and this much of their goal they realized. But so far as making headway around the mountain, they found that the nearer they got to Mawenzi, frustratingly, the more chasmic the valleys became and the more inpenetrable the undergrowth.

From a point on the ridge that formed the southern wall of the Great Barranco, they had a superb view across to the precipices of the East Face: "These stupendous cliffs dive down on the one hand into the depths of an abysmal ravine, the bottom of which could not be seen, and on the other hand rise to the magnificent skyline of the summit ridge of Mawenzi." Two of the party scrambled into the ravine, hoping to reach the foot of the East Face and forge a route over the mountain, but to their dismay the sides of the ravine steepened dangerously and dense shrubbery soon rose above their shoulders. They never even saw the riverbed, let alone attain the head of the Great Barranco.

Four years later a Sheffield University team joined with the Geological Survey of Tanganyika to make a comprehensive survey of the Kilimanjaro massif. As part of their reconnaissance, Professor C. Downie and Peter Wilkinson succeeded in dropping into the Great

a circular tour of Mawenzi. Following a subtle line of Firmin's down precipitous gullies and along narrow ledges on what Howard later described as the "rottenest of rotten rock," it took three hours to reach the valley floor and they vowed nothing would induce them back up that slope of tottering rubble. They bivouacked at the head of the barranco, a chaos of crumbling rock spires, and next morning climbed onto the East Face. They reached a ledge about 1,000 feet up, in a "sensational position." But progress was halted after another wall and some steep gullies brought them to a hopelessly friable section of cliff. The circuit it would have to be. Here, they had better luck. Crossing the divide between the two barrancos, they forced a way out to the north, to Mawenzi Tarn, on the third day. They promised them-

SATURDAY One of the first things you notice on an expedition is how dry your skin gets. Nothing heals. You get these cracks on your fingers, which start as little splits at the edge of the fingernail, then widen into crevasses, going right over the point of your finger. I think they call them "nail-bed splinters." You can't put on enough cream to stop it happening. Heidi, who usually has the most pampered hands in the world, has come off worse than anyone on this trip and is in agony when she tries to buckle her rucksack with her wounded hands. David has been supergluing the cracks together for her, telling her that's what real expeditioners have to do. Good thing we're not in the Antarctic for six months. Our hands would just shred into fly whisks.

Barranco from Three Kings Valley on the southeastern rim. They scrambled around at the upper end of the gorge, climbing some distance up the face below Latham Peak. Here, they discovered a plug of diorite at 14,000 feet with a diameter of about 300 feet, which they recognized as the major volcanic vent of Mawenzi. It confirmed that what remains today is the remnant of a highly eroded stratiform volcano, from which little, if any, of the original crater rim has survived. The whole east side of the mountain had been lost to erosion—not explosion. The two barrancos have demolished the bulk of the original mountain.

In September 1954, Arthur Firmin carried out further reconnaissance of the East Face with John Howard. They hoped either to find a route up the face or to make

selves another go at the East Face one day, but it was not to be. Firmin, who'd been the inspiration and driving force of East African mountaineering for at least 15 years, died tragically in Nepal in May 1955.

More sorties were made into the barrancos by MCK members during 1955 and 1956, rather to explore further traversing possibilities than to tackle Mawenzi's great organ-pipe face, which had come to be known as the Eiger of Africa. The East Face was not attempted again until October 1964 by two British RAF men stationed near Nairobi. On a reconnaissance with friends some weeks before their climb, it had struck them that the key to descending into the Great Barranco was to strike down into it as near to its head as possible, much nearer than Firmin and Howard had gone. They marked the spot with a cairn for easy re-identification. RAF Station Workshops meanwhile made up special equipment for their venture, including steel stanchions, pegs, étrier hooks, hammocks, haul bags, and nylon slings.

They began zigzagging into the barranco, lowering their kit bags. Apart from "two dicey abseils" it proved easier than they'd dared hope. The slopes at the bottom were thick with giant groundsels. The two climbers, John Edwards (aged 30 at the time) from Shrewsbury and William Thompson (28), a physical training instructor from Prestonpans in Scotland, began scrambling up the increasingly steep headwall, gaining height easily until reaching a small ledge with a deep gorge on one side and fantastic exposure, which may well have been the same point reached by Firmin and Howard. From here they traversed right over crumbling basalt, and spent their first night out in an improvised hanging bivouac below what they believed must be Point Latham.

Above, the wall looked absolutely hopeless, and in any case was far left of their desired direct route to the summit. Next day they climbed a right-slanting chimney with one appalling pitch halfway along toward the Downie Ridge, where a heavy rainstorm deluged them. After two hours, they'd have been happy to find any route out—and began descending into the Lesser Barranco. "This was risky," Edwards reported. "Two near vertical 100-foot pitches, with appalling exposure, bad rock, poor belays—very frightening." After more than five hours abseiling and scrambling they found themselves at the head of the Little Barranco, looking up into a steep, wide gully. It mounted the East Face for some 1,000 feet to emerge on Mawenzi's ridge between the main summit, Hans Meyer Point, and the next peak along to the north, Nordecke. Though icy, it appeared far and away the best option they'd had all day and they began climbing. Two hours saw them into a scree-filled corrie high on the face, from which another, more difficult, gully issued, ice-choked in its upper section. That could wait for tomorrow. They bivouacked again, but it was so cold that before dawn they were on the move by the light of headlamps. The last long, difficult, and twisting gully brought them finally to Hans Meyer Spitze. Shattered, but delighted, they had bagged the first ascent of the East Face of Mawenzi.

Four years later a strong MCK team, led by Ian Howell, fought its way through successive waterfalls up the Great Barranco valley from near Tarakea, hoping to reach the East Face. Roger Higgins, one of the party, has told how finding camping areas big enough to accommodate eight men was an enormous problem, and all the time they worried about the weather. "If it rained on the mountain we could expect to be flushed from the Barranco like rats from a sewer," he said. They'd been fed tales of 20-foot walls of water crashing down this gorge. Higgins describes how, from their highest camp, Howell and Iain Allan went ahead to scout the way, only to stagger back later that day, soaked through and shivering:

Between sips at their brews [teas], they reported that they had climbed six more waterfalls above our previous high point, in appalling conditions. They had finally been turned back by cold and the threat of exposure after a swim of nearly a hundred feet through the water—at 20,000 feet. No wonder they looked sick!

Next day they tried again, but it was no good. They weren't going to make it through to the East Face: There was simply too much cold water. To the best of my knowledge, nobody has ever managed to do so.

Back in their camping meadow above Tarakea, most were ready to quit, but Howell and Higgins still hankered after the East Face and went back into the barranco. Instead of following the riverbed, they clambered onto Downie Ridge, which gained height fairly evenly until it struck the East Face some thousand feet below the summit. They ascended an elegant new line following a complicated system of gullies and ramps. "It seemed as though one sneeze could send the whole mountain down onto the plains like a pack of cards," Higgins said. "Once or twice we enjoyed the thrill of climbing on really solid rock and the odd peg or two comforted us, but for the main part we groveled and clawed over horribly loose rubbish."

There were a handful more ventures on the east side of Mawenzi over the years, but an article in a recent issue of the *Mountain Club of Kenya Bulletin* doubts if more than 30 people have ever descended into either of the mountain's barrancos. Its author, Julian Bedale, remarked that he'd been advised by Kilimanjaro's Chief Park Warden in 1999 that the Nanjara Route, shown on maps as starting from near Tarakea and following the Little Barranco to the mountain's northern slopes below Mawenzi Tarn Hut, was not a recognized route, and unlikely to be opened at any time. You could get a fine view of the lost barrancos, Bedale said, from the bottom of Tarakea village, where you may also see the summit of Kibo appearing over the northern shoulder of Mawenzi.

THESE WERE THE halcyon days of East African mountaineering, when a very active group of mainly Nairobi-based mountaineers were grabbing new routes throughout Kenya and Tanzania. The Mountain Club of Kenya had broken away from that of East Africa in 1949. There seemed no end to its members' energy and enthusiasm. Many classic routes on Mount Kenya's twin summits, Batian and Nelion, had been climbed in the early years by Arthur Firmin and his friends and, as we have seen, forays to Kilimanjaro and other peaks were not uncommon. The mid-1950s were the years of the Mau Mau emergency, when Kenyan peaks were officially out of bounds—although in practice the authorities sometimes turned a blind eye to climbers entering this closed area, as when Robert Caukwell and Gerald Rose snatched the first route on the icy West Face of Mount Kenya in January 1955. Injection of new talent came in the 1960s when Barry Cliff and later Ian Howell arrived from England and pushed up climbing standards dramatically. Ice climbing received its great boost in the 1970s under the influence of Phil Snyder, who was resident Park Warden on Mt. Kenya. These MCK men were supremely fit, as instanced by several marathon ventures such as that pulled off in 1964 by Barry Cliff with Rusty Baillie.

They had set themselves the target of standing on the tops of Kilimanjaro and Mount Kenya within 24 hours, and planned to start from the third cave above Loitokitok Outward Bound School on the northern slopes of Kilimanjaro. That should allow them to be on top of Kibo by midday. Unfortunately, after their hectic preparations, they overslept on their first morning, putting themselves behind schedule before they'd even started. Noon found them still struggling up awful screes, and it was 2:00 p.m. before they staggered around the crater rim to Uhuru Peak. Already they felt exhausted but, as Barry reminded himself, they were committed now: People were lined up along the way to ease their progress. They were to be paced down the mountain by the fittest of the Loitokitok instructors. Putting on a brave face, they bounded down the scree to where he was waiting. On they jogged, anxious to be out of the "game-infested" forest before it was dark. More friends ferried them back to their car, which they'd left having emergency repairs made to a damaged fuel tank. At breakneck speed they drove nonstop to Kenya, where another volunteer was waiting. By 2:00 a.m. they were slogging up Kenya's infamous "vertical bog."

At Klarwill's Hut we stopped as dawn approached and I felt so hungry that I ate an old sandwich we found there. I was immediately sick.... We eventually reached Top Hut at 7 am, made a brew and left to cross the Lewis Glacier at 8 am. What a relief it was to be on rock and we both got a second life. Climbing solo, we quickly reached Mackinder's Gendarme and roped for Eric Shipton's Rickety Crack. At 10:30 am we were on Nelion and 11:40 on Batian (17,058 feet). (Barry Cliff)

They'd made it in 21 hours 40 minutes from summit to summit. And there was Kilimanjaro, just visible above the cloud 200 miles away. They had been on the move for 42 hours from the Third Cave before they reached a friend's house in the early hours of the next morning, where Cliff took the bath he'd been dreaming of for most of those hours. Before he'd finished, Baillie had fallen asleep in all his mud. Next day, out of curiosity, Cliff looked underneath his car to see what

LEFT: HENRY BARBER POSES NINE MONTHS BEFORE HIS TRIP TO KILIMANJARO WITH ROB TAYLOR. ABOVE: IAN HOWELL BELAYS
BILL O'CONNOR ON THE FINAL ICE-PITCH DURING THE FIRST ASCENT OF KERSTEN GLACIER DIRECT IN DECEMBER 1975.

THE GREAT EAST FACE OF MAWENZI

IAN HOWELL
BRITISH-BORN, NAIROBI-BASED CLIMBER

WHEN I LEFT England for Kenya in 1967, my ambitions were fixed on Mount Kenya. But talking to resident climbers I soon heard of other attractions. Iain Allan, then a schoolboy but already a keen climber with an eye for a line and new places to climb, fired my imagination with talk of the enormous and complex East Face of Mawenzi. It had been visited, he said, and the top 2,000 feet scaled in 1964. This ascent by Edwards and Thompson was a fine achievement. But why climb just the top? What about the other 6,000 feet that fell to the headwaters of the Great Barranco?

To get to the foot of the face you'd need to find a way into the gorge at the bottom. Iain was excited at the prospect of going where no one had been before, as was I, but we'd need a bigger team. Soon we had a party of twelve—four climbers and eight in support. A flight over the Barranco revealed the daunting size of this gorge, whose depth was impossible to gauge; you couldn't see into it from above. Fred and I made a quick reconnaissance on the ground, discovering that you could enter the gorge some ten miles from the face, near a small village called Tarakea. At last, in July 1968, with rations for eight days, we ventured in.

For the first two days things went well and we managed to scale the waterfalls cascading down the gorge. In places we carried up trees from the forest to use as ladders for surmounting the steeper torrents. But the farther up the gorge we went, the higher the waterfalls, and the wetter and colder we got. We should have taken wet suits to climb in. We carried firewood, and at night could warm up and partly dry our sodden clothes. We stuck it out for six days, until the gigantic East Face was in sight above us. But it was still a mile higher than we were. With disappointment, we descended our fixed ropes and came out of the gorge to see the sun for the first time in almost a week.

Most of the team just wanted to go home, but three of us didn't. We still had time and food to do something. The obvious choice from here would be to follow the ridge separating the Great and Lesser Barrancos, which would lead us up and onto the East Face of Mawenzi. After our week in the river, this seemed highly attractive, though was not without its own excitement. It became frighteningly narrow in places, and one quartz dike, 18 inches wide, had to be traversed for 100 feet with thousands of feet dropping away on either side. We couldn't have foreseen this as no one had ascended the buttress at that time. Fred and I left our meadow camp; a serious ear infection drove Iain Allen back to Nairobi for medical attention.

The first day we forged upward through a barrier of endless bush. We were too tired to talk and both of us were extremely thirsty. By now, we' had rationed our drinking water and longed to get higher to find snow and ice for melting. Next day the bush thinned out, to be replaced by scree and weird rock formations that sometimes had to be climbed over or around to gain height. Our next bivouac was under a slightly leaning dike wall that offered meager protection from the elements. A trickle of water oozing out of the rock supplemented the dwindling supply we had carried up.

Mawenzi is the remains of a much older volcano than Kibo. The whole east side of its crater at some stage had been eroded away. Our second bivouac was thus inside the original crater. Dike walls of hard rock held up scree, like coal bunkers. Next day, as we traversed around these walls, we started to run into snow and ice gullies that had to be climbed without ice equipment. With our rock hammers, we cut steps where they were most needed. Around lunchtime we reached the mountain's final 1,500-foot headwall directly below Hans Meyer Peak, the highest point. We chose a left-slanting ramp that led up to better rock, which we followed, at about Severe grade, to the summit of Borchers Peak, some 100 feet lower than the main summit. The traverse to the top was slow, as it was difficult to find good anchors to abseil into the gap between the peaks. We arrived on the summit and bivouacked close by as the sun set.

sort of repair had been done on it. "There it was...stuck up with a piece of soap!" He looked for that mechanic for years afterward.

In 1972 Ian Howell and Phil Snyder decided to make an unsupported traverse of Kilimanjaro's two main summits, the sort of venture climbers like to refer to as lightweight because it does not involve the full paraphernalia of an expedition. They brought food for seven days and a full complement of rock climbing and snow and ice equipment, plus what Howell calls "fairly serious bivouac gear." Having hitchhiked to Moshi, they had one last hearty meal before catching a bus to Umbwe, from where they would hike through forested farmland up to the Umbwe trail. On the fourth day they were bivouacked in a cave below the Breach Wall at 14,500 feet. Lacy clouds came dancing over the top of Kili, pressaging bad weather and, as they plodded up the Little Breach Glacier, thick clouds crept in to smother everything. Before they'd climbed a thousand feet it was snowing, and they pitched camp on a rocky spur.

The storm blew itself out by evening and the sun forced its way through the clouds. The nearby Breach Wall looked beautiful with its ledges and little holds picked out in newly fallen snow. They identified a fine-looking route right up the middle, a really impressive route, but it was out of the question in snow. They decided to continue up the Little Breach Glacier—considerably bigger in those days than now—and climb into Kibo's crater by the Western Breach. This was all straightforward, apart from struggling over collapsing wind-sculpted ice flutings to gain the crater. From Uhuru Point, an easy descent by the popular route brought them to Kibo Huts, where unacclimatized tourists, suffering severe loss of appetite, readily handed over great platefuls of food to the hungry climbers.

"Boosted by a proper meal and a lie-in," Howell wrote in his diary of the trip, "we trotted off to cross the Saddle to Mawenzi Hut, each of us secretly imagining that some food would have been left there by somebody else." They hunted in vain. As the sun sank, they realized that if they didn't get outside quickly the water supply, which in this hut came from meltwater, would have frozen for the night. Out they dashed with mugs, bottles, and spoons to rescue what they could of the dwindling supply.

Next day, their eighth since leaving Nairobi, was the big one, the crux of the traverse. They'd climb Mawenzi and descend by its friable East Face. Howell had been worrying about this ever since they'd agreed to do it. Usually, if you abseiled, it was out of unwanted necessity since this was the greatest cause of fatal climbing accidents. Yet here they were, choosing to abseil down one thousand feet of insecure rock. It was crazy. But what alternative did they have?

He suddenly remembered the RAF East Face climb. Those men followed a steep ice couloir to the notch between Hans Meyer Peak and Nordecke. That could provide the answer. From the ridge, they peered anxiously into the intimidating void, then—armed with pegs, ice screws, and prussik loops on the rope—they descended carefully, watching out all the while for loosened stones and jamming ropes. One overhanging ice pitch presented two problems. "First the rope, cutting into the ice lip, tended to jam, and secondly, on swinging in over the lip, my feet came up against large rotten icicles which at a touch dropped off and clattered down on top of Phil, who was belayed to an ice-screw seventy feet below."

Two hours and six abseils saw them down what had become known as Thompson's Horror (the name given to it by the RAF men) and onto easier ground. Passing through the goblin country of the upper barrancos, they made for Downie Ridge where they bivouacked. One last day of descent, which left them weak from lack of food and water, took them through the trailless giant heather until, in the forest, they came upon a woodcutter's track leading back to civilization at Tarakea and thence to Loitokitok. It had been a great adventure.

BACK ON KIBO, during the early 1970s the Great Breach Wall had become the big magnet, along with its associated glaciers. The straightforward lines on the Little Breach, and the Heim, Decken, and Kersten Glaciers had been climbed. Now the extreme routes were being sought out, routes that were never considered feasible by earlier mountaineers, and again MCK climbers were the major players. Howell, with Britons Bill O'Connor and John Cleare, bagged the Kersten Glacier Direct at the end of 1975, which, Cleare reported, "involved spectacular aid-climbing on a hanging icicle." The route was graded VI A1. A few weeks later South Africans Paul Fatti and John Moss put

ARTHUR FIRMIN, THE DRIVING FORCE OF EAST AFRICAN MOUNTAINERING FOR 15 YEARS, DIED IN NEPAL IN MAY 1955 WHILE BEING ASSISTED BACK TO POKHARA AFTER BREAKING HIS THIGH ON HIMALCHULI.

in a new direct start to this climb, effectively a separate route because the two lines came together only in the easier upper sections. Then, in July 1976, Iain Allan and Mark Savage found an eloquent Grade V line in "perfect" condition on the right side of this glacier. The Kersten is the steepest of the large southern glaciers—"steepest and most chaotic hanging glacier on the mountain, a tumbling heap of ice with three great barriers of seracs," according to O'Connor. Like the Heim, it satisfyingly delivers you almost onto Kibo's summit. The Heim received its direct route, grade VI, in 1977 by R. Barton and D. Morris, and remains to this day the most popular glacier on the mountain. In 1978 the first guided ascent was led by Allan and Vince Fayad via the Standard Route, and today commercial groups regularly make the climb.

Since the early 1970s, climbers had been eyeing the Breach Wall. Howell and Snyder harbored designs on

end of the wall a promising gully system beckoned, leading almost to the summit. They fell for it, only to find the traverse across the top of the ice field alone took almost the whole day. "Ropelength after ropelength, on front points most of the time, rarely hard climbing, rarely easy. We became even more impressed by the scale of things. Nowhere along the whole of the Upper Wall did we see anything resembling a line of weakness. Just massive vertical, smooth cliffs."

They reached the gully to find a waterfall coursing down it, and the bottom section overhanging. A steep, shattered chimney to the right looked ghastly, but might just be possible. Another wet night was followed by a nightmare of a day wrestling with rotten rock, falling stones, meltwater, and evil gray ice—"too much ice to make the rock easy, but not enough to hold a hammer pick firmly." Temple, who has four children, was fast coming to the opinion that this was no place for a fam-

> **SATURDAY** Imagination runs riot up here. I noticed a small lump on the palm of my hand and immediately thought, "Oh, my God, a blood clot. I'll be dead this time tomorrow." Two days later it's still here—and so am I. So, I've pushed it from my mind.

it in 1972 before the snow deflected them to their grand traverse. A Swiss climber, Fritz Lörtscher, started the ball rolling in January 1972 with a couple of mixed rock and ice climbs at the far western end of the wall, based around the Breach glaciers. In December 1974, climbing with Tony Charlton, John Temple found a mixed route on the eastern end of this massive wall, which crossed the Balletto Icefield and finished up at the edge of the Heim. He was back a few months later with Dave Cheesmond and a much more ambitious project in mind.

Climbing steep rock, they reached the Balletto Icefield in cold, wet weather, aiming for the prominent ice pillar, by which they hoped to gain the Diamond Glacier above. That first night they slept beneath what we now know as the Breach Icicle, with fine powder snow from the Diamond gently sifting down and drifting into their shelter. It looked intimidating and surely would take a day at least to get up, whereas at the far eastern

ily man, and he could recognize the surrealism of Cheesmond trying to inch his way up a waterfall: "He stood in a sling with water running off all points of his crampons. I should have taken a picture but at the time it was a scene I wanted to forget. I pressed myself back against the rock and wished I wasn't there."

Progress was slow and another long, damp bivvi had to be endured before boots were thawed over the stove at dawn and 600 feet of plodding saw them on the summit at last. The route appears in guidebooks now, graded VI, with a recommendation to allow three days for it. But John Temple's account of the climb, when it appeared in a magazine in August 1976, reinforced the word in the climbing fraternity that the Breach Wall with its eye-catching Icicle was the great challenge of the day.

In October 1977 the celebrated British pair Doug Scott and Paul "Tut" Braithwaite found the face under constant bombardment and the ice too mushy and dangerous for the direct line they were planning up the gullies below the Icicle. For a week they hung about in the Great Barranco, soaked to the skin, before heading off to make a fine new climb on Mount Kenya's East Face instead.

Next to arrive were two Americans from New England. Henry Barber was one of the boldest rock climbers of the day, and in great demand as a lecturer, equipment consultant, and demonstration climber. Alert and talented, he was working his way through some of the toughest climbs, making a habit of arriving in a climbing center and tossing off without effort the hardest route there. "Oh, no, here's Hot Henry," the local climbers would groan in jest, "come to show us how it's done!" The apparent spontaneity and effortlessness of his climbing was underpinned by constant practice and observation, and he steeped himself in climbing lore. Yet, for all his meticulous planning and drive, there was a romantic side to his nature, and he was passionate about his climbing. He felt particularly at home in the British mountain-climbing scene. Rob Taylor was perhaps more typical of a laid-back age—more openly emotional, not pushy, a dreamer and lover of nature, photographer, writer. Mountains had beguiled him as a boy, and he felt freed by them. At 17, he left America for Scotland, where—with a short break following an avalanche accident—he lived for a number of years in Glencoe, climbing, guiding, instructing, assisting with rescues, and working for and with Hamish MacInnes and other legendary Scottish mountaineers. If Taylor lacked the flair and confidence of Barber, he too knew how to read mountains, and he'd acquired superb craftsmanship on ice. These two, then, Barber and Taylor, created a formidable partnership, their experience imbuing it with the widest possible range of technical expertise. Their differing outlooks and temperaments were of less certain benefit, but as the more forceful of them, Barber usually pushed through the decisions; so far this had worked well for them. They'd enjoyed a very successful trip to Norway in 1977, making 10 or 12 first ascents, which included the 1,000-foot Vettisfossen, considered one of the most rigorous ice climbs anywhere in the world.

Both were in their mid-20s and neither had been to Africa before. Barber had been building up his alpine and ice experience steadily—New England, he says, teaches you about cold, but you can't get your legs and your lungs there—so he'd pushed farther to Alaska, and then the Caucasus and the Tienshan, climbing peaks up to 17,000 feet. African ice seemed a logical next step for himself and Rob. He'd heard about the 4,000-foot Breach Wall, with its vertical ice pillar at around 17,000 to 18,000 feet, from Iain Allan, whom he'd met in Yosemite. He'd not seen pictures of it, any more than had Rob, but the kind of contenders it was attracting gave a sense of its aura. After the Vettisfossen, Barber felt they could climb the hardest ice in the world. "It seemed feasible that we could—and we knew that if we did something like the Breach Icicle, it would probably be one of the hardest technical pitches climbed at altitude anywhere in the world."

They planned on getting into shape with an ascent of the prized Diamond Ice Couloir on Mount Kenya, and this they achieved within 48 hours of landing in Nairobi. Looking back, Henry can see it was a "really, really stupid" way of going about things, and they suffered terrible headaches. But it gave them a sense of tropical ice and bottomless, granular snow. "We didn't really understand how hideous that could be; nor how ice can deteriorate so quickly in a fog." Still, they'd moved fast and efficiently, and tackled the steep crux pitches without much difficulty. Things were looking good. They'd be much more fit when they got to Kilimanjaro. Meanwhile, Barber put in some rock climbing with MCK friends at Lukenya and Hell's Gate. He was committed to being back in the States for a sports show appearance in a couple of weeks, but he didn't see this as a tremendous problem and packed as much as he could into every moment.

The Kenyan border with Tanzania was sealed at that time and reaching Kilimanjaro Airport involved flying by way of Ethiopia, which was a nuisance they could have done without. In Addis Ababa they found themselves caught up in a military emergency: Ethiopia was ten days away from invading Somalia and planes had been commandeered for ferrying troops and equipment. An unscheduled stop there left them with just nine days of holiday when they eventually reached Kilimanjaro. They hitched a lift around to the southwest of the mountain and immediately began the long trudge up the Umbwe route. As the walls of the forest closed over their heads, it was suddenly borne in on them how wild this valley was, and how vulnerable they were in the alien landscape. They had bypassed the park authorities, and no one knew they were there. Their

FRANK CANNINGS, ON THE HEIM GLACIER, LEADS THROUGH PAST AN ICE CAVE IN A CONFUSED SERAC BAND.
FOLLOWING PAGES: EVENING FALLS AT 18,000 FEET ON THE HEIM GLACIER ON KIBO'S SOUTHWEST FLANK.

friends in Kenya had been plying them with horror stories about snakes, killer bees, and big cats. Two Dutch climbers, they'd been told, vanished without trace from the Umbwe trail—only their tents and gear were ever found. And a hang glider pilot came down in this jungle leaving no trace at all. Here, too, a Cape buffalo forced Rusty Baillie to spend a night in a tree, and Iain Allen said he and two friends had to keep a persistent leopard at bay by throwing rocks at it, lighting fires, and yelling all night. His party was so spooked, he told them, they hiked out at first light—and there was the animal, bold as you like, on the trail watching them. No way did Rob and Henry fancy "bivouacking with leopards," and they stepped up their pace to gain the steeply inclined Umbwe Ridge. Soon they were on a narrow rocky walkway above the trees, which led into the giant heather and finally to the open plateau, where they thankfully pitched camp. They'd climbed more than 7,000 feet that day, and in the morning continued to the Barranco bivouac, a cramped tin hut near the head of the Great Barranco.

Now they got their first real look at the Breach Wall rearing above them. Decades later, Henry was still marveling at the scale of the thing, and how deceptively wide it was: "You know, when you come from the Umbwe and you're seeing that whole ice face from the Heim over to the Icicle, it looks like a beautiful line, and of course you don't realize that it's 2,500 feet to get over there, half a mile of decent climbing. It's like seeing the North Face of the Eiger from that little train to Kleine Scheiddegg, it's so wide."

They climbed up to take a look at the Heim, but rain set in and they retreated back to the Barranco hut and remained pinned there for the rest of that day. The sheer scale was still impressing itself on them: not just the great width of the wall, but its height, too. The summit was a vertical mile and a half above them. It was staggering. Next morning, they could afford to wait no longer. Heading up the broken icefall onto the Heim Glacier, they circumvented the first rocky tier of the Breach Wall. There would be no time to tackle that if they wanted to get to the Icicle.

They climbed the tongue of the glacier and the initial headwall and by 10:00 a.m. were on the Window Buttress, a rocky spur separating the Heim from the Breach Wall and its Balletto Icefield. But with the whole face now muffled in thick fog, the consistency of the snow was deteriorating—hard-packed névé turning to slush, leaving nothing for their crampons to bite on. They were forced to let another afternoon tick by in inactivity as they sat on tiny bivouac ledges, listening to avalanches rumble past.

It was almost as nerve-wracking as their perceived threat of leopards in the forest, but all that sitting, dozing, and brewing up drinks was to some purpose: After a good night, during which they slept well, they were able to make an early start next day, rested, rehydrated, and feeling fit.

"We did a couple of thousand feet in three or four hours of simo-climbing," Henry said, "deciding which point we were making for, then climbing diagonally and

recollection. Rob afterward wrote a raw-edged account of the entire trip, spelling out his dissatisfaction with the way events were turning well before reaching the Icicle; but that was the moment when for Henry everything went cool. Should they turn back? They discussed it. Rob urged prudence, recalling that Temple and Cheesmond had bivouacked under the Icicle; they could do that, he suggested, or retreat 300 feet and sit it out under overhangs.

Already, clouds were moving in. Clearly they had to move up swiftly or wait another day. Rob is of the impression the decision to go ahead and try it was Barber's, who, with cracking patience, he says, was arguing that it would be crazy to wait when they could be on the summit by dinnertime. Henry remembers the hemming and hawing, and saying he'd be more than happy to give it a whirl; they could always back off. (Henry prided himself on being able to downclimb anything.)

SUNDAY You sometimes read in survival books that if you run out of water on Kilimanjaro's arid slopes, you can drink the liquid trapped in lobelia reservoirs. Has to be dubious advice, that, because lobelias contain lobeline, a highly toxic alkaloid that kills cats and dogs, and us too probably. The only people I know who tried it, Ian Howell and Phil Snyder, found it viscous, tasteless, and home to colonies of little worms. They decided to keep searching for the real thing, however long it took.

simultaneously toward it." They'd put in some protection before climbing vertically for three or four hundred feet, switching leads, until they got to the next natural diagonal line. In this manner they traversed the ice field toward the Icicle really quickly. Henry remembers it as one of the high points of the trip, when they worked very well together. At that point he still hoped it would be possible to finish the climb that day, but the slope had steepened and the fog was back by the time they reached the Icicle.

"It was so sugary," Barber recalls, "like the side of a snowbank on a warm winter day after it's been hit with road salt, the dripping sugar snow icicles hanging off it. Touch it with your finger, and it collapsed. It was rotting. The fog was almost like sea fog, as if it had salt in it—that's how rotten it was."

After such a good morning, the complexion of the enterprise altered in seconds—at least that's Henry's

Or, they could finish up the Heim Glacier, whatever.

Taylor still *wanted* the route. "I'll give it a whirl," he said.

"If you don't feel happy about it, let me go first."

"No, I'll go." To Rob, frosty stalemate had concluded with him deferring to Henry, as usual. He cautiously probed the delicate ice, telling himself he'd just have to put in more protection than usual:

The ice on the icicle is the worst I have ever encountered. To a depth of three feet, the surface is composed of fragile latticed striations of rotted ice crystals which collapse at the slightest touch. For each tenuous placement of the ax, this sugary surface must first be cleared away. It is a strenuous task at this altitude, and I quickly find myself fully extended just trying to stay in contact with the decomposed vertical sludge.

Placing his first ice screw some 20 feet above Barber, he was surprised how reassuringly solid it appeared. But the ice above was poor and, to reach what looked like a better section up to the left, he made a layback move on a projecting cauliflower-head of ice. When he lunged and all his weight came onto this projection, it snapped off. Taylor fell backward in space. With the screw in place, it should have been a short fall, but he came to rest, revolving gently on the rope, to find he was looking up at his partner. He had smashed feet first into the sloping ledge below Henry's belay. There was a sharp pain in his left leg, and he was aghast to see, instead of the top of his red-and-blue supergator, the 12 points of his crampons and the sole of his boot. The arch of his foot has been wrenched around so that it brushed his inner calf. In disbelief, he looked up at Henry, "My ankle's broken," he said.

Henry lowered him down to where it was less steep and out of the way of falling ice. "I'm sorry, I'm sorry, I'm sorry…," was all Rob could mumble, as he took in the horror and helplessness of his situation.

"Let's get over to that spot," Henry indicated shelter. "We can bivouac there, and we'll take care of it." There's no dressing up with Henry, he's a plain talker, and there'll have been a few obscenities as he geared himself for the task ahead. "C'mon, let's get on with it," he said. (He's the first to admit he has no bedside manner.) From their different standpoints, both sourly reflected that they'd half expected something like this: Taylor never believing Barber appreciated the seriousness of their undertaking, was always too nonchalant in his decision making; Barber seeing Taylor as overanxious and too eager to succeed. He wanted that route too much, it had occurred to him earlier. "This climb was seeming to possess him."

Such thoughts were of course not helpful. Now that they were in this mess, they had to do and endure what needed to be done. It was up to Henry to get his companion down, and he had to stay calm and concentrated for that. Any stress or emotion he felt he had to bottle up for now to stay on top of the job. And he'd need Rob's cooperation, too, so he must keep prodding and prompting him. There was no gain to be had in coddling the patient, to his mind, even if that were his style. He had to keep him alert and fighting.

Rigging Rob's injured leg in a sling to enable him to use the knee as a substitute foot on steep ground, Henry

back-climbed 300 feet up to the right in order to bring his partner into the cave to assess the situation. Blood, they now noticed, was oozing out of Rob's gaiter and staining the ice. It could mean only one thing: Rob had sustained a compound fracture. Broken bones had pierced the flesh. And they had only two painkiller tablets with them.

Taylor's ice tool and a screw had been lost in the accident—how was he to be brought off the face? Chances of rescue, as Barber well knew, would have been infinitely better on the popular route of the mountain. You heard of people being evacuated from near the summit in a few hours, but what options were open on this remote cliff? The only chances of finding help, it seemed, would be to get onto the standard Marangu route, or down to one of the villages to the south of Kilimanjaro. Here, at the mountain's west end, even if you reached the roadhead by going back down the Umbwe, you'd still be miles from anywhere and unlikely to find someone with a vehicle. Abseiling directly down the Breach Wall was a nonstarter with its 2,000 feet of unknown, loose, and nearly vertical lava; they hadn't the rock hardware for this. In fact, they were very short of gear altogether.

Rob, with his paramedic experience, knew the risks he faced. "Shock is immediate death," he reasoned, "in fighting I have at least a chance." He could splint the leg as it was, and risk having no foot by the time he reached the nearest medical help, just a black gangrenous mass waiting to be cut off. Or he could set the fracture and chance nicking an artery with the bone-ends, to die in a pool of his own blood in minutes. It was a stark choice. Henry marveled at his courage. "He got into his leg and started moving the bones around," he recalled. At that time, he said, the two of them were occupying "different spaces." Rob was lost in his pain and the magnitude of the problem, while Henry was busying himself getting water going, cutting open pack belts to secure foam for splinting, carving their ice ledge to afford a flatter platform. But for the gruesome task ahead, they came together once more.

He made the decision that we had to set this thing, and talked me through it. We were organized. We took apart a crampon to use for a splint, we used a hammer that had a broken pick as a splint, we used the pack belt stuff, the crampons straps—we really worked as a team, and he helped me manipulate the foot. It was grisly. Really grisly… we could hear the bones move.

Now Rob was anxious to get down, but Henry could see no sense to leaving while it was still foggy and the ice was clattering down. It had taken three hours to come across this 2,000 feet; it would take a minimum of six to get back, and they were virtually certain to get "whacked" by falling ice if they left now. Also, he needed to work out the best way of handling the descent. They had six ice screws to get them down 3,000 feet, and he knew he should keep two or three in hand for the head-wall. It could be done, he figured, with some solo climbing, but he wanted to play and replay the various scenarios to himself—also, to prepare himself mentally for the task. He had the fortitude, he knew, and didn't believe they were in danger of dying; he just wanted to be sure he'd covered everything. They started the following morning, Henry belaying Rob and cajoling him back across the Balletto Icefield and down the Heim Glacier.

"I'd lower him, then he'd kind of swim across, using his ice ax to move along," Henry explained. "He'd be there with just an ice ax belay or something, and I'd solo down a couple of hundred feet, then get way over to the right of him, so that he could let go and start swimming again. He'd sort of pendulum slingshot himself across the wall." In this manner they had to abseil only once or twice down the hardest ice. It was very efficient and, though in great pain and at times semi-delirious, Rob managed to stay conscious and controlled, handling the ropework well. "The courage that guy had is unbelievable," Henry said.

Once down the glacier, after their second bivouac, Henry carried Rob a couple of hundred yards to a big rock where he could be relocated more easily, and gave him most of what little food remained. Both were exhausted, and Henry is right to say, as he did afterward, that probably only a handful of American climbers could have done more than he did. It was a stu-

RIGHT: ROB TAYLOR CLIMBS THE ICE PILLAR OF THE BREACH WALL, JUST BEFORE HE FELL. BELOW: AT THE BIVOUAC AFTER BREAKING HIS ANKLE, TAYLOR RESET AND SPLINTED HIS LEG WITH THE AID OF HIS PARTNER, HENRY BARBER.

pendous effort. Yet Rob would grow increasingly resentful over time at what he perceived as Henry's lack of compassion, even while acknowledging that he owes his life to him.

After making Rob comfortable, they review their options one more time. Unwilling to face a night alone in the Umbwe forest, Henry settles on traversing eastward around the mountain to the Horombo Hut, which he believes has a radio. It's around noon, and the hut must be some six hours away. If anyone's there, Rob should see help that night or the next day. Henry packs all the loose gear and valuables and sets off, intending to run most of the way. But soon it starts raining, and the fog is back. He slows down. He can't afford to fall: Rob is depending on him. God, he wishes he'd taken time to study a map or guidebook before he'd come. God, oh God, he thinks, Rob will die if I screw up.

He loses all sense of time. There's a trail going off, labeled Mweka Route, and he's pretty sure there's a hut down there, too, so he heads down toward it. Almost immediately he wonders if he's made a mistake. It's steep and rocky. Slipping and sliding, he finally comes to a tin hut, but it doesn't look as if anyone's been there for months. It's all locked up. And he's back in the heather forest now, where all his fears of wild animals return with a vengeance. He has to get inside that hut, and he scrabbles with his ice ax to dig a hole big enough to crawl through. Once in, he refills the gap so nothing can come after him. Scared, soaked, cold, he would say afterward that this was the lowest point of the whole experience. And what's hap-

pening to Rob? It's been raining hard for ten hours now; higher on the mountain, Rob must be under loads of snow. Henry feels he's failed him.

Unsure where the Mweka track comes out, he spends the night racked with indecision. By morning he's convinced himself he must climb back up to the split in the trail and keep heading toward the Horombo. All he can think is that Rob will die if he doesn't hurry.

He continues traversing around the mountain, clambering in and out of its radiating valleys. Coming into what was perhaps the eighth valley, he notices movement above him, which at first he takes to be a hyrax. Then he catches sight of a creature, which looks to be three feet high. His worst fears have come to life. "It was intermittently slinking along. I would see it,

then wonder why I wasn't seeing it, but it must have come to a boulder or something and scurried across. Then I'd see it peering out again. After a few minutes I realized I was walking toward a leopard and it was 100–150 yards away. It sent chills up my spine. It still does 23 years later."

There is no mistake; he can see the spots. He's in a trap, because he needs to cross this valley, and it means walking toward the creature, then away from it. All the while, the leopard contours around above him, "moving very sleekly, with shoulders scrunched," and matching his movements, stopping when he stops. "The thing just scared the [ ] out of me, tracking along with me like that. I took off my pack and wrapped my ice ax leashes around my hands, walking like that for

his instincts are urging him to go. It's hard to think straight. He heads down. Fine at first, the track gets rougher and more incised, and the vegetation is "denser than the jungle on the Umbwe." Scared to death by now and exhausted, his feet and muscles wrecked, he hobbles or runs on his heels for what must be 12 miles before stumbling into a "woodcutter's camp." An old man shows him to a mission where two clergymen arrange for him to be taken to the park office. At 7:00 p.m. on the fifth day since Rob's accident, he is able at last to raise the alarm.

NORWEGIAN CLIMBERS Odd Eliassen and Ulf Prytz were working in Tanzania, building huts and amenities in the national park. They immediately mustered a rescue team, which Odd drove up to the Shira Plateau, reaching the Breach Wall the following afternoon. Would they find Rob alive after all this time? They hardly dared hope it. But there he was, warm and dry inside his sleeping bag, and in surprisingly good spirits. Not, of course, that that's how Rob remembers the nightmare of his long wait, when he despaired of ever seeing anyone again and his leg festered. It took another two days getting him off the mountain and into the local hospital. The first thing he wanted to know when he woke up after the initial treatment was, "Where's Henry?" Henry, he was told, had left upon learning that Rob was safely in hospital.

Emergency surgery saved Rob's by now gangrenous foot from amputation; two months' hospitalization after his return were followed by a further eight months of immobility, but finally Rob was back on his feet. He'd retain a limp, but he would return to his mountains, even go back to Kilimanjaro.

And the Breach? The infamous Icicle was climbed within weeks of Taylor's and Barber's attempt by the South Tyrolean super-climber Reinhold Messner and his partner, Konrad Renzler. They made the complete direct ascent from the very base of the Breach Wall, and because of its tendency to shatter, they forswore ax and ice screws on the Icicle itself, climbing it free. The plum route on Kilimanjaro had been plucked.

an hour and a half, my knuckles white." He sees no reason to charge to his death, and walks slowly, backward, away from it, keeping it in sight. "I was so freaking scared. There was heavy mist, a shroud; it was creepy—if a rock fell, I was really petrified, just about in tears...."

At last it stops coming with him; he must have left its territory. Henry crashes through the undergrowth to get back onto the trail. By now the landscape's broadening out, becoming more arid, and the dome looks to be turning back around. Again he's reminded just how big and broad this mountain is, but surely now he must be almost at the Marangu Route? The path forks. Which way? He is certain the hut is to the left, but the right-hand track heads downhill, the way ◆

CHAPTER NINE

VOLCANO

We were turning into geezers. Ratty beards sprouted.
Fingers swelled. Faces grew puffy and wrinkled.
Our rest steps slowed to funereal pace. We got gaseous....
Why do people put themselves through this wringer?

TOM DUNKEL, 1996

WE DECIDED TO LEAVE

the Great Barranco by taking the gentler path along the edge of the stream, avoiding the eroded zigzags. Even so it was a pull. I started out first and finished last, which seems the natural order of things. Adamson, my porter, looked after me very well, carrying my rucksack as well as his, along with my kitbag of bedding. So I had no excuse for being so slow, except that it was very warm, and there was a lot to look at. Up on the barer ridges traces of snow lingered in some sheltered hollows, and the earth raking was particularly marked. The ice needles were just melting, making the ground quite sloppy in places and the mud ooze down the hillsides. At the top we stopped for a tea break: Freddie was waiting there with his welcome thermoses and mugs spread out ready. Hunkered down among the rocks, you become aware of pocket-handkerchief-size alpine gardens in the gaps and crevices, mainly comprised of tiny helichrysums, white arabis, and yellow daisies. But really this is the realm of lichens. The boulders appear to be wearing threadbare fur coats from the flowing tufts of tawny, black, and green lichens. Other skin-tight varieties in brilliant reds and oranges blotch many of the rocks; they seem to radiate neatly from the center,

PRECEDING PAGES: IN KIBO'S CRATER, HEIDI AND ROGER EXPLORE AN ICE CUL-DE-SAC OF THE FURTWÄNGLER GLACIER.
LEFT: THE FILM CREW PAUSES IN MOONLIGHT TO ENJOY THE VIEW FROM THE WESTERN BREACH.

maintaining a near round or oval shape. Then there are crusty, flaky ones in gray, green, and black that crumble as you touch them. At least 120 species of lichen have been recorded on Kilimanjaro, and scientists cannot say they've discovered them all yet, nor that they fully understand the role they play in water catchment. They tend to grow more prolifically on the southern sides of rocks and cliffs, facing the mist-carrying winds.

Soon we dipped down into an intervening valley, before clambering up the steep slope on the other side through an eyelet of rock and a narrow, windy defile into Lava Tower Camp. We reached camp toward midday, with the sun still shining. Nevertheless, it was a bleak and breezy spot. There were very good views of the route ahead and down the slopes of the mountain to the plains, but it was not long before these were blocked by the incoming mists, and it grew cold and dreary. We retreated thankfully into the mess tent.

The Lava Tower, at 15,000 feet, is a prominent feature on the southwestern side of the mountain, standing at a point where the summit dome begins to steepen. As the name implies, it is a volcanic column rising more than 200 feet. The darkly orange rock is blocky and loose, as the many boulders around its base testify. At least one hut here, tucked in at the foot of the tower to be out of the wind, was squashed completely flat by rockfall. To one side of the tower, a sandy, soccer-field-size patch of flat ground walled in by right-angled dikes of lava serves as the campsite now. I imagine that it is not immune from rockfall either. Respectable toilets have been erected behind one of the dike walls, though these are very exposed to the wind, and it's clear from debris around them that the structure blows down and has to

HEIDI, HANSI, AND ROGER PAUSE TO REST AT THE TOP OF LAVA TOWER, A LOOSE VOLCANIC COLUMN NEAR THE FOOT OF THE WESTERN BREACH. FOLLOWING PAGES: CLIMBERS SET UP A WINDY CAMP BELOW LAVA TOWER AT 15,000 FEET.

be replaced fairly frequently. Still, it looks directly up into the cirque of the Western Breach and on to the summit when it's clear enough—inspirational, or sobering, according to your mood.

The lava dikes are impressive, too. Like Inca walls, 10 to 20 feet high, jointed rock, you either clamber over them to get to the "wash room," or sidle along a cleft where one of the joints has opened up.

The younger members of the expedition were interested in the rock as raw material for climbing and soon we saw Monica and Joey waving from the top. Our Sherpas, meanwhile, recognized the innate holiness of a site like this and scrambled to string prayer flags from the lower rocks of the tower, while Wongchu quietly intoned Buddhist prayers.

Around dawn, I needed to get up and visit the loo. Clambering back across the lava dikes, I gazed out over

notic—breathing, thinking, movement all at one with the mountain and the mountainscape. I picked up the tune and hummed it inside, and only some while later came out of my semi-trance and recognized what it was. "We are climbing Jacob's ladder."

We-are-cli-mbing-Jacob's-ladder... we-are-cli-mbing-Jacob's-ladder... I laughed. We certainly were. And you couldn't ask for a better climbing mantra. I doubt if I'll ever toil uphill again without that tune drumming unbidden in my brain.

"Do you ever get tired of climbing this mountain, Jakob?"

He grins; he's a shy man and he does a lot of grinning. My dad was the same. No, he says at last, he doesn't find it difficult and he loves the plants and animals. Of course, he'll retire one day, and then he thinks he'll expand the little shop his family runs in Machame-

---

MONDAY We have a rushed breakfast about sixish and are away by 6:45, the film team preceding us. You can't really call this an early start because we'd been in our tents since eight o'clock yesterday evening. Not long after sunset a nearly full moon rose over the Barranco Wall and lit up the dome of Kibo. It was absolutely stunning. I had a comfortable night but didn't want to get up this morning when the alarm went off—not because I hadn't had enough sleep, just because I was so snug and cozy in the tent.

---

the plains just being touched by the morning sun behind the mountain. The center of my field of vision was still in shadow, but the edges were bright, and I suddenly realized what I was seeing. A giant shadow was being cast across the landscape. Kilimanjaro. I had read about mountain shadows before, but I'd never seen one.

Later, as the camp was being struck and more of our group were climbing the tower, I set off slowly with Jakob and some of the porters for our next camp at Arrow Glacier, only a few hours ahead. The path zigzagged up a steepish slope and it was definitely a case for "pòle, pole." Soon we had the rhythm going, climbing without undue stress and still having enough in reserve to enjoy the view, which was getting better and wider by the minute. Jakob was humming softly, a slow, lilting regular hum that helped to maintain the slow, regular placing of feet. It was hyp-

Foo village. But he's not ready yet, and besides, he adds, there are still children at home. Guiding pays better than shopkeeping.

"How many children do you have?"

He grins again before answering proudly, "Eight kids. The oldest is 21, the youngest is only 1." It turns out that his first wife died leaving him with six children; he's had two more with his present wife. Jakob is very anxious that his sons at least should all learn good English to assist them in their careers, and that means they need good schooling. It's expensive to educate children here. He has three sons and five daughters. One of his sons is with us on this trip, he tells me, as a porter—a rangy young man who looked very like Jakob.

"Have you climbed other mountains?" I ask him. No, he's traveled a little around Tanzania, but he does cherish a dream. He'd love to see Everest, to trek up to its

Base Camp. "But," he adds sadly, "I can't see how it would be possible for a man like me."

Once more, one is aware of the gulf between us. Some things are possible and some not. And far more things are possible for westerners than they are for Tanzanian mountain guides. I may have had to wait till I was 50 to see the Himalaya, 60-something before I saw Africa, but I have seen them. I didn't think I could reply brightly to Jakob, "Oh, I went there. It's lovely!" I say merely that I sincerely hope he'd manage it one day. Then, as the slope gets steep, I lapse back into my rhythmic plodding, as dozens of heavily laden porters steam past me on the stony trail.

MAPS REFER TO the Arrow Glacier Hut lying at almost 16,000 feet. There is no hut there now. It was demolished by rockfall back in the 1980s, but the name lingers, as it does for Lava Tower Hut and goodness knows how many other prefabricated refuges at high level on this mountain. Once a hut, always a hut. By the time I tramped in here, around midday, a village of tents had been set up by our porters. They were still going up, even though we are whittling down now and squeezing more people in together to save on gear. We were going to have only one mess tent tonight, instead of one for the trekkers and one for the crew, so we'd be eating in relays.

Arrow Camp occupies a boulder-strewn slope, with one or two flatter spots upon it for tent platforms; these will have been leveled off by the porters, and if more are needed they set to it and construct more. We're right at the base of the Western Breach here, a very steep, snow-covered scree slope, crowned and surrounded by tiered cliffs. It's a huge amphitheater, the near-vertical cliffs wrapping in a semicircle around the screes, which in the center appear to reach almost to the top. The cliffs are deeply fissured, with isolated icicles in the deepest of the cracks. The exposed surface represents a section through the sequence of lava flows, and it ranges in color from gray to red. The brighter colors, Roger says, are merely the more weathered surfaces where various elements are leaching out. He couldn't wait to begin investigating, as this is one of the few places on the mountain where you get a good section like this. So he's off, clutching his fossil hammer, to see what he can find. But first he wants to get some markers on the shrunken Arrow Glacier in the center of the Breach, to get an idea

of its movement and melting rate. It will be a busy afternoon for him.

The camera crew, too, is busy taking scenics and interviewing the trekkers. I take a little turn around the basin, but it's hard to know where to walk to be out of shot. Rocks are the main interest here. We're pretty well above the plant line, except for a few, very scrawny little individuals huddled under rocks, and the lichens of course. In an hour or so Roger returns, his hat full of rocks. Now it's obvious why Englishmen wear "such funny hats," as David put it; a baseball cap makes a very poor basket when it comes to collecting mineral samples. Roger pulls out his pocket lens and shows us his treasures. He's particularly pleased to have found some really ancient rocks, packed with large crystals of nepheline, which have been spewed up from the Earth's mantle.

Major climatic changes over the past million years produced a series of glaciations on the mountains of East Africa No less than five glacial episodes are recognized for Kilimanjaro alone within the past 500,000 years, interspersed with volcanic activity. The precise extent of these has proved difficult to determine since each successive glaciation or eruption overlays, to a degree, evidence of previous activity. Scientists have been marrying research on the ground with aerial photos in their quest to identify and date moraine deposits, glacially smoothed and striated rock surfaces and lava flows. Still they argue over the likeliest sequence of events.

The glacial maximum, we can be fairly sure, occurred around 20,000 years ago, coinciding with the great ice age in temperate latitudes. Ice borings tell us that the oldest ice remaining today dates back some 10,000 years. But there is little if any fresh build up, and many believe that under present climatic conditions the hypothetical level for sustaining permanent ice at this latitude lies above the height of the mountain. Over millenia, Kilimanjaro's ice will have waxed and waned many times, and may have disappeared on occasion. Factors governing this are intricate and incompletely understood. Global warming is unlikely in itself to be responsible for the recent dramatic retreat. Thermal activity, or a drop in precipitation at the end of the 19th century could just as easily have played a part.

A sharp wind blows in with the mist and, by mid-afternoon, most of us are driven to the refuge of the mess tent where there are thermoses of hot tea, and someone has unearthed a packet of ginger nuts—which never tasted better. Most of the camp food has been supplied with the idea of catering for an American palate, but Arabella tucked in a few goodies so that the three Brits would not feel forgotten. We drool extravagantly over Marmite and marmalade and ginger nut biscuits to everyone else's bewilderment. The Sherpas follow our culinary wars with great interest, try out everything on offer, and out-consume all of us when it comes to chili sauce or Bombay spice tea. One's sense of taste lacks its fine tuning up here, and with appetites depressed as well—another altitude effect—it takes a great effort of will to eat and drink at all. It's the bold and salty flavors that win through.

I saw high-altitude trekking described by Tom Dunkel as "taking a long walk toward senility. Body and mind slowly crumble." Human beings can make

Our bodies struggle to effect the right balance. Despite our excessive drinking and urinating, water is often retained in the tissues, swelling up fingers and faces. At the same time, weight drops off us. I don't know when I've seen my tummy so flat in a long time, an effect I could enjoy were it not hidden under these multilayers of clothes we have to put on to keep warm. Our duvet jackets only caught up with us at Great Barranco, and we're very grateful for them here at Arrow.

There is a sobering reminder at this Arrow Camp of how dangerous it can be to come to this elevation when you are not used to it. On the rocks beside my tent lies a battered plaque in memory of a young 27-year-old from Dayton, Ohio, who died here during the 1970s. No further details are given, but it's safe to assume this young man would have been a victim of severe altitude sickness. It is hard to get an idea of just how many people up

TUESDAY There's a tremendous contrast between this camp at Arrow Glacier and the ones we've been in before. It's bleak and barren, with few plants. We had mist and hail this afternoon, which made the whole place so dismal and cold, but Roger was in his element, scampering around, chipping rocks, and collecting bits of spewed up mantle. Tonight, though, it's beautiful here at 16,000 feet, looking over a sea of clouds at sunset, and there's a great sense of anticipation.

modest physiological adaptations, enabling them to survive and function at altitude, although the degree to which they can do this varies from individual to individual. The highest permanent habitations on Earth are around 17,500 feet. If people need to work higher than that on a daily basis, they tend to come down to sleep and climb up again in the morning. In most cases, these high-livers will have had a lifetime to acclimatize, yet that doesn't exclude them from sometimes being smitten with acute debility. Most of the rest of us lowland beings will need to start making our physiological adaptations from around 10,000 feet. Principally, we are looking to increase our red blood corpuscles in order to maintain sufficient oxygenation of the tissues. Because this is not itself without danger—of clogging up our circulation—we mustn't forget to drink and drink and drink to keep up our fluid levels.

here succumb to cerebral or pulmonary edema, the most deadly of the altitude-induced disorders. No figures are published, but it could be as many as one a month.

The fact that no technical climbing difficulties are involved in most of the routes up Kilimanjaro does not mean that anyone should assume they'll get up without a problem. Tom Dunkel, who climbed the mountain in the mid 1990s, was told a cautionary tale by one of his guides. On one trip, this guide, Remmy Damion, was offered an extra $300 by an American doctor to make sure he got him to the summit. The client was overweight, but absolutely determined to bag Africa's highest summit. Gamely, he huffed his way up the Western Breach, the route that faced us in the morning. "Breathing like a buffalo, he was," Remmy recalled, imitating an

FOLLOWING PAGES: A FULL MOON AND KILIMANJARO'S SHADOW HANG ABOVE THE SHIRA PLATEAU AT DAWN.

exaggerated wheeze. "I advised him to turn back, but he refused." So Remmy guided him up the Breach, as ordered—but that night the doctor died of a heart attack. Dunkel was shown the man's business card, which Remmy still carries in his wallet as a reminder that nobody can buy their way up this mountain.

That evening in the mess tent David produced a pulse oxymeter, a little device that clips onto a finger and measures oxygen saturation in the blood. We took it in turns to see how we were faring. Most of us recorded percentages in the 80s; I was about 83 percent with quite a high pulse rate of 80 or 90. But one of our fit young porters was producing an oxygen uptake, up here at 16,000 feet, of 95 percent and his pulse rate remained at a steady 50. That's acclimatization for you!

Most of the trekkers and film crew have slowed down a bit at this altitude, though no one is really poorly so far, thanks to our slow progress in getting here. Arabella, who'd come up later and rushed about a lot more, was off color this morning, but improved dramatically with a cup of tea and a Diamox. I've been holding off taking the Diamox, as I've never been sure of its effectiveness when I've used it before. It makes your extremities tingle violently—at least that's one of the side

than others; perhaps, when it comes to the latter condition, some people's brains are a tighter fit within their skulls, particularly when young. Oldies, like me, whose brain has doubtless shrunk over time, maybe have a little more wiggle room inside the skull cavity. Who knows? The most effective treatment for either disorder is to get the sufferer to a lower altitude quickly. These days, this can also be achieved artificially by putting the patient in a pressurised Gamov Bag, which can be pumped up to simulate lower altitudes. And there is great excitement at the moment following Swiss claims that the use of vasodilaters can be beneficial for pulmonary edema.

Our chief guide, Allen Philemon Mbaga, has been quick to reassure me that I need have no worries. If anyone collapses at this camp, he could have them down to the roadhead in a couple of hours, and nowhere on the mountain would they be more than seven or eight hours from intensive care.

We don't sit up very late as we are all anxious to get our day bags packed for the morning. After two days of light walking, we now face a much longer haul into the crater, where we will camp tomorrow night.

"You're to set your alarm early," David advised me as I retired to my tent with my mug of Sleepytime tea. "I want you away first in the morning. Your porter knows to be ready." I sighed, start first, finish last, I know the score—wouldn't it be nice, just once, to find a sudden reserve of energy and surprise everyone.

IF ANYTHING, the steep scree slope was getting steeper. It was disorienting to have the ground sweep away from your feet like this, and all the landmarks you'd looked up to before, such as the Lava Tower, become mere specks beneath you, merging into the background. The belt of forest looked dark and inviting down there, but only a fraction of its size. Farther out, we could see lakes on the plain and firesmoke, which the porters said was coming from a sugar cane plantation. The ground has been dry so far; in only one place did we have to cross a tongue of snow, but Douglas, our safety rigger, cut a neat line of steps across, and it really wasn't very far. Even so, it was wise not to look down too often. One slip here and you'd be right down

effects for most people. And you don't realize till that happens that your nose and cheeks are among those extremities; it's a most peculiar sensation. Too high a dose and you can hallucinate. The couple of times I took it going to Everest in 1986 and 1996, I noticed no significant improvement and only began to feel better once I stopped. But it's a personal thing, and it's good to know it's around if you want it.

Pulmonary edema is when your tissues leak fluid into your lungs, which eventually can drown you; and cerebral edema is a buildup of water on the brain. It's hard to know why some people should be more susceptible

KILIMANJARO'S VOLCANIC HISTORY

ROGER BILHAM
ASSOCIATE DIRECTOR, COOPERATIVE INSTITUTE FOR RESEARCH IN THE ENVIRONMENTAL SCIENCES

KILIMANJARO is the tallest of the African volcanoes and the most isolated, and just why it should have risen three miles above its base in this particular setting is not at all clear. Indeed, it may once have been even taller, because the edifice is much eroded, and because a vast ice cap of unknown thickness added to its skyline summit. The immense weight of this 50 by 25 mile pile of volcanic rock has depressed the African surface by as much as 600 feet, causing a topographic dimple with a radius of more than 100 miles. The depressed area surrounds Kilimanjaro like a moat but is now clearly discernable only north of the mountain. Wells drilled into the southern moat in search of water reveal the existence of the moat beneath layers of lavas and ash.

Although the clues to its early history are buried deep within the volcano, it is probable that less than a million years ago Kilimanjaro did not exist. The volcano has grown 50 miles from the East African Rift, along cracks that represent a relatively minor splinter in the African crust. Three vents played a dominant role in constructing the volcano. The western and earliest of these, beneath the Shira Plateau, formed an isolated volcano 750,000 years ago, before a loss of pressure in its underlying magma chamber caused its center to collapse. Magma subsequently welled out of the edges of this cone-shaped collapse fissure, forming minor volcanic piles near its southern rim. The plumbing that fed these later volcanoes were three-foot-wide cracks now exhumed by erosion

A BIRD'S-EYE GLIMPSE OF KILIMANJARO'S SUMMIT AREA REVEALS THE NEARLY PERFECT RING OF THE REUSCH CRATER AND THE SUNKEN ASH PIT AT ITS CENTER.

as walls of rock known as volcanic dikes. Among the interesting rock types on Shira is one that includes chunks of the green crystal, olivine, propelled there from the Earth's mantle 30 to 50 miles below the surface. The volcano Mawenzi, on the eastern end of the Kilimanjaro massif, may have started erupting soon after Shira's extinction. Perhaps a half million years ago, having constructed a volcanic cone similar in height to Shira, eruptions on Mawenzi also fizzled out. Mawenzi is now in an advanced state of decay, with its core carved into shreds by erosion.

About 360,000 years ago a massive vent between the two earlier volcanoes erupted, building the central mass of Kibo and flooding Shira's central plateau and the flanks of Kibo with a black lava full of huge rhombic-shaped crystals. Numerous parasitic cones line up with these three major vents indicating the path of the crustal crack that underlies Kilimanjaro's volcanic centers. The highest peak of Kilimanjaro, Uhuru Peak, roughly 300 feet above the present vent, is a remnant of a yet higher structure on Kibo that collapsed long ago.

Unlike the flanking volcanic piles of Shira and Mawenzi that are now quite extinct, the vent that formed Kibo was weakly active some 400 years ago, tossing out volcanic bombs and ash but with no evident lava flow. Hot gases, rich with sulfur and other minerals, rise from fissures near this most recent vent. These hot gases provide a microclimate for grasses and flowers that survive in sheltered rock crevices at elevations of more than 19,000 feet. The gases keep the summit warm at quite shallow depths, so that the ice cap on Kilimanjaro has most certainly been melted from below. Contorted laminations in the remnant ice sheets suggest that this basal melting has been uneven, being faster where the ice is on rock than where it lies on layers of insulating ash.

Kilimanjaro is a dormant volcano, meaning that it is quite possible that it will erupt again. From the chemistry of its lavas, we may speculate how a full-blown eruption might proceed. In shape, Kilimanjaro looks quite unlike the graceful volcanoes, formed from fluid lavas and ash granules, of Japan and the Aleutian islands. Their flanks are concave and crowned with peaked summits, whereas Kilimanjaro has a bulbous summit and convex flanks. From afar, it resembles an inverted pudding bowl. This signifies that its lavas are viscous—and thereby dangerous. The reason for alarm is that viscous lavas tend to plug their vents like toothpaste in a neglected tube. Squeezing the tube can clear the block but cause a sudden rush of toothpaste. In the same way, Kibo may in times past have plugged its vent, to be subsequently cleared in giant but infrequent explosions. These explosions may have had enough energy to blow the top off Kilimanjaro. It is more likely though that explosive eruptions were localized, and that Kibo's missing summit has foundered deep into the mountain along cracks similar to those that now surround the vent that has filled the caldera floor with ash and lava flows. Its highest point, Uhuru peak, is a surviving flank of this earlier summit. For the past 10,000 years eruptions of Kibo have been somewhat subdued, yet they indicate that the central vent, a resurgent dome, is attempting to reconstruct the former summit edifice. Whether it succeeds or not will depend on the availability of new magma deep beneath the volcano. The supply of gas and lava fluctuates and is presently at a low ebb, judging from a ring of collapse fractures that rim the present vent, but it would not take more than a modest future eruption to bury these beneath fresh lavas and ash.

...just why it should have risen three miles above its base in this particular setting is not at all clear. Indeed, it may have once been even taller...

While many of the crystals in the rocks of Kilimanjaro are small because of the quenching action of lavas when they erupt, Kibo's dominant rock types (porphyry) tells us that the magma chamber erupted in the act of slowly freezing. It takes many thousands of years to grow crystals an inch or more across, yet in the porphyry from Kibo giant and perfectly formed crystals of feldspar have been frozen in the act of growing yet larger. In some places crystals are embedded in black, glassy obsidian. On the edges of Uhuru peak it is possible to scoop up handfuls of these crystals, which must have splashed out of a bubbling lava lake that once ponded near the summit.

All over the summit area you see traces of the most recent eruption—volcanic bombs that were thrown from the vent and smashed on the ashy summit floor. They lie between the towering ice cliffs of the once continuous ice sheet that used to feed numerous glaciers on the flanks of Kibo. The relict glaciers on Kibo's flanks convey little of the power that their ancestors clearly possessed deep in the past ice age. Huge valleys were carved into the edge of the volcano exposing its interior structure. Glacial moraines of volcanic debris were pushed relentlessly downward into piles for later dismantling by gravity and stream action.

The activities of ice retreat and advance have been recorded in ancient soil layers beneath frozen lava flows. This dangerous mix of fire and ice in the past million years produced another of nature's menaces—lahars—flows of hot water, mud, rocks, and tree stumps that have ploughed catastrophically to the base of the mountain. Moshi and villages to the southeast are built on some of these ancient mudflows. Former lahars can be recognized by the huge boulders that now litter the fields of the apron of gently sloping land surrounding the mountain. An awakening of Kibo and the reactivation of new mudflows would of course be devastating to the large populations that now cluster at the base of Kilimanjaro.

THE TEAM SETS UP TENTS BESIDE THE FURTWÄNGLER GLACIER INSIDE THE CRATER.

the basin to the boulders at the bottom. Soon we had reached a lava spur, blocky and broken, and climbing became a hands-and-feet affair, with no shortage of handholds. The rock was loose and the sense of exposure still with us. The real danger was to the porters, who were scrambling up with really awkward loads balanced for the most part on their heads. One or two porters have adopted rucksacks, but heavy boxes and tied-up bundles are invariably consigned to the head. The Sherpas were impressed; they had long since taken to backpacks themselves. You still see the forehead tump-line used for load carrying by country people in Nepal. It may look strange to outsiders, but does not require such a feat of balance as climbing rocks with a head load.

About two-thirds of the way up, we found the film crew lying in wait for us. What a time for an interview, when we were barely drawing enough breath to keep ourselves alive. I heard David ask Hansi what sort of day he was having. The answer was hard to discern amid the gasping breaths. "Myself," Hansi said, "I think today

has been a very terrible day. Long, hard, and the weather's messy. You can't see where you're going. And my legs are going to finish me off...."

"What's the matter with your legs?"

"My knee hurts. I've twisted it or something. It's the one I hurt playing soccer before we came. I hope it's not far now. I just want to get into camp and have a sleep."

"Oh, it's not far," David reassured him.

"Huh?" Hansi would take some convincing. He recalled the time in the forest when, as he said, his feet were screaming. All he'd wanted then was for that day's hike to end. "Most of the guys were telling me, 'We'll be at camp in 20 minutes.' I walked for 25 minutes, and I saw another porter who said, 'Just 30 minutes, and you'll be there.' A little later I saw another guy and asked him how far the camp was. 'Oh,' he said, 'something like an hour and a half.' I got so mad!"

"No, Hansi, *really*," David promised. "It isn't far now." Then it was my turn in front of the camera.

"There was a time about halfway up," I confessed, "when I began thinking *What the hell am I doing here?*

And right then I was pretty certain this was going to be my very last climb. But now, if we really are nearly at the crater, and there's every possibility the weather will brighten up later, well then … I'm not so sure I am ready for retirement just yet. I guess I'm in for some more of this yet."

"You know," David told me quietly later. "You don't have to go to the summit if you don't feel like it. The porters won't go over the top; they'll walk around from the crater camp to reach the path down. You could always do the same, if it gets too much."

I dearly hoped that wouldn't be necessary. Maybe the summit isn't everything—that's what we're supposed to say to ourselves—but it would be a tremendous pity to miss it, especially after getting this high.

Back at Arrow Glacier, when we were gazing up at this Western Breach, I remember David remarking that what we could see as the top of the cliffs really was the

kept rolling. "Oh, my god, It's no good…." Nevertheless I kept going, fighting between gritting my teeth and gasping for air. I had fallen behind the others now, who seemed to have found new energy and were simply swarming over the rock ahead. "Maybe I've dropped out of shot altogether," I thought hopefully. "I've got… can't take any … gotta…stop…." But with one last effort, I heaved myself over the steep lip of rock before flopping to the ground on the other side, wrenching after breath. I felt sick.

Once the roaring inside my head had subsided and my chest was heaving a little less violently, I began to take in what I was seeing. It was astonishing. We were in an utterly different world.

Hemmed in by the lip of rock, we were inside the vast circular crater of Kilimanjaro. It was filled with rusty-colored gravel, from which rose elegant walls of turquoise-tinted ice, sculpted into the most exqui-

> **WEDNESDAY** Kilimanjaro is throwing its whole repertoire at us today. We set off this morning from our glacier in chilly dawn. Really, really cold, it was, but very clear with views to the distant horizon. Then the sun came out and life was wonderful on the warm rocks, but a couple of hours later in rolled the mist, and now we're getting snow and rain, and cannot see more than a few yards ahead of us.

crater's rim and not a false summit. Give or take an intervening bulge or two, I suppose it was, although surmounting those upper tiers was taking far longer than expected. From below the effect of distance and foreshortening diminished them considerably. The ground up here was loose with rolling gravel, and you had to tread carefully. I was very glad of the ski pole I'd brought as an extra leg, but I refused an additional one kindly offered me by one of the guides. I needed one hand to clutch at rocks for some feeling of security, however illusory.

The big lenses were once more focused on a stretch of rocky scrambling ahead, and as we approached we heard, through the IMAX camera's mighty *whirr*, the command *"Action!"* I took a deep breath and tried to match my pace with the climbing figure in front. It was an effort. "I can't keep this up, I can't, I can't!" I was longing to hear the magic word *"Cut!"* But the cameras

site shapes. These may represent only a shadow of the former ice cap, yet still the scene takes your breath away. It really was a magic fairyland. And suddenly we were hugging each other, jigging about, laughing and crying at the same time; we'd made it to the Roof of Africa. Okay, not yet to the tippy-top, but we were on the cone, on top of the iced pudding, and very much aware of the sky arching overhead. The richest blue— all trace of sleet and mists vanished—and the low sun was casting a golden wash over the gravel and ice. It was an emotional moment, and one that affected us all. We simply gazed around in wonder. "What do you feel, what are you experiencing now you're here," the hungry film rolls desired to know. We were struck dumb for want of lofty thoughts. Or of ways to express them.

Roger tried a piece to camera. "So, today, we've walked up a half a mile vertically," he began, breath-

lessly, "...which means we're now three and a half miles above sea level." He paused for another deep breath and muster of thoughts. "And, uh, one thing we've found very noticeable...is the difficulty in speaking long sentences. There's not a lot of air up here.... And there's not a lot of plant life either. In fact...all that seems to be up here is a vast, desolate plateau of rock and ash left by the last eruption...punctuated by large sheets of ice, which are

obviously retreating quite rapidly...." All of which was true, but it did no justice to the transcendental beauty of these fugitive glacial forms. Later that evening in camp, after he and Heidi had rushed out to explore the nearest glacier, the Furtwängler, Roger put the scientist in him aside, and had another go at describing these evanescent marvels.

"The shapes of the ice were quite fantastic with the sun shining through them," he enthused. "Magical. The

◆ THE INNER, OR REUSCH, CRATER IS THE VOLCANIC HEART OF KILIMANJARO; ITS CONCENTRIC ASH TERRACES MARK THE MOST RECENT PERIODS OF ACTIVITY.

glinting teeth, or fins, or they would be sailing boats, transluscent castles—the shapes were endless. Inside the ice were darker stripes that Roger identified as traces of ash from former eruptions. Beauty and history crystallized together.

It was as if the ice gave these two energy, for they scrambled about like children till the light was almost gone, while most of the rest of us sank into our tents, whacked out and fading fast. Again, I felt nauseous; the cup of tea that was meant as a reviver had the opposite effect. I didn't want to eat tonight. The youngsters had done amazingly well to get up here today. I wondered how many 12- or 13-year-olds had ever made it this far. Admittedly, Hansi arrived in some pain from his knee: He was given a fireman's lift around the edge of the Furtwangler into the camp, which was up and waiting for us under the final cliff to Uhuru Peak. Now everyone was rallying round, giving him massage, painkillers, special knee supports. I felt sure he'd be all right after a good, long sleep. It was clearly tiredness more than anything that had really overwhelmed him. Exhaustion hit Nicole differently; she was still giggly and bright. But it had been a tough day for her dad, with so much steep, uphill work. He looked a little gray.

After the euphoria of finding ourselves inside the crater this afternoon, we'd all grown a little subdued and merely pecked at our dinner. Apart from little Nicole, that is, who was ravenous and excited. She was still feeling lyrical that evening as she wrote in her diary: "The sun set very gracefully, like a spoon of red liquid gently melting into a glass of clear water. It just melted away."

It was a star-studded night and very cold outside. I kept warm enough in the tent I now shared with Arabella, but I noticed she'd raided the stores and was wearing two duvet jackets inside her sleeping bag. I had to keep reminding myself, "I'm in the crater! Really in the crater! Not far now." And then I'd warn myself not to build hopes too high. Just cross fingers that I wouldn't feel sick in the morning, or I might yet find myself taking the shortcut down with the porters.

deep blue color of really old, compacted ice, devoid of bubbles, melting away in the late evening sun. It's strange to think that these forms could be changed by the next day and take on ever more elaborate shapes and colors.... Nature in transient form."

He and Heidi couldn't resist the lure of clambering up onto what they both now saw as a momentary work of art, sculpted by wind and sun, and tinted by the red dark rays of sunset. The ice pinnacles took on the form of

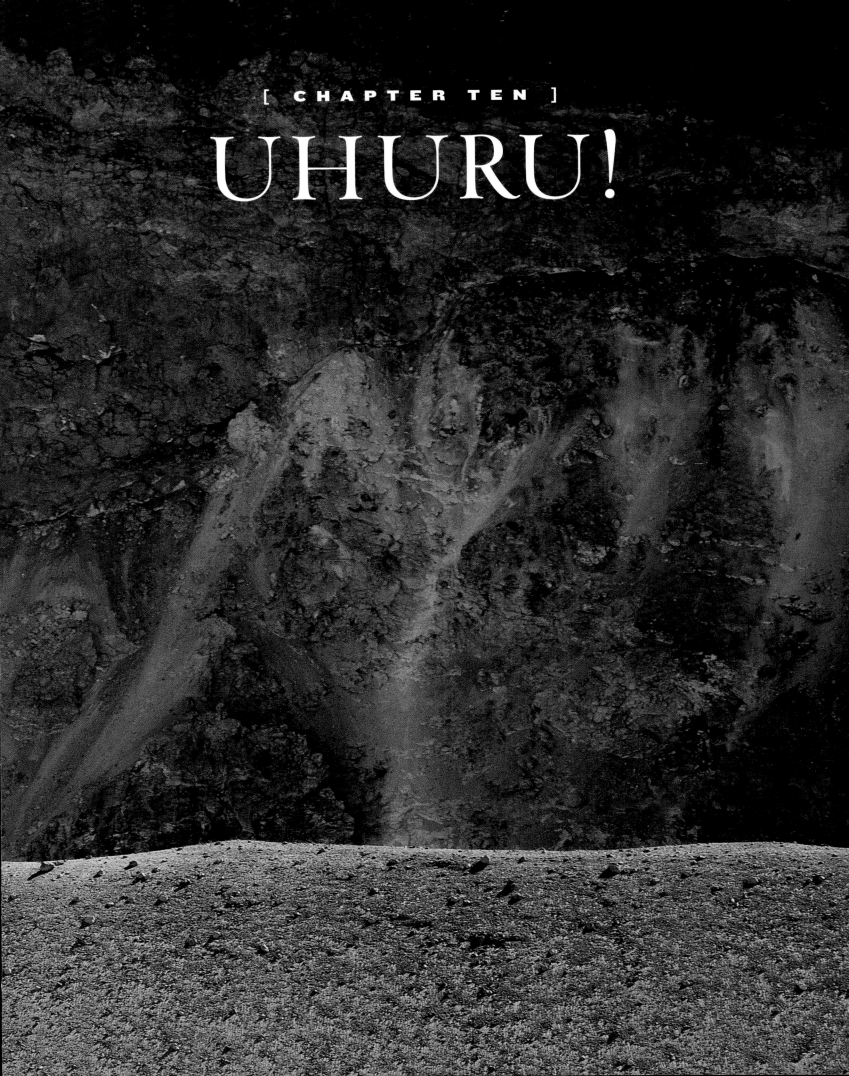

[CHAPTER TEN]

UHURU!

...and then the earth opened up there before us, revealing the secret of Kibo: Taking in the whole upper part of Kibo there opened up a giant crater with steeply precipitous sides....

HANS MEYER, NEARING THE SUMMIT OF KILIMANJARO, 1889

ROGER SET HIS ALARM to get up early. Before we started for the summit he wanted to trek across the caldera and take a look at the inner crater, the powerhouse of this volcano. Even though sleep comes so fitfully up here that you spend half of the night awake, it takes a supreme effort of will to turn out into the darkness and cold. The temperature had dropped to 8°F that night. Steeling himself, Roger stepped outside to rouse Jakob, who would accompany him to what is now known as the Reusch Crater. They trudged off in silence. It wasn't far—just around the end of the Furtwängler Glacier and up a gentle, rolling, little hill that, at 18,700 feet, has the power to rack you with breathlessness. ∾ There was a serenity to the scene, as if this was how things had been since the beginning of time. Yet, as Roger well knew, nothing here was permanent. A carapace of ice once covered this whole summit area, including where our tents were now standing. Meyer's photographs from the end of the 19th century testified to glaciers spilling from an overladen crater to extend well down the sides of Kibo's dome. Jakob could remember there being continuous ice across the main crater floor when he first started climbing the mountain, but now they were crunching through deep gravel and ash.

PRECEDING PAGES: ROGER AND JAKOB WALK AROUND THE RIM OF THE ASH PIT.

LEFT: HUTS SUCH AS THIS SHELTER CLIMBERS ALONG THE ROUTES.

In the past 30 years more than half of the glaciers Jakob knew had disappeared, leaving truncated remnants like stranded icebergs on a beach.

It didn't take long for the two to reach the top of the hill, which proved to be a cone of cinders and ash that the volcano had spewed out over the last several thousand years. Gasping, they found themselves gazing into a deep circular pit, measuring half a mile or so across and penetrating some three to four hundred feet into the ground.

The sun was just coming up, painting the relict glaciers a warm gold. Roger was about to scramble into the crater for a closer look when Jakob called his attention to the wider view. It was glorious. Mawenzi and Shira were lit up in the first rays of sun, and in the distance Roger could see what he recognized as the rift zone about 50 miles away, a receding chain of stupendous volcanoes. Kilimanjaro marks the end of the southward

"It's amazing to think that it's only a few hundred years since this volcano last erupted," Roger remarked to us later over breakfast. "That means temperatures of about 2,000°F. Difficult to imagine, huh?" It was, huddled there in our down jackets. "Think of the violence that could throw up a volcano like this—and how young it all is." No one was exactly sure of the date of the last eruption, he said. Legends appeared to refer to it, but we hadn't been left any contemporary eyewitness accounts as there had been in A.D. 79, when Pliny the Younger recorded Vesuvius erupting to bury Pompeii and Herculaneum. Still, it was very obvious to Roger that he and Jakob had been examining an exceedingly recent volcanic form—geologically speaking. There'd been hardly any erosion since the last active phase. "We were looking down into the furnace that created this mountain," he said. After months of reading up about it and its significance in connection with the

THURSDAY It was windy when we woke up this morning. Young Nicole came rushing into the dining tent as if she were chased by demons. "I had to go fast," she explained breathlessly. "If I walked slow, I'd have been knocked over by the wind." There's certainly no weight to her at all; it's a good job the wind dropped soon after, or we'd have had to anchor her down.

propagation of the eastern or Gregory Rift. Having gotten as far as here, the rift could get no farther, and shortly afterward the volcanoes Meru and Ol Doinyo Lengai erupted to the southwest. Meanwhile, farther west still, another branch propagated on the far side of Tanzania and went on heading south, then southeast to Mozambique. Eventually it may cut off the whole eastern side of Africa, separating it from the rest of the continent by a new ocean.

Spectacular as the view was, they found it impossible to ignore the viciously cold wind buffeting them on the exposed rim of the crater. Roger peered once more into the Reusch Crater, where concentric terraces of different colored ash marked the most recent stages of volcanic activity. Wreaths of vapor were emanating from the crater's walls. These were the fumaroles, or hot-gas vents, from magma chambers beneath the ground.

African Rift, he'd found it thrilling to be standing on the cone from which all that molten rock had poured forth, and to be staring into the dark hole at the bottom, the central vent, which was its main conduit from the bowels of the Earth.

Around the fumeroles, patches of lighter material could be made out. These were deposits of sulfur and carbonate, left by the gases as they escaped. Roger and Jakob began walking around the crater rim when Jakob suddenly vanished from view. It seemed that he had a mission of his own: He was after some of the mineral deposits beside the outpouring fumeroles. Later, we discovered that collecting this residue is a bonus all the local guides and porters seek to exploit when they're up here, for it fetches a good price down in the villages. I had heard of *ikati*, a special white "salt" found high on this mountain, and supposed this must be it.

"He knew exactly where to find it," Roger said, "and I was amazed at the purity and the quantity he was able to gather in just a few minutes."

"I know *ikati*," Freddie told me when we were talking about it later. "You collect it from the Reusch Crater, or hanging under large rocks in caves and hollows. It's a very white salt—I don't know the English name."

"But, what's it for?" I pressed.

"Oh, it can be used many ways," he said. "Women are fed it to make them have abortions. Very small amounts can be mixed with glucose and given to babies who keep crying for no reason. If someone gets food poisoning, *ikati* makes them vomit. Or when a cow gives birth and the placenta doesn't come out properly, *ikati* helps with that too." It sounded a very versatile substance. I made a note to research it further when I had the opportunity.

Down at the fumeroles, Roger had found that there were telltale smudges of greenish yellow around the vents, which proved to be pure sulfur and the emissions themselves were giving off a truly noxious whiff.

"Look!" Roger said, diving into his pocket and pulling out a large chunk of the sulfur he'd picked up close to one of the smelly vents. We passed it around the table. Its color was characteristic clear primrose. I was at once whisked back to childhood, when sulfur tablets were a mainstay in our medicine cupboard. Horrible things. Well, strange anyway, for if the taste wasn't exactly repellent, it certainly wasn't nice. Nor was their effect. I sniffed at the lump, remembering.

"It hasn't got a smell in its pure form," Roger said. "It's the sulfur dioxide and hydrogen sulfide in the gases that pong. It's really unpleasant up there, I tell you. We're lucky the wind is blowing the smells away from this camp." The hot gases were an indication that this quiescent volcano was not dead yet, as formerly thought.

"It was pretty sobering seeing that gaping hole waiting to eject more magma." Roger added. "And you know something else? When we got to that crater both Jakob and I had very cold feet. But as we walked down inside, toward the fumaroles, we found ourselves sink-

ROGER AND JAKOB DESCEND THE SULFUROUS ASH INTO THE REUSCH CRATER. THE SULFUR IS A RESIDUE FROM THE ACTIVE GAS VENTS. FOLLOWING PAGES: OUR CAMPSITE IN THE CRATER PROVIDED A RARE TREAT; MOST NEVER CAMP AT THIS LEVEL.

ing into soft sulfurous deposits that were baking hot. We stood there for a bit to let our feet warm up. But you couldn't stand in one place for long, or you'd bake like a potato. I think that was the most dramatic indication of all that we were actually walking on what is still an active volcano."

It is curious that, although the writings of the pioneer climbers reveal they found hot springs at 13,000 feet, or, in the case of Hans Meyer, observed that the top of the "central parasitic cone" of brown lava and ashes stood proud above the ice sheet, they never doubted that Kilimanjaro was extinct. Meyer was categoric: "The volcanic activity of Kilimanjaro is now a thing of the past," he pronounced. "There is no trace even of fumaroles."

This remained the accepted wisdom for more than 40 years, even though the mountain was regularly climbed. Either people bypassed the Reusch Crater, or we have to assume this was an especially dormant phase in the peak's history. In 1933, the British mountaineer H. W. Tilman, upon reaching the summit on his own, decided to investigate the volcano's workings. "Sulphurous fumes rose from the lip, and pieces of sulphur lay about," he reported in *Snow on the Equator*, the book of his African travels. Tilman himself drew no special inference from this, nor indeed did anyone else for almost a decade. Then the young Arthur Firmin of the Mountain Club of Kenya camped within the caldera and photographed the gushing fumaroles. Vulcanologist J. J. Richard also paid visits in 1942 and took the temperature of rocks around the inner crater, which proved surprisingly warm in places. Struck by the strong sulfurous smell, he regretted not having with him the right instruments for testing gases. But he did find himself growing exceedingly drowsy. He warned future visitors to take due precautions "in case such gases should prove deleterious."

By now, public attention was well and truly ignited and a series of articles and letters in *The Times* and *Illustrated London News* proclaimed the "recrudescence" of Kilimanjaro's volcanic activity and urged the governments of Kenya and Tanganyika to institute periodic monitoring of the situation. A major geological survey was undertaken in 1953 by Sheffield University scientists, in association with the Tanganyikan government, and another, on their own, in the International Geophysical Year, 1957. Arthur Firmin, who

revisited the crater in 1954, remarked that things still seemed to be hotting up: The fumaroles were far more conspicuous on this trip, and had spread farther around the crater. Readings taken at the mouths of the fumaroles in 1953 over a period of 77 days indicated temperatures ranging between 170°F and 220°F, in other words hovering around the normal boiling point of water. Within any one day a variation of up to four degrees might be observed.

"So, you really think Kibo could erupt again?" Hansi sounded anxious.

"It's hard to say," Roger told him. "This may well be the last phase—the volcano's death throes—we simply don't know. It's just that further eruptions can't be ruled out. Kilimanjaro could blow its top once more at least, sometime in the next several hundred years." Even if this were only to pelt the summit with more volcanic bombs and add another ring of ash around the Reusch Crater, it could still be a serious business for the countryside around. As well for Hansi that we didn't pursue this line of prediction. It was time to set off on the final stage of our climb.

Our tents at this last campsite had been tucked in a rocky alcove at the edge of the caldera, almost directly below the highest part of the surrounding rim, Uhuru Peak. There remained only some 400 or 500 feet to climb to the summit, though this was up a very steep and airy track—if it could be called that. Zigzagging tightly, it would deliver us onto the rim, from where the going should prove easy. We just needed to crest a couple of undulations and we'd be there. It was hard to believe after a week on the mountain that we almost had it in the bag. We might be a bit exhausted, and battered, our skin held together with sticking plaster and superglue, but we were still all here and on our feet. It turned out I hadn't been the only one feeling sick at the end of yesterday. Heidi's energy in the crater, which I had so envied, was almost totally the product of her excitement and relief at having gotten so high. She confided that halfway up from Arrow Camp she'd found it difficult to breathe and had become extremely scared. Her diary entry last night recorded headache, pain, nausea, lack of appetite, breathlessness, lightheadedness, sore feet, and tiredness. All she wanted, she told me, was to sleep forever. Much the same as me, then—and Hansi, too. Until now, Hansi had been coping amazingly well—not just with the rigors of the climb, but with being among strangers and away from home. We'd seen his confidence inflate: He was so thrilled at being a real mountaineer. No friend of his, no boy he knew, had been to the crater of Kilimanjaro, let alone had slept in it. If and when he stood on that summit, his dad and mum were going to be so proud of him, and his little sister so jealous. He could hardly wait to tell everyone of his adventures. When yesterday took so much out of him and homesickness welled, his summit prospects looked bleak. I was relieved at breakfast to see that his appetite had returned. Mangos, sausages, and scrambled eggs were being consumed, and now and again the glimmer of a smile crossed his face. It was going to be all right. He'd managed to speak to his dad on the radio telephone late last night, which bucked him no end, and then he'd had a good, long sleep. Things looked a hundred times better this morning.

away. The camera crew was ahead of us, but not quite ready for our arrival, so we sat down to wait and enjoy the view, idly dribbling the small pebbles through our fingers. But this was no ordinary gravel. We'd been thoughtlessly crunching through drifts of crystals. Roger and Nicole began scrabbling through them eagerly, trying to outdo each other in a quest for the biggest, most perfectly shaped crystals.

"What are they?" Nicole wanted to know. I guess we all did.

"Nepheline, I think mostly. And some feldspars. But really big."

They certainly were, giants, some almost two inches long. We learned a new word: mega-phenocrysts, that's what such large, well-formed crystals are called. They are more striking than beautiful, and come in various dun-colored shades, with a glassy sheen that catches

THURSDAY From the soup bowl of the crater, filled with its rusty gravel, it was a short, sharp pull up to the summit ridge. Hard to breathe, but quickly over; really, it was surprising how quickly we got up. And now, here we are, on top of Africa. It's amazing! All of us, looking out over this pearly sea of clouds to the horizon. We can see the craters, see that magnificent fleet of glaciers. We're so happy. And, for the moment, put from our minds any thought of the long, long, long trudge down.

The Furtwängler's ice cliffs were dazzling under a cloudless sky and sunlight washing across the floor of the crater as we left the tents. The cliff we had to climb was still in shade. Even if that meant a cold start, it was no bad thing, for we soon worked up a head of steam. Now that we were on the move, my queasiness passed. Each breath had to be fought for, though, and I wobbled a bit on my legs, adding a certain spice to what was already a vertiginous climb. Gradually our camp dwindled in size as we looked back, and the porters packing up the tents became as small as insects scurrying about. The ravens, which had been croaking at us to leave this morning, had moved in now to see what morsels we'd left behind.

Before long, we pulled over the top of the cliff and began shuffling through what I took to be gravel as we headed toward the summit, now only a couple of humps

the light. Some were perfectly coffin-shaped. They were formed in the late Pleistocene period—almost 12,000 years ago.

"But why are there so many?" I wanted to know. "Have they weathered out of those rhomb-porphyry lavas we read about?"

"No, more probably they were tossed out of a bubbling lava lake up here." Roger took some to analyze properly when he got back to his laboratory.

We'd become quite absorbed. "I can see you're going to be a geologist." Roger told Nicole, who grinned widely. We were drawn from our inspection by a shout from above.

"Come on troops, we're ready for you," David called. We dusted off the Pleistocene grit and scrunched up the last few yards to the summit—all of us—with the cameras to record the moment.

We stood atop Uhuru Peak, formerly Kaiser Wilhelm Spitze—the summit of Kibo, the summit of Kilimanjaro, and the Roof of Africa. It was an emotional moment. We were way above the clouds that spread in rumpled billows to the horizon. Whichever way we looked, we were cut off completely from the world of people below. Only Meru pierced this cloud ocean to become a distant companion in our own bright, celestial world, a world comprising solely the summit, the crater, the glaciers, the clouds, and the great blue sky.

Marking the summit was a newly carved sign proclaiming "Congratulations! You are now at Uhuru Peak, Tanzania 5,895 AMSL. Africa's Highest Point, World's Highest Free-standing Mountain, One of the World's Largest Volcanoes. Welcome." Beside it, among the stones on the ground, a battered metal box carried a further inscription:

The Tanganyika Flag and the Torch of Unity were first raised here on the 9th December 1961.

We, the people of Tanganyika, would like to light a candle, and put it on top of Mount Kilimanjaro which would shine beyond our borders giving hope where there was

despair, love where there was hate, and dignity where before there was only humiliation.

Julius K. Nyerere

Nyerere, the mountain was climbed once more. Then the flag was moved to its rightful place on the summit proper, which was renamed Uhuru (or Freedom) Peak. The image of Lt. Alex Nyirenda planting the standard in the summit snows has become one of those enduring icons of history, appearing on commemorative postage stamps and frequently reproduced.

Hansi insisted on carrying the flag aloft like Lt. Nyirenda in his summit picture. Once more he rang his dad, and read out to him the words on the summit notice-board. His proud father passed the phone around his office so that everyone could share the moment. Beaming and happy, Hansi sat now with his binoculars, trying to make out his home village over on the slopes of Meru.

MANY AFRICAN MYTHS center on the twin peaks of Kilimanjaro. One, involving the summit of Kibo, builds on the legend of Solomon and Sheba, which we know from the Bible and other ancient writings. Makeda was the virgin queen of Sheba and Ethiopia, who crossed the burning desert of what is today Saudi Arabia with all her courtiers and a phalanx of elephants to pay her famous state visit to Judah. Once there, her beauty captured the heart of a monarch famous for his superior wisdom. The story goes that she repeatedly resisted the king's advances until he, in some exasperation, demanded to know what it would take to gain her surrender. Nothing, she told him imperiously, would make her change her mind. "Aha!" said Solomon, as his famous intellect set to work. "But supposing you stole something of mine, couldn't I then claim what I wanted in recompense?" Maybe, she conceded, but it wouldn't happen. Never would she take anything belonging to him without asking.

That evening, on Solomon's orders, a banquet of highly spiced and salted food was laid before Sheba. Later, when she went to her chambers, such a raging thirst came upon her that she could not sleep. Finding no jug of water in her room, she tiptoed outside. Through the open door to the king's quarters she could see a large ewer on a table, just inside. "If I'm careful," she thought, "I can pour a drink without waking

Snow conditions up here at the end of the year in which Tanganyika received its independence were so bad that it was impossible to walk safely around the crater rim. The new nation's flag, its symbol of freedom, had to be raised at Gillman's Point rather than the higher Kaiser Wilhelm Spitze. But the following year, 1962, when Tanganyika merged with Zanzibar to become Tanzania under its first president, Julius

ETERNAL ICE AND SNOW?

Douglas Hardy, Ph.D.

RESEARCH SCIENTIST, GEOSCIENCES DEPARTMENT, UNIVERSITY OF MASSACHUSETTS

CROSSING THE VAST summit crater of Kibo en route to the Northern Icefield, my oxygen-starved brain struggled to interpret environmental observations that weren't fitting together. Ahead loomed the glacier's imposing vertical wall, yet where was the snow required to nourish the glacier? Joining sun-blistered colleagues at the ice, dripping icicles quickly replenished our empty water bottles, yet we knew the fantastic ice fins, spires, and cliffs on Kibo signified the dominance of ablation processes other than melting. Our expedition's purpose was to begin a new study of glaciers and climate at Kilimanjaro's summit focusing on the recent retreat of these glaciers. As we set our packs down on the warm volcanic sand, the intellectual equivalent of warning lights were beginning to flash in my head: Don't expect any simple explanations.

Hindsight reveals that a severe drought was under way throughout East Africa in February 2000, when we joined Lonnie Thompson and his team from Ohio State University at the summit. Thompson spent four weeks there extracting six ice cores from several different glaciers, which are yielding a record of climate and environmental change spanning millennia. The history of these glaciers, provided by the ice cores, extends right up until the day each is drilled. The interface between Thompson's work and ours is here at the surface where, through automated weather, snow, and ice measurements, we are documenting how the glaciers record. Studying the past and present, we are working urgently to understand the dramatic retreat of glaciers currently underway on Kilimanjaro before the evidence—and the historical record—disappears.

Glaciers today cover a tiny fraction of Kilimanjaro relative to their extent during the last ice age. Kibo alone had probably 50 times more ice than today. There may also have been intervals with less ice than today in the roughly 20,000 years since the Last Glacial Maximum. Direct observation of Kilimanjaro's glaciers began in 1889, with the explorations and first ascent by Hans Meyer. His prolific and eloquent accounts are both fascinating and invaluable. Glaciers encircled the summit and filled much of the crater, covering an area ten times greater than today. By the time of Meyer, modern evidence indicates that the retreat, from a minor advance phase, had been underway for several decades. Continuous ice recession was documented through the 20th century by photographic mapping and satellite imagery. While we were on the mountain with Thompson in February 2000, less than one square mile of ice remained—representing 18 percent of that mapped in 1912, and 67 percent of the area covered only 11 years earlier.

The rapid decrease in glacier area during modern times (since 1889) has led many to ponder how long the ice will endure. Indeed, upon ascending the mountain nine years after his first climb, Meyer speculated that the glaciers of the Kibo crater would disappear within 20 to 30 years. The latest assessment of ice area in 2000 attracted attention and concern both within Tanzania and around the world, and very few news accounts could resist linking the retreat of Kilimanjaro's glaciers to global warming. Without adequate diagnostic evidence, however, this linkage is on thin ice; we must recognize that the mountain's glaciers have little in common with mid-latitude Alpine glaciers and accept that simple explanations are not always possible. Kilimanjaro is a mountain that defies expectations and shatters assumptions.

On a global scale, glaciers are in widespread retreat. From records of area and length, recession of mountain glaciers has been documented worldwide with few exceptions. In tropical mountain areas particularly, there is abundant evidence that the retreat is accelerating. For example, Thompson has made long-term observations on one glacier in Peru where the rate in 2000 was 32 times faster than in 1978. According to the World Glacier Monitoring Service in Zurich, mountain glacier recession during the 20th century is a response to climate change, initially probably natural but which may now "…contain an expanding element of anthropogenic [human-induced] influence."

Glaciers and bank accounts are both entities that grow, shrink, and provide storage, governed by the balance between credits (accumulation) and debits (ablation). On mountain glaciers mass accumulates primarily through precipitation, while ablation is dominated by melting and sublimation — a rather mysterious process through which water molecules are transferred directly from the solid phase (snow or ice) to vapor. From measurements of accumulation and ablation, each expressed as water equivalence, we can establish a glacier's mass balance, which is intimately tied to the glacier's health. Mass balance studies are complementary to those mapping changes in area and length but remarkably, no mass balance measurements exist from Kilimanjaro prior to those we began with Thompson in 2000. Considerable debate took place within our tents that February as to whether the Northern Icefield would gain or lose mass over the next 12 months. Over the past century however, the overall net balance has clearly been negative.

Sublimation deserves further discussion, for in dry tropical areas this mechanism of ablation can result in significant mass loss. It has long been known to promote growth of *nieve penitentes* high on tropical mountain glaciers, which are strange, east-west oriented blades of ice, pointed at the sun and sometimes several meters high. Sublimation from snow and ice surfaces is a difficult process to measure, but can be calculated from meteorological measurements at the glacier surface. Recently, a French group working on Zongo Glacier in Bolivia found that nearly all the energy available was consumed by sublimation during the dry season, leaving almost none for melting. Why is this distinction between sublimation and melting important? One reason is that the process consumes tremendous energy that might otherwise be available for melting — a whooping 8.5 times more, for the same mass of snow or ice. Secondly, the balance between sublimation and melting is principally controlled by humidity. Therefore, relatively subtle changes in any atmospheric variable related to humidity (e.g., cloudiness, wind direction) will have an amplified impact on a tropical glacier's mass balance. Until now, there has

been insufficient meteorological data from Kilimanjaro's summit to determine the disposition of energy (i.e., sublimation vs. melt), but we believe that sublimation is the dominant mechanism of ablation through much of the year.

Lewis Glacier on Mt. Kenya (200 miles north), the best documented glacier in the tropics, provides an analog for mass balance processes on Kilimanjaro. Although the mountain is lower in elevation, 17,058 feet (5,202 meters), and considerably smaller at high elevations, mass balance measurements and analyses made over a number of years by Stefan Hastenrath and colleagues are relevant. They attribute the initial retreat of glaciers on Mt. Kenya to a late-19th century precipitation decrease, along with an associated reduction in cloudiness; together these changes decreased accumulation and increased ablation. Warming in the 1920s caused further retreat, but temperature change alone cannot account for ice wastage since 1963. The smoking gun according to Hastenrath is held by humidity, a slight increase leading to reduced sublimation and therefore increased energy available for melting. Our new measurements and Thompson's ice-core record will help establish the degree to which these results apply to Kilimanjaro, where the mountain and its glaciers extend higher into the cold, dry tropical atmosphere.

Kilimanjaro's glaciers are situated more than halfway through Earth's atmosphere, and herein lies their great value to science. As an island in the sky, rising 19,340 feet above the East African plains, Kilimanjaro provides a unique perspective on the present and past global climate system. A better atmospheric measurement platform would be hard to design.

A great deal remains to be learned from Kilimanjaro's glaciers, and I look forward to visiting them for decades to come. But we cannot alter, within decades, the relationships between the glaciers and the global climate, and we cannot ignore that the area covered by ice is steadily diminishing. In future years, snow will continue to grace the cone of Kibo through much of the year, and the mountain will appear as Hemingway saw it: "…great, high, and unbelievably white in the sun." However, if the ice disappears, so too will the historical archive from this irreplaceable vantage point on our planet, and our chance to document how that history is recorded. We have much work to do.

AN AERIAL VIEW OF KILIMANJARO, LOOKING DIRECTLY INTO THE REUSCH CRATER, SHOWS UHURU, THE HIGHEST POINT, AT THE TOP OF THE PICTURE.

anyone." But just as she lifted the filled cup to her lips, she felt a hand on her arm. She had broken her pledge and taken a drink without asking. To redeem her honor, she surrendered herself to the king. That night, the future Menelik the First, great emperor of Ethiopia, was conceived.

No long-standing, happy union followed, however. The sovereigns exchanged elaborate gifts before the young queen—whose beauty is said in some sources to have been marred by a single blemish: the webbed foot of a goose—returned to her Sheban homeland.

Menelik grew brave and strong and exhibited all the wisdom and wiliness of his distant father. Some legends do tell of a tearaway period in adolescence when he was sent to see his father and stole the Ark of the Covenant, but in his reign as King-of-Kings he was a popular and successful monarch. He extended his kingdom well into eastern Africa, absorbing Shoa, Somaliland, Kenya, and the area around and beyond Kilimanjaro. Ethiopian Christians tell that, as he was returning home after these great conquests, with all his men and the spoils of war, he stopped to camp on the Saddle of Kilimanjaro, between snowy Kibo and jagged Mawenzi.

Menelik was no longer a young man, and that night a great weariness washed over him. Recognizing that death was near, as a great king he wished to die like a king. Outside his tent, the glistening snows beckoned, and at first light he started climbing up the snowy dome of Kibo with some of his war lords. They were accompanied by Menelik's personal slaves, bearing all his jewels and treasure. That evening the war lords retreated down the mountain without their king, telling the waiting company that Menelik, his slaves, and treasure had disappeared inside the crater, there to sleep forever.

Tradition holds that one day an offspring of the royal house will arise and restore the glory of Ethiopia, re-conquering all of the land to the Rufiji River. This sav-ior will climb Kilimanjaro, retrieve Menelik's fabled hoard and the Seal of Solomon, the mystical ring responsible for that celebrated wisdom. With this on his finger, the heroic spirit of Menelik and the sagacity of Solomon would work their wonders once more.

As late as the 1920s, there were Ethiopians who found it hard to believe that men had really climbed to the summit of Kilimanjaro because no one had come back saying they'd found the great king or his jewels. This story is also known in Tanzania, and it is hard to tell whether it was handed down the generations all of a piece, or if it is an amalgam of different tales. It could explain the references 19th-century travelers picked up of precious stones on top of the mountain. What strikes me as fascinating is that to cross the flanks of Kilimanjaro by way of the Saddle does not appear to be taken as anything remarkable. I suppose I should never have supposed it was, for that would be to fall into the trap of considering the early European explorers the first on the scene, which is clearly nonsense.

to the conclusion, therefore, that the former tenants of our cave must have belonged to the Wa-ndorobbo, parties of whom are known to follow the chase into remote districts of the mountain, though we had not before suspected that they penetrated thus far.

The Wa-ndorobbo (now Dorobo), he goes on to tell us, were the "semi-serfs" of wandering Masai, whose livelihood was gained solely by hunting. With no cultivation on the northeastern slopes of the mountain, and a much scantier forested zone, herds of eland would frequently come up from the plains to graze on the Saddle. Meyer had seen them there. The Masai steppe extended north and south from the mountain's foot, but the Masai were not hunters. Although they would hunt lion as ritual proof of manhood and to eliminate the chief predator of their livestock, they abhorred the consumption of

---

THURSDAY Every day on this climb I've thought, "This is fantastic. I've never seen anything like this." I was absolutely transported in the forest, and then we got into the higher heathland, seeing so many flowers and birds and I thought, "Nothing can top this." But we came up into the crater and it, too, was beautiful in a very austere way. I wish I'd climbed to the Ash Pit, like Roger, but we had great fun today, picking up the crystals. It really did feel as if we were on the roof of the world.

Coming in from the southeast, the 19th-century travelers found Chief Mandara's men wary of venturing out of the forest and onto the Saddle, though it was clear they did so on occasions. But their reluctance was for fear of tangling with warriors from other tribes, particularly the Kibosho, who regularly visited the upland territory. Johnston tells us that every day he spent on the Saddle the Wa-kiboso (or Kibosho) came to trade. And Meyer reported reaching a cave at 15,390 feet, close to a feature he named The Triplets and below what is today known as Gillman's Point, to find that he and Purtscheller were by no means its first occupants. From the "fossil remains" lying about, he saw at once that this was not the scene of any former European encampment:

It was equally certain that none of the Wa-jagga tribes would have ventured thus far up the mountain. We came

wild animal. Yet they had need of animal by-products, such as eland skin for sandals, straps, and water carriers, and this is where the Wa-ndorobbo came in.

If the Saddle was regularly visited by different tribesmen, it's hard to believe that there were not venturesome souls in some generations whose curiosity drove them higher. When we sat near the summit, Roger was saying that he couldn't believe the urge to get to the top dated only from the last 130 years. "This volcano must have appeared in fits and starts," he said. "Early man, watching from the plains, would have seen it grow. Perhaps for ten years it would erupt and grow a few thousand feet. Then everything would go quiet again. Surely the people would want to know what had been going on—all that lava and ash and volcanic bombs blowing out of the top, and huge surges of mud flowing down the sides of the mountain—they'd have gone up to look, wouldn't they?"

ABOVE: THE FILM TEAM AND TREKKERS, THEIR SHERPAS, GUIDES, AND PORTERS SMILE ON THE ROOF OF AFRICA.
FOLLOWING PAGES: TWO CLIMB NEAR THE SUMMIT AT DAWN ON TOP OF STELLA POINT.

And then, he went on, there'd have been times when the mountain was covered in ice. "During several glaciations in the past the ice cap would have extended 3,000 feet lower than now, and the glaciers would have come right down below 12,000 feet. It would have looked absolutely magical from the plains. Just think, for almost a million years our ancestors will have looked at it and enjoyed it. Of course they'd have come for a closer look as soon as they could."

THE CHAGGA, who inhabit the slopes of Kilimanjaro now, may not have been around to see the growth of Kilimanjaro. They are believed to have migrated into the area within the last four or five hundred years. Nevertheless, they have great respect for the mountain, especially ice-decked Kibo, and their folklore includes many stories of how the mountain came into being. One tells of an arrogant individual named

Tone, who lived in this land before there were any mountains here at all. He was no respecter of his fellows, any more than they cared much for him. One day he fooled Ruwa, the supreme god of the Chagga, into inflicting a terrible famine on his people. When the others learned of his scheming, Tone's life was not worth living. Everyone was after his blood and he had to flee. At last he found sanctuary with an old herdsman who offered him protection as long as he agreed to guard the man's two prize cows—Tenu and Meru. Tone agreed. At the beginning he never let them out of his sight, knowing his very survival depended on his vigilance. Even so, in time he became careless, until one day, when his mind was off elsewhere, the cattle escaped. Sick with apprehension, Tone scoured the countryside. All the way to the horizon he searched, but he could find no trace of Tenu and Meru. Weeks went by, and still he searched. He'd almost given up hope when one day he spied Tenu in the distance and

charged toward her. In the blazing sun his lungs almost burst with the effort. He did not know the old man's cows had the power of magic. When she saw him coming, Tenu mischievously created an enormous hill between herself and Tone. And she kept casting hills in his path, one after the other, as he ran toward her. The more desperately he searched, the higher were the hills that whirled through the sky to land at the feet of the gasping man, whose cockiness and selfishness were by now completely crushed. Tone struggled on until at last he believed his quarry was cornered, only to hear Tenu laugh triumphantly as she slammed down a mighty volcano. It was the highest mountain in all Africa. The last anyone knows of Tone and his errant charge was the cow running playfully down into the volcanic crater closely followed by the demented man.

that counts, not the ice upon it. I do know that this mountain "shrank" between when we first talked about climbing it, and when we actually arrived here: A reevaluation of the height of Kilimanjaro, employing the latest GPS technology, was undertaken in 1999 by a team from the University of Technology in Karlsruhe, Germany. The results suggested that Uhuru Peak should be downgraded slightly.

It's impossible to say if the mountain has really lost or gained height since it was measured in 1952 using vertical-angle measurements. The closeness of the results of the two surveys merely serves to underscore the accuracy of the earlier triangulation. Observations then were possible only in good weather with bright sunshine for the heliographs to signal to the theodolites, and the surveyor K. T. Pugh found himself having to climb the mountain twice in 18 days to get these results.

THURSDAY I'm sitting here on a wonderful evening with real air to breathe, and I can't believe the day we've had. It's been magic. When I got up this morning I felt sick and wretched and half inclined to give the summit a miss. But it turned out easier than I thought. It was brilliant. It's the first "real" mountain I've climbed, and I'm so delighted to have done it. I was walking on air after, but I'm footsore now.

This story was collected in 1924 by Charles Dundas. The legend of Menelik's death in the crater was picked up at around the same time by missionary Dr. Richard Reusch, often referred to as "the little Cossack," who was then living and working in Moshi. It's impossible to say how old these stories are, or whether there was cross-fertilization between the two. Nor can we know if either story was related before Europeans had confirmed the existence of the crater.

STANDING HERE on the Roof of Africa, living our own stories, we photographed ourselves beside the sign saying that this was the highest point of Kilimanjaro. Yet, strangely, it didn't seem to be quite the top. The dome of ice at the heart of the Southern Icefields, looming beside us, definitely looked higher than we were. Whether that was an optical illusion or not I can't say, but in any case it is the height of the bedrock

OUR EUPHORIA AT reaching the top, with all the whoops and hugs and jigging around, had mellowed to simple enjoyment. Photographs all taken, we wrote our names on the summit record, then sat and absorbed the view. All too soon it was time to think about going down. Though we were reluctant to leave, many hours of descent lay before us, and the weather could yet deteriorate as it so often did in the afternoons. We'd be heading off in the opposite direction, to make our retreat by the more direct Mweka Route, which drops almost due south to Mweka village, and from there to Moshi. Our aim tonight was to reach the Mweka Hut campsite at 10,170 feet.

WE CONTINUED, counterclockwise, around the crater rim. Now we had a fine view over the Southern Icefields, which were even more impressive looking back. We know that Kilimanjaro's snows are melting

THE OLD MAN OF THE MOUNTAIN

AUDREY SALKELD
AUTHOR, MOUNTAINEERING HISTORIAN

WHEN HANS MEYER climbed Kilimanjaro in 1889, one of the guides supplied to him by Chief Mareale was a tall teenaged boy, Kinyala Lauwo, whose family were elephant hunters. The lad knew the forest like the back of his hand. One hundred years later, Tanzanian newspapers carried the story of a centenarian living in Marangu, who had "led Hans Meyer and Ludwig Purtscheller to the highest point of Africa." It seemed unbelievable; how could anybody be alive from so long ago? The old man, Mzee Yohana Kinyala Lauwo, was invited to the centennial celebrations that year when a plaque was put up at the Marangu Park Gate to honor six local men who accompanied Meyer and Purtscheller on the mountain. Lauwo's name was at the top of the list. In recognition that he had been the first mountain guide on Kilimanjaro and that the momentous ascent in 1889 had given local tourism its initial boost, a grateful national park authority presented the old guide with a fine new house on a ridge below the mountain.

In those years, when colonialism was just taking grip, the young men of Chagga were being called up for road construction, but Kinyala Lauwo tried to dodge the draft, preferring to go on hunting for ivory, honey, timber, medicine, and colobus monkey skins. He was caught and brought to Mangi Mareale's palace for trial. By chance he arrived when Meyer was visiting the chief, requesting permission, guides, and porters for his climbing attempt. The Mangi's advisors spotted the

KINYALA LAUWO GUIDED HANS MEYER IN 1889.

boy, knew the reputation of the Lauwo clan as experts of the forest, and recommended him as a guide.

I could find no mention by name of Lauwo or his five companions in the English translation of the expedition book. Meyer reserves his descriptions for his favorite, Mwini Amani from Pangani, and his three Somalis. The Chagga, when they appear in the narrative, are usually recalled as huddling, half frozen, over spluttering campfires; but he talks of sending "the five men who had thus far accompanied us" back from the Saddle. Mwini, we know, camped higher, but didn't go to the summit. However high Kinyala Lauwo climbed, it is right that the Chagga pathfinders should be honored for their contribution to the mountain's exploration. Roger Bilham and I drove around to Marangu to see Lauwo's name on the plaque. There it was, at the top of the list. Yohana was the Christian name he adopted on his baptism after the climb—Johannes, in other words, just like Meyer.

Lauwo's assistant guide on that first Kilimanjaro climb was Jonathan Mtui, and the porters: Elia Minja, Tom Mosha, Makalio Lyimo, and Mamba Kowera.

Lauwo went on to guide many people up Kilimanjaro for more than 70 years. He was awarded an O.B.E. (Order of the British Empire) for bravery after saving a climber's life on the mountain. He died, aged 125, on May 10, 1996.

The first Wachagga known to have reached the summit of Kilimanjaro were two guides Oforo and Jonathan in 1925, credited with the 11th and 12th ascents.

into history, that only a tiny percentage of the original ice cap is left; some scientists believe as much as 80 percent has disappeared since the early years of the 20th century. As on Mount Kenya, whole glaciers have vanished along with the ice climbs they supported. What remains is the deep heart of what once was here. These Southern Glaciers, comprising the heads of the Heim, Kersten, Decken, and Rebmann Glaciers, constitute a third of that remnant. Reduced to statistics like that, they sound merely sad and diminished, but though they be shrunken, these glaciers are exquisitely beautiful still. Tumbling in a sequence of fretted steps, they come alive under the

play of light. This is one reason why climbers of the Marangu Route set off at such an hour on their summit day, to be beckoned upward by the vision of this ethereal stairway, flushed sugar pink and lavender in the dawn's glow. Well, that was one vision we'd have to leave to the imagination, but even in the harsh light of mid-morning this was a crystal cascade. We passed the subsidiary landmarks known as Elveda Point and Hans Meyer Point to reach Stella Point, from where our trail headed downhill. We did not take in Gillman Point, which at 18,650 feet (5,685 meters) is often accepted as the token summit for those trudging up the Marangu Route and who do

had dropped almost 4,000 feet before coming over a buttress of rock; the Barafu Hut came into view just below us at 15,092 feet. This spectacular spot cannot be described as welcoming. The hut and assorted tents are sprawled over an exposed and very rocky ridge. Rocks and tents look as if they've been shaken out of a sack to tumble in a heap. We were told that many fatal accidents have occurred here over the years on the awkward ground. I supposed the many oxygen-deprived, somnambulant trekkers setting out at midnight for the summit, their minds in a fog, were most at risk here. Already tonight's batch of hopeful summiteers was gathering.

Freddie was waiting for us with his reviving thermoses of tea. Other porters had laid out an appetizing spread of picnic goodies for lunch, which we fell upon hungrily. But welcome as it all was, it was a mistake to stop and let muscles tighten up. Afterward, it took sheer willpower to move on, and all those little sore, rubbed places on the feet became full-fledged blisters in moments. We picked our way over delicately poised rocks, which moved and clanged hollowly as we scrambled across them. It looked like a wasteland, with the only consolation being we at last had a good view of Mawenzi, it's many fingers thrusting into the sky.

And then, under one of the seesawing rocks, there was a flower, a scruffy little yellow daisy. A few steps farther and we saw two or three more. Dusty, frowzy little things on bent and blackened stalks, but so welcome. However scrawny, they were leading us back to the world of vegetation. Before long they were joined by wispy grasses, tiny little arabis, and occasional everlastings. Imperceptably, almost, as we marched on, the ground gradually supported more life. Before we knew it, we were walking among low clumps of tree heather and could feel a damp warmth in the air. All afternoon we had been passing trekkers on their way up, toiling, red-faced, puffing... and with so much still ahead. All that scree. We sympathized, but couldn't help feeling rather smug and superior, too. We'd been there. To the top. Only a few hours before, but already so far into the past. Euphorically, we swung on down the trail.

not wish to add an hour or two's extra struggle to gain Uhuru Peak. Recognizing the effort it takes to get even here, the national park authorities issue a Gillman's Point certificate.

Dropping off the ridge we plunged into gravelly scree, deep and yielding. Suddenly we had seven-league boots. Every step taken produced at least twice its length in distance gained as we skied on a rolling carpet of pebbles. It was tough on the knees, but so exhilarating once you'd learned not to resist the slide. In no time we had left the Rebmann Glacier behind. Gradually, the angle eased; we continued to cover ground quickly, but there was so much to cover. We

CHAPTER ELEVEN

KILIMANJARO AT THE CROSSROADS

The reliance of rural African communities on natural products
cannot be denied, or denied to them by conservation-minded European
academics who unaccountably place an intrinsic value on forest weeds,
and collect and cart them away as dried specimens.

JOHN M. GRIMSHAW, 1996

THIS WAS A LOVELY SPOT, our tents set amid tall feathery tree heather. But we were appalled to see how much felling of the heather had been done to clear the campsite, far more than was required to permit a few level tent platforms. For the most part, the stumps were left in the ground and will, if given the chance, sprout once more. A gardener might consider this the best way to maintain vigorous growth, but it would be to encourage one species at the expense of others. This ericaceous vegetation of Kilimanjaro supports a particularly rich assemblage of "lower plants," the bryophytes and lichens. Not just the forest floor, but trunks and branches of tree heather are home to colonies of liverworts and mosses, whose importance is only now becoming fully appreciated. On Kilimanjaro these lower plants play a critical role in water catchment, so any disturbance or degradation is potentially serious ∾ The Hungarian ecologist Tamas Pócs has been investigating the cryptogams, or flowerless plants, of Kilimanjaro for more than two decades. He identifies almost 600 species of bryophyte and about 120 different lichens, some so specialized, so narrowly endemic, that they are restricted to a single spot on the mountain—like *Pocsiella hydrogonoides*,

PRECEDING PAGES: THE FILM TEAM SETS UP EQUIPMENT AMONG THE HEATHER OF THE MWEKA ROUTE TO FILM THE DESCENDING PARTY. LEFT: FATHER HERMAN TAIIMO, PRIEST AT KILEMA MISSION, STANDS IN FRONT OF HIS CHURCH.

which is known to live only on the dripping volcanic rock inside the climbers' first bivouac on the Umbwe Route. They are found in all of the mountain's vegetation belts and, compared to other types of plant, they have a particularly high biomass, giving them far higher "interception capacity." In a single rain storm, Pócs estimates, the moss-lichen cover can sop up more than eight times as much water as canopy foliage; this is what makes this cover so important in terms of regulating the water flow and reducing loss through evaporation, especially from the soil surface. The cloud belt, where some of the highest precipitation occurs, not unexpectedly, is also one of the richest and most complex of the bryophyte zones, which places the highest concentrations of mosses and hepatics between the altitudes 7,200 and 9,200 feet in the upper forest that we were just about to enter.

ALTHOUGH THE flora of Mount Kilimanjaro, including its bryophytes, has attracted more study than that of other East African mountains, it is still imperfectly understood; species and subspecies continue to be

THE TEAM BEGINS THE JOURNEY DOWN. FOLLOWING PAGES: ZEBRA BROWSE AMONG THE ACACIA IN THE NGORONGORO CRATER, RENOWNED FOR ITS TEEMING WILDLIFE. MOST AFRICAN ANIMAL SPECIES APART FROM GIRAFFES LIVE TOGETHER IN THIS CRATER ALONG WITH 400 KINDS OF BIRDS.

very long intervals, but that begs the question of whether anyone came seriously looking in between those flowerings.

Mweka Camp is at 10,170 feet, low enough for us to register tremendous benefit in the amount of oxygen available to us. We drank in the rich, soupy air, and all slept remarkably well, to wake with raging appetites. The views back to Kibo from here, over the Southern Glaciers, are particulary fine and give little clue that the snows of Kilimanjaro are disappearing at such an alarming rate. Our old friend, Meru, is back in sight, too, almost due west of here. Really, this is a most attractive spot—or is the unaccustomed oxygen just switching our vision from monochrome to full technicolor? The sun rose behind Mawenzi this morning, at first merely lightening the sky to throw the famous rooster-comb into misty silhouette. Then, for a moment, the orb lodged in one of the peak's skyline notches and rays of golden light streamed through. It lingered barely long enough to point the camera at it before the whole world was alight and it was radiant day once more.

My goodness, it was heaven to feel fit. You might expect the climax of a climb like this to be the summit—which of course it is, one of the climaxes at least. But the icing on the cake is to have a day like this, with its outcome more or less assured. A day you know will be energetic, but with no uphill and no straining after breath, a day with new things to see in a fresh part of a fairy forest when the euphoria of success still buoys you along. Your enhanced senses are appreciative of every living thing, so that you get almost drunk on the greenness of it all. Perhaps that sounds too idyllic. It wasn't going to be a day without pain. Muscles had certainly tightened after so much descent yesterday; toes that had hammered long and relentlessly into the fronts of boots were sore and, for some of us, blister-raw. Getting started was excruciating, but before too long the surroundings shouted louder for attention than aching flesh.

Heidi's feet were giving her trouble. She thankfully grabbed an extra pole for support and, when it came to

discovered. As recently as the early 1990s, John Grimshaw, in the course of three years' fieldwork on the northern slopes of Kilimanjaro, discovered three new plants—plus one subspecies of giant lobelia that, as he says, was hardly inconspicuous. Even where species are known and named, their exact cycles have not necessarily been studied. Until Grimshaw's sojourns on the mountain, little continuous research had been done. For instance, details of pollination are scarce for any but the most visible plants such as the giant lobelias. Some plants are said to flower only at

the steep, rocky patches with lethally slippery roots creeping across them, she accepted all the help that was generously on offer. At one such patch, as the Sherpas were handing her gently down between them, Wong Chu looked up to see I was following close behind. Though his hands were full, his sense of responsibility was on red alert. Waving a ski pole in my direction, he shouted to the world at large, "Help the mummy! Help the mummy!"

The mummy made this particular descent without mishap, but there would be several times in the oozy forest below when she and the others skidded ignominiously to finish butt-down in the mire.

The Mweka Route drops steeply south to Mweka village, and thence to Moshi. It is the most direct and shortest route on the mountain, but because of its gradient is used mainly for descent. What seemed so amazing to me was how different it is in character to the Machame/Shira Plateau route we had followed coming up. We were only a little way around the mountain in distance (two streams away, that was all) and yet we were seeing a quite different association of plants. In particular, and what gave me special pleasure, the proteas now revealed themselves. In fact they made up one of the basic ingredients in what had become a thick covering of shrubs of a little over a man's height, and extending over a wide, undulating swathe of countryside. *Protea kilimandscharica* is a handsome plant. Its stiff, leathery leaves are oval in shape and gray-green in color with a red central midrib. The stalks, the new shoots, and the fat flower buds are scarlet-tinged, too, as are the undersides of some of the leaves, while the flowers are a plump pincushion of creamy white—except the pins are so close together that the effect is of froth. How strange that there should be such a vigorous society of these here when there appeared to be none coming up from Machame. It emphasizes the influence exerted by aspect and the subtle changes in climate from one place to another, even close at hand. Whether or not the area has undergone burning in the past also plays a part.

Protea bushes can grow to 15 feet tall, and maybe away from the path they do so here. The other predominant shrubs in this community are heathers and brooms. We were following one of the mountain's ridges, overlooking an ocean of green. Down in the valley, a couple of hundred feet below, we could pick out the line of the watercourse from the architectural leaf canopies of giant groundsels, presumably the thin-barked forest variety, *Dendrosenecio johstonii*, which favors growing along stream beds. They were too far away to investigate but served to remind me that there had been a scarcity of other tree senecios on this flank of the mountain. We stopped at a sunny patch on some rocks to make interviews for the film. Someone picked up an animal skull.

"Klipspringer," the porters said with conviction, which if true would mean it had to be quite old. This little antelope, still listed in some Kilimanjaro guidebooks as resident here, was last reported on the mountain back in 1944, and even then may have been misidentified. Zoologists are pessimistic about the long-term future of many of the mammal species in Kilimanjaro's montane forest, partly because of human disturbance or fire damage, but especially because of the mountain's increasing isolation from other wildlife habitats. Looking over these rolling foothills, this shrubby belt appears extensive, and between the ridgetops doubtless is little visited. But the dominance of the young tree heathers, I am told, is indicative of previous burning, which puts many species at a disadvantage when it comes to regeneration, particularly in the shorter term. Every loss to an area's biodiversity, however small, reduces the choice and plenitude of what creatures who live there have evolved to expect. There is a little Kilimanjaro moss that is said to make its home exclusively on leopard droppings. Leopards are endangered here these days, possibly because of heavy poaching in the past; when it comes to farewell *Panthera pardus* in this part of the world, doubtless it will spell doom also for the mossy colonies of *Tetraplodon mnioides*.

The extent of this youthful ericaceous regrowth brings home to you how serious brush fires can be up here. Fires are a natural part of life on volcanic mountains. Thus it's no coincidence, John Grimshaw tells me, that so many of the Afro-montane trees are pioneers on disturbed ground. To an extent, localized fires can boost the ecological cycle, promoting a diversity that may be lacking in a mature community where certain species dominate. But if this burning takes place too often in the same place, then regenerating vegetation is continuously destroyed. This is what's been happening on Kilimanjaro. For the past 20 years

A SIGNPOST TO THE REBMANN MEMORIAL LIBRARY, NEAR MACHAME, COMMEMORATES THE 19TH-CENTURY MISSIONARY
WHO FIRST "DISCOVERED" KILIMANJARO.

sections of forest and the shrubby land above it have been alight at least twice every year. In February and March 1997 fires raged unchecked in several places around the mountain, destroying nearly 10,000 acres of forest and heathland. Despite the best efforts of firefighters, they were only completely extinguished when the Long Rains came that April. This disastrous conflagration followed on the heels of a particularly severe drought; indeed there is evidence that some fires may have been burning since August 1996. It was easily the worst instance in living memory. But two years later, after another dry spell, Kilimanjaro was ablaze once more. Further acres of precious vegetation were devastated. Experts predicted ecological disaster. It galvanized environmentalists and forest managers to reassess ways of monitoring the situation, and reacting more promptly once fires were spotted.

When only the crowns of trees are damaged, plants suffer but there's a degree of regrowth. Where vegetation has been totally destroyed along with leaf litter and the soil beneath, the seedbank probably has been obliterated also. Slow regeneration will occur from incoming sources, but it takes half a century for the first forest trees to appear, and up to 200 years for some cloud forest species to return. The same association of plants will never be replicated, and it may take thousands of years for a forest to be as rich as before. Above Mandara Hut on the Marangu Route there's been extensive grassland at least since the beginning of the last century, yet clumps of giant heather and hagenia trees in a few sheltered spots indicate that the area would support heather forest, were it not burnt so often. One of the principal effects of Kilimanjaro's regular fires has been to pull the upper edge of the forest downhill.

The first plants to recolonize burnt areas are the mosses and algae, then come grasses, followed by bushes (as here), and eventually trees. Ecologists have learned to read the burn history of Kilimanjaro's slopes from the mosaic pattern built up by growth of different ages. Until trees reestablish, the fire risk to new vegetation remains high in dry seasons. Frequent widespread burning clearly puts rare endemic species and biodiversity in jeopardy. But by far the most serious

EARLY MAN

Chris Stringer, Ph.D.
Head of the Human Origins Group, London Natural History Museum

Over the last 15 million years, the face of East Africa has been transformed, and that transformation has been critical, both in catalyzing human evolution and in preserving the record of that evolution. Over the same period of time, the Earth's climate has gradually cooled, and in Africa this has been reflected by a change from a preponderance of forests to grasslands and, at certain times and places, to deserts. East Africa is gradually splitting away from the rest of the continent, and that process has opened up deepening and widening basins of lakes, rivers, and gorges that have acted as sediment traps. Those sediments also accumulated fossils that provide evidence of the changing environments of the region, and of the creatures that lived there, including our ancestors. In turn, the continuing rifting process has helped to expose the accumulated sediments so that they can be studied, and this process has also been accompanied by volcanic activity that allows scientists to accurately date the geological events and associated fossils.

Still the most famous site in the region, Olduvai Gorge, is cut into the Serengeti Plain of northern Tanzania, about 120 miles from Kilimanjaro. The gorge is about 30 miles long and its exposed sequence of lake and river sediments preserves portions of the last two million years of East African prehistory. Olduvai Gorge became world famous in 1959, when Mary and Louis Leakey discovered a skull that was at first called *Zinjanthropus boisei* (Boise's East African Man, after Charles Boise, who was a benefactor of the Leakeys). Its huge back teeth also prompted the nickname of Nutcracker Man. Further study showed that it was in fact similar to creatures fossilized in South African caves, known as robust australopithecines, and like them it is now assigned to the genus *Paranthropus*. While the South African forms are classified as *Paranthropus robustus*, those from East Africa are now called *Paranthropus boisei*. As well as massive jaws and back teeth, these creatures had ape-size brains, but nevertheless walked upright much as we do. The wider group to which they belong, the australopithecines (Southern Apes), were first identified by Raymond Dart in 1924 from the remains of a child found at Taung in South Africa, and assigned by him to a new kind of manlike creature *Australopithecus africanus*. As we will see, East Africa has provided many more fossils of this diverse and long-lived group, which is now also known from countries like Kenya, Ethiopia, and Chad.

Louis Leakey at first assumed that *Zinjanthropus* was the long-sought maker of primitive stone tools found in the oldest deposits at Olduvai, and dated about 1.8 million year old, but over the next few years remains of a more humanlike form began to be found in the same levels. These remains were assigned to a species of human, not australopithecine, called *Homo habilis* (Handy Man, in recognition of its presumed tool-making skills) in 1964. This species had smaller back teeth and a somewhat larger brain size than contemporaneous or older australopithecines.

Just as scientific attention had switched from South Africa to Tanzania with the Leakeys' finds, it switched even farther north to Kenya and Ethiopia during the 1970s. The sedimentary basin around Lake Turkana (formerly Lake Rudolf) in northern Kenya became a focus for research by teams led by Louis and Mary's son Richard. Here, further remains of *Paranthropus boisei* were discovered in layers about the same age as those at Olduvai, and there were also stone tools; as a result, scientists speculated that *Homo habilis* would be found there, too. This seemed to be confirmed by the discovery of skull KNM-ER 1470 (Kenya National Museum—East Rudolf find number 1470), which had a brain larger than any other habilis finds. However, its face was distinctively flat, with deep cheekbones, and many scientists now refer it to a different early human species called *Homo rudolfensis*. And in Ethiopia yet another kind of australopithecine called *A. garhi* was discovered in 1999, perhaps associated with the earliest evidence of tool use and meat-eating in the human lineage at 2.5 million years old.

In Ethiopia, even older deposits in the Rift Valley were being examined by French and American teams, and work at Hadar led to rich discoveries of a more primitive australopithecine called *Australopithecus afarensis* (after the Afar region), about 3.5 million years old. The most famous of these fossils was the skeleton of a young female, who became known as Lucy. She must have been little more than a few feet tall, with the brain size and body shape of an ape, yet her hip bone showed that she walked upright. This species was also recognized from fossils found by Mary Leakey's team at Laetoli, near Olduvai, in Tanzania. Even more remarkable was the preservation of floors of volcanic ash at Laetoli on which were many tracks made by the creatures living there 3.6 million years ago. Included were footprints made by a creature walking on two legs, assumed to be *A. afarensis*. However, in 2001, a distinct kind of apeman was discovered in northern Kenya, in deposits of about the same age as those of *afarensis*. This creature was dubbed *Kenyanthropus platyops* (Flat-faced Man of Kenya), but its relationship to the australopithecines and to us is still unclear.

RICHARD LEAKEY DISPLAYS SKULL FINDS FROM NEAR LAKE TURKANA. THE THREE ON THE RIGHT ARE *HOMO* SKULLS; ON THE FAR LEFT IS A ROBUST AUSTRALOPITHECINE.

Where did *afarensis* and *Kenyanthropus* come from, and when did the human line split from that of our nearest living relatives, the bonobo and common chimpanzee? In the last few years a possibly ancestral species to later forms, called *A. anamensis*, has been identified from northern Kenya. It is dated to about four million years old, but an even earlier creature called *Ardipithecus ramidus* has been discovered in deposits at Aramis in Ethiopia, around five million years old. *Anamensis* was clearly bipedal, while the results of the study of a partial skeleton of *Ardipithecus* are eagerly awaited to confirm that this creature, too, walked on two legs. Even more ancient, and controversial, are the remains of a six-million-year-old creature called *Orrorin tugenensis*, found near Lake Baringo in Kenya. The scientists describing *Orrorin* believe it, rather than *Ardipithecus* or *anamensis*, is the earliest human ancestor yet found. However, most scientists remain cautious about the earliest stages of human evolution while they absorb the details of these new finds.

And what happened in human evolution in East Africa after the time of *Homo habilis*? Well, by 1.8 million years ago a new and much more advanced species called *Homo ergaster* is also known to have existed from deposits in northern Kenya (*ergaster* is sometimes regarded as just an early form of a species called *Homo erectus*, known from sites in Asia). Its brain size and tool-making abilities were initially little different from those of *habilis*, but the skull and body shape were definitely more like our own. This species is also known from deposits of similar age at Dmanisi in Georgia, and thus *ergaster* is the first humanlike form found outside our ancestral homeland of Africa. However, its evolutionary origins, whether from something like *Kenyanthropus*, *garhi*, or *habilis*, are currently unclear. By about 700,000 years ago, *ergaster* had apparently evolved into the species *Homo heidelbergensis*, known from regions as far apart as South Africa and England. By about 300,000 years ago, *heidelbergensis* had given rise to the Neanderthals (*H. neanderthalensis*) in Europe, while in Africa sites such as Guomde in northern Kenya and Omo Kibish in Ethiopia record the early evolution of our own species, *Homo sapiens*. From about 100,000 years ago, *Homo sapiens* began to disperse from northeast Africa, and eventually colonized the world. In doing so, our ancestors replaced the surviving descendants of *Homo heidelbergensis* (such as the Neanderthals) and *Homo erectus*. After four million years of evolutionary complexity, we are now the only human species on Earth.

ABOVE: NO ONE KNOWS WHEN THE CHAGGA STARTED CONSTRUCTING THEIR COMPLEX SYSTEM OF WATER CHANNELS, BUT IT HAS
BEEN AN ONGOING PROCESS. RIGHT: KILIMANJARO RED HOT POKER, *KNIPHOFIA THOMSONIII*, A SHOWY PLANT FOUND IN
WOODLAND CLEARINGS AND AMONG SHRUBBY ERICACEOUS GROWTH, WILL REESTABLISH ON BURNT GROUND. FOLLOWING PAGES:
MERU, SEEN AT DAWN ON A PINK BED OF CLOUDS, SEEMS TO FLOAT AS VIEWED FROM NEAR MACHAME CAMP.

long-term threat is that, with the reduction of forest and heathland cover, delicate bioclimatic balances will be affected. Reduced precipitation could be one result; its interception another. Experts believe it is highly likely that the 1996–1999 fires will have changed the mountain's water holding capacity.

These fires are almost without exception induced by man. Theoretically, lightning strikes could account for a few, even the burning-glass effect of water droplets, or the friction action of trees against each, but no evidence exists for natural forces being involved, beyond offering tinder-dry conditions. Some blazes are started by carelessness, but most are attributed to the activities of honey hunters in smoking out bees, or poachers and hunters setting fire to bush to flush out

animals. Charcoal burning and the deliberate clearance of lower forest for settlement are also culprits. They are so hard to extinguish because the organic topsoil and buried tree stumps and roots can smoulder away unnoticed, the fire even traveling underground before bursting into flame anew.

Policing illegal activities on the mountain, and fighting fires, are not helped by the fact that different government departments are involved within the fire-risk area, which falls also under the control of four regional administrations. Traditionally this has made concerted action difficult. Fires on the mountain are usually tackled on a cooperative basis by park and forest reserve personnel, with extra assistance from the army and others, including volunteers from the general public. Help has tended to be given willingly enough, though calling it out is often too slow. The authorities recognize that individuals brought in to fight fires need to be compensated for their time, but this can be counterproductive. When they're out of work, local people may start fires just to get a square meal.

As WE LOST HEIGHT, the nature of the woodland changed. Trees pressed in more closely now. At first they were quite low and spindly, their twigs snapping easily as you brushed against them. Once more we were seeing trailing lichens and tree mosses and the ground grew thick with club mosses, all holding aloft their cudgel-shaped fruiting bodies. I don't think I had stopped to think before how they came by their common name, but it was obvious now, seeing them there like armed regiments. In clearings, the gladioli and red hot pokers reappeared. I was stopped in my tracks by a different, more slender giant lobelia, *L. gibberoa*. In the shelter of the forest it had no need for such tight and mechanical rosettes as its higher cousins. Its leaves were altogether more floppy, though it still bore the curious conical flower spikes with their bird-perch bracts.

Something had been making a good meal of it, despite the lobeline (poisonous ingredient). I knew that lobelias regularly featured in the diet of hyraxes. Mount Kenya hyraxes have developed a taste for tourist scraps, and their numbers have gone up dramatically, but whenever there's a hiccup in tourist numbers, the associated hyrax-damage to giant lobelias is marked. Here, on Kilimanjaro, the hyraxes have to watch out for themselves. They, too, are tasty, and in great demand among the locals, who set snares to catch them; hyrax fur has always been prized here for capes and blankets.

Before long, the characteristic busy-lizzies were

back, *Impatiens kilimanjari* and *pseudoviola*. But what really took your breath away, as trees grew taller yet still allowed shafts of light to filter through to the undergrowth, was a haze of heavenly blue. This came from the flower heads of a tall forest sage-like plant, *Plectranthus sylvestris*. Individual flowers were widely spaced on their spikes, but collectively they built into a delicate blue mist.

Soon we found ourselves on steeper ground and began slithering into deeper, darker forest. There was more than ever to see, but you had to keep your eyes on your feet as well. My bet is that none but the surest-footed porters got all the way down Kilimanjaro without plastering themselves in mud from one or more slips. We were soon even dirtier than we had been coming up. This is a precarious descent, hell for heavily laden porters, and made all the worse by the deeply incised channels that run just where you expect the path to go. At first we tried detouring around them, thrashing our way through tangled undergrowth to avoid the watercourses, but that offered little advantage. Soon we plunged into the ditches, paying little heed to ankle-deep water and thick yellow mud.

These channels were collecting the percolating water from the mossy forest above. At last we began to appreciate what is meant when people say that Chagga irrigation is a wonder of the world. All the early explorers remarked how like a garden Kilimanjaro was, and lauded the Chagga for their ingenuity in collecting, sharing, and putting to good use the water coming off their great mountain. New said, "The watercourses traverse the sides of the hills everywhere; and I now understood what I had been told upon the coast, viz., that the Wachagga make the water in their country to run up hill!"

In each chiefdom water was diverted into a series of

channels and conduits and conveyed to reservoirs, from where it was fed to the different fields and homesteads. Wooden frames and stones were used for support pipes, where necessary, and tree trunks fashioned into aqueducts to carry water over the rockier slopes. The mangi decided how the water should be allocated, and he had the power to sever the supply, too. It is still told in Moshi how Mandara used to cut off the missionaries' water whenever he was displeased with them. Not far from the Marangu Gate is a waterway known locally as the Canal of Blood. It dates back to when the Rombo people, desperate for water, began diverting some from headwaters that served neighboring Marangu. They did their best to keep their canal-digging secret, but the Marangu got wind of it and crept in to butcher all the Rombo workers.

Late in the afternoon, we had descended to within a couple of miles of the trail's end. Needless to say I'd fallen to the rear of the group, tramping along with my porter, Adamson. We were surprised to see a vehicle waiting up ahead, having driven some way into the forest. Then we saw Freddie inside and learned that he and the driver had been sent to pick me up. The gesture was meant kindly.

"Do you *want* to ride down?" Adamson asked.

"Well, I'd have preferred to finish on my own two feet," I whispered.

He went up to the two men, telling them firmly, "My gran doesn't need a ride. She'll be walking down. With me." All the same, he took the opportunity to throw in the heavy pack so that he could relieve me of my day bag. No point in us carrying principles too far. Thus light-

LT. ALEXANDER NYIRENDA OF THE TANGANYIKA AFRICAN RIFLES (TAR) RAISES THE TANGANYIKA NATIONAL FLAG ON TOP OF MOUNT KILIMANJARO ON DECEMBER 9, 1961.

ened, we swung down the last bit, past lush *shambas* to rejoin the others at the grassy reception area at the end of the track.

We were filthy, tired, and hungry, but above all we were jubilant. As we drove back to Arusha, the mist cleared and Kilimanjaro loomed beside us in evening light. There was a glow on its distant snows. Eagerly, we picked out the familiar landmarks—the Western Breach, the summit, the line of the Mweka Route. I turned to Hansi, who was sitting next to me. "Can you believe we've just been up there? That we were on top yesterday?" I could hardly believe it myself. Hansi's smile was wide and luminous.

THERE IS A ROAD junction just outside Arusha, with a crude four-way signpost. Nowhere on Earth could offer more promise. Fingers point to Kilimanjaro, Olduvai Gorge, the Serengeti, and Ngorongoro Crater. All your dreams of Africa can be realized, it seems, from this unprepossessing spot. If only there were time to explore them all. Most of us had allowed ourselves some days before flying home, and we took off in all directions, several to go on safari, Hansi to catch up with his school friends—and his soccer and bike riding and hamburgers. Roger would shortly be away to conduct his routine monitoring of the African Rift, but meanwhile there were errands here he and I had set ourselves. We booked a vehicle and followed the now familiar road past the airport, to Moshi.

For some time Roger had been speculating that Kilimanjaro must be considerably larger than the mountain we see. Its tremendous weight, he says, has dimpled the Earth's Archean surface, so that a considerable portion of it now lies below ground level, rather like the submerged base of an iceberg. How could he test this? Who would know the depth of the lavas beneath Kilimanjaro's slopes? Mining companies might keep records. After the discovery of the gemstone tanzanite in the late 1960s, a flush of small mining claims had sprung up between Arusha and Moshi, as Kilimanjaro has the only known economic deposits of this rare form of zoisite. But the scattered nature of the individual mines, and the expectation of a certain degree of professional secrecy, was going to make this too difficult a line to pursue in the time available to us. What about the Water Authority? That surely had boreholes all over the area. Perhaps they'd tell us how many hit the Archean Layer.

was filled with an impressive map of Kilimanjaro and its many springs, streams, and channels; I eyed it enviously before we were passed on to the Regional Hydrogeologist. From him, Roger obtained useful information to support his ideas. I, with a vaguer agenda, did less well.

Next, we wanted to check out the Rebmann Memorial Library, which I'd seen signposted near Machame. It was open only on Monday afternoons, we'd discovered, and, as this was Monday, we headed there and took the overgrown turning into the banana groves. The sign said 1.2 kms, but it seemed a great deal farther before we came to a cluster of buildings among the trees. In the center of this settlement was a grave-like memorial inscribed in German: "In Remembrance of the Discov-

MONDAY I fretted that we had seen only a small slice of this great mountain. There isn't time to go right around it, but I'm seeing how far I can get with a day and a half, a landcruiser, and an urban Masai guide. Once past Meru, we leave the metaled road and head into the *serenget*, the Masai steppe, which seems barren at first. But soon we're seeing Thomson's gazelle, ostriches, and jackals, perfectly camouflaged in the honey-colored landscape. Zebra and giraffe hang around the occasional thickets of scrub and candelabra euphorbia, but I don't think I'll ever spot anything ahead of Kirimbi, my driver and guide. He's so sharp-sighted. We are close to the Kenyan border here.

I wanted to learn more about Kilimanjaro's water supply in general. Global warming and increased demand have resulted in a decrease in dry season run-off from the mountain—so I'd read. Streams that used to be perennial now flowed only intermittently. And was pollution a problem? How long could Chagga remain a garden, and what could be done to conserve as much water as possible? Kilimanjaro's water, after all, not only supplies inhabitants of the immediate area, but also is a critical factor in the hydrology of all of northern Tanzania because it feeds the Pangani River Basin.

With Freddie as our interpreter, bold as brass, we dropped in on the Senior Hydrologist. If a little surprised, he received us graciously. One wall of his office

erer of Kilimanjaro, Missionary Rebmann." That seemed a bit rich here, where Kilimanjaro has never been lost or unknown. I wondered what the locals made of it, but perhaps they didn't read German, or had lived with it long enough for it to be just part of the fabric. The library was closed. Not many tourists find their way to this off-the-road village and in no time at all curious villagers clustered around us, followed by a lady with a key to show us inside.

We hadn't known what to expect, but fantasized that some African missionary papers might be stored here—or a copy of Rebmann's journal. Maybe a photograph of the good reverend hung up in there—at the time I'd been unsuccessful in tracking down any likenesses of him. Well, it wasn't like that. A table and some chairs

KILIMANJARO: STILL A MOUNTAIN OF CONTRADICTIONS

W. A. RODGERS

CROSS BORDERS BIODIVERSITY PROJECT, UNITED NATIONS DEVELOPMENT PROGRAMME

KILIMANJARO HAS long been a symbol of Tanzanian identity—of freedom, of dignity, and of development. And this of course despite attempts by Kenya to either annex it (as in 1924 by white settlers who petitioned the colonial office) or more recently by tour operators who pretend the mountain is actually in Kenya. But Kilimanjaro is more than a symbol. It is also a microcosm embodying all of the contradictions and tensions so typical of Tanzania's development process today. The tensions and institutional rivalries behind the tension serve to prevent real development with sustainable resource utilization. Many people believe that conservation contradicts development.

At its most simple the mountain is sometimes synonymous with Chagga-land, that is to say with the Chagga farming culture and its three-tier home garden system of shade timber trees and bananas over coffee over beans and sweet potatoes. But the drier foothills are peopled by pastoralist Masai herdsmen and hunters whose movements around the mountain are determined by the grazing patterns of their cattle. Decades of tribal rivalry culminated in the marginalization of pastoralism by colonialism, as dry season grazing gave way to settler estates and forest reserves. Ethnic and class tensions continue today, partly as population pressures force cultivators downhill and pastoralists uphill. This is accentuated by ill-defined water rights, with the upstream users reducing water availability to those lower down. This exacerbates the cultivator-pastoralist divide.

Water is the keystone resource of the mountain, and Kilimanjaro falls squarely in an arid part of East Africa. Mountain catchments on volcanic ash soils do not produce major rivers but give rise to a system of seepages and springs around the mountain (best exemplified by the Amboseli and Kitwana Swamps in Kenya). Aquifers are depleting, water is more scarce especially in the dry season, and water quality decreases with industrial and agricultural pollution. This is the biggest problem on the mountain and in the dry surrounding areas that are dependent on mountain water.

The breakdown of traditional systems, and a breakdown in civil service regulatory capacity means water rights are abused. The rich and powerful dominate over poorer interests. This rich-poor divide over water is mirrored by the schism between subsistence villages and commercial estate agriculture.

Much of the lower forest adjacent to pastoralist lands was developed by colonial estate agriculture, initially for coffee, and later for arable crops on West Kilimanjaro. The size of the coffee estates led to much investment into coffee research with eventual spinoff to smaller farmers through extension services. But the estates, with foreign ownership, become an anachronism for Nyerere's socialism, and many were nationalized after 1967—most with no compensation to the former owners. The new national owners, mainly government parastatals or village cooperatives, prospered at first, but proceeds rarely went back to the land and production decreased year after year. In recent years government has, perhaps rather reluctantly and slowly, welcomed private owners back into the area to rehabilitate moribund estates. This understandably has angered those who benefited from poor management, but many workers have welcomed the chance to be paid again. But coffee's present prices are the lowest in over 30 years, and scarcely cover picking and drying costs.

This coffee dilemma affects the small-scale farmer and the traditional Chagga. Coffee does not pay so many people are uprooting coffee and growing more food crops or fodder for stall-fed cattle. "No," says the government, which needs the foreign exchange, "grow more coffee." "Pay us properly," say the farmers. Slowly government reforms and private enterprise improve—but it is probably too late. Acreage and so production continue to decline. An alternative cash income is in fact coming from plantains, which are exported to Kenya. This informal agricultural export sector is growing. Chagga entrepeneurship is behind that, but the government loses its multitude of export levies and taxes.

Another cash crop is marijuana (hash or bhangi), grown on small farms or in clearings in the forest. Prevention—growing marijuana is illegal—is not easy, and there is cynicism against the government's inability to control, promote, or regulate.

Tensions exist across all institutional boundaries, whether they be pastoralists to cultivator (accentuated by century old tribal divide), or estate to peasant cultivators, or government agencies to the farmers themselves. But all these tensions are within the agricultural sector.

THE DIVIDE BETWEEN cultivator and forest reserve is a source of conflict all over the tropics, and Kilimanjaro is no exception. People want land, want timber, want fuel, but do not want the crop losses associated with monkeys, buffalo, and even elephants coming out of the depleted forest. Numerous solutions were tried; most have failed. One infamous failure was the Taungya or Shamba System of forestry. This arose from the government's clearance of large areas of logged natural forest and replacement with exotic pine plantations. One easy way to grow such trees is for people to tend the young tree crop in their maize fields.

Once the trees grow and shade out possible crops people should move, according to the system—but in practice people did not move. People stayed, maize flourished, and trees dwindled. People obtained political support to stay on "their" land (trees cannot vote – unfortunately). More tension developed.

Higher up still is the divide between the forest sector and the national parks sector of the mountain. Both organizations are there to conserve natural resources, both are in the same Ministry—but there has been 20 years of antagonism. Park staff see poachers, encroachers, and fires coming out of the poorly conserved forest estate. "Give us the forest to manage and we will improve it," say the parks people. "Give us your level of funding and staffing and we will do even better," say a very under-funded and jealous forest service.

And finally at the top, the National Park protects the moorland, Afro-alpine scrub, and the ice cap itself. Surely here within a single organization there should be agreement and common purpose. But what is this common purpose of Kilimanjaro National Park? Is it to conserve or to develop tourism? How much tourism can you have before conservation suffers? How many routes, how many huts, and how many visitors per day? But visitor revenue does not stay on Kilimanjaro, it goes all over the country in supporting other less visited parks and only a quarter or so feeds back into community conservation and development initiatives around the park.

Is there a way forward out of this complex set of tensions? Many of us believe that answers will only come when all stakeholders agree that there is a problem and face up to the need to seek a solution. We who write about Kilimanjaro must broaden the debate from just parks and forests to this living ecosystem with a million plus people.

Global conservation thinking is changing (albeit slowly), and now talks of the ecosystem approach to integrate resource management. This attempts a cross-sectoral planning and implementation process across all sectors, with a strong emphasis on participatory planning from the bottom up, with targeted research, adaptive feedback, and more objective monitoring. In theory this sounds good, but is this sufficient to bring Kilimanjaro back to its past unity and development?

There are now five times as many people as there were at the start of the last century, wanting more out of a less resilient ecosystem. There are more stakeholders each with different demands and wants. We lack a unifying vision, an all-embracing goal for stakeholders to rally around. Until that happens, I cannot see a bright future for Kilimanjaro, its resources, or its people.

There are now five times as many people as there were at the start of the last century, wanting more out of a less resilient ecosystem.

TINGATINGA ART BEGAN IN DAR ES SALAAM IN THE 1960S WHEN EDWARD SAIDI TINGATINGA FOUND A READY MARKET FOR HIS EXHUBERANT CANVASSES OF VILLAGE LIFE AND LOCAL ANIMALS. ONE CAN NOW BUY TINGATINGA PAINTINGS ALL OVER EAST AFRICA, AND STYLIZED IMAGES OF KILIMANJARO'S TWIN SUMMITS OFTEN FEATURE. THE FACT THAT MOST OF THE ARTISTS LIVE ON THE COAST AND MAY NEVER HAVE SEEN THE GREAT MOUNTAIN EMPHASIZES ITS IMPORTANCE AS A SYMBOL OF TANZANIAN IDENTITY.

stood neatly in a simple room, and around the walls leaned a few flimsy bookshelves. They bore the oddest, most random assortment of dog-eared books imaginable—books that even the poorest thrift shop at home would throw out without a qualm. It was so sad. Here was a fine watertight building barely used, and a few yards outside children were doing their lessons in classrooms with no windows and rain puddles on the beaten-earth floor. No doubt a library seemed the perfect way to commemorate a bookish scholar, but what a

pity that the well-intentioned folk who raised money for it didn't see the real needs in a village like this, and give the building wider scope and better books. Poor Rebmann! He never saw much reward for his labors during his lifetime, and even in death somehow he misconnects. And yet, how surprised he would be if he could see Chagga now, and know the real and lasting influence missionaries made there.

Missionary schools were subsumed into the state system after Independence. Roger and I went next to take a brief look at Kilema, Rebmann's first port of call on the southeastern slopes of the mountain. This region had come under the influence of Roman Catholic missionaries—the Spiritans or Holy Ghost Fathers from Alsace-Lorraine, who had put up a fine large church. Some of the mission buildings, amid their avenues of jacarandas, now housed a Teacher's Training College, which we were shown around by a member of the staff. Later, I was to meet a Tanzanian academic who'd been born in Kilema and now had returned there to work as an educator and project leader. He'd been recommended to me as the greatest living spokesman on the Chagga—a university big shot who'd grown dispirited with the professional rat race, armed himself with a laptop and mobile phone, and gone back to his roots. He describes himself as Tanzania's first *in*patriate development officer—soon to be one of many it is to be hoped. The Catholic missionaries were more tolerant of Chagga traditions than were the Lutherans, he told me. The Lutherans had this obsession that all native customs were pagan and needed eradicating. Traditional dancing, music, and rituals were obliterated. My new friend, Canute Temu, went on, "You know, the first converts were not from the nobility, but people from the margins of society who had nothing to lose. The very last conversions were among the kings and the nobility." He smiled. "You can see why? They didn't want to let go their power, nor their wives, to join a church which advocates humility and says you must live with just one woman all your life!"

The eventual acceptance of Christianity in Chagga and elsewhere, he had no doubt, was the result of collusion between the colonial government and the missionaries. "It's only now," Canute says, "when fortunately most of the missionaries are black, that we are rediscovering our cultural roots. At baptisms or burials these days, the priest conducts the European liturgy, then we add our own rituals. Either the priest goes away and we enact them, or, where I come from with a Chagga priest, we continue in front of him and he understands."

The Chagga are traditionally monotheistic; their God is Ruwa. And their Trinity, if you like to call it that, Canute explained, comprises Ruwa, the departed spirits, and man on Earth. Spirits who have died most recently are the closest to the living and are believed to have power to influence human life.

Because good people become good spirits, people pray to them to intercede with Ruwa—appeal to their ancestors to help them."

There was a duality now, he said. "Suppose you fall ill: You say mass, you go to hospital. But if those fail, what do you do? You go back to the spirits; perform whatever ritual the elders recommended. Then, if all fails, you await your fate. You see this nowadays with the AIDS epidemic. People come to the villages from Dar es Salaam at Christmas and Easter to do the rituals—there's no other help available, no way of explaining this terrible thing."

What was important, in his view, is that the days are gone when people had it dinned into them at school how uncivilized they were. "We are no longer ashamed of our culture. Even some of our dances are coming back." Two dances, the *iringi* and the *rosi*, are now performed on Kilimanjaro—with modifications and in modern dress.

"There's another traditional sexual dance, the *masanza*, which was never danced in my youth," he told me with obvious delight. "Now it's danced openly—just by women, when there's a wedding." It's danced in two circles, apparently, one inside the other, by women representing the bride and the groom. Then the circles penetrate, and the climax has one woman from each circle dancing together inside, to celebrate the sexual union. "Unthinkable a few years ago, now it's danced at weddings and the guests video it! People feel liberated now to express themselves."

WHAT WAS GOING to happen to Kilimanjaro? I kept coming back to that question in the months after returning home. Here was this unique, important, beautiful, fascinating, and eminently fragile place being assaulted, it seemed to me, by just one damned thing after another. Global warming; population pressure with its concomitant problems of hunger, poverty, unemployment, poor health, housing, and education; aquifers drying up and at risk of pollution; inconstant rains. Its forest and national park suffered encroachment and plunder, some of it by organized syndicates poaching for the bushmeat business, perhaps even with the connivance of local officials. There was hunting, illegal settlement, grazing, deforestation, wild fires, erosion.... Meanwhile, increasing numbers of species of flora and fauna become extinct or are lost to this area. The list seemed endless. Time was running out. Wildlife was running out of room.

There is no shortage of concern. Government departments, aid workers, ecologists, sociologists, animal welfare, and conservation organizations abound. Regular symposia and workshops are held, involving as many stakeholders and experts as possible, endlessly commissioning studies and turning over the problems in the search for answers to the near insoluble. Identifying problems is one thing. What has come out of it all beyond brave new theories and buzzwords?

It's all too easy to become cynical and gloomy. And, yes, those who live locally have developed a sense of alienation from the authorities, with too many decisions and prohibitions made over their heads. Faced with fences and fines, it's easy to see how resentments can build up among those for whom Kilimanjaro is home and provider. They come to believe they are no longer considered a valuable part of the ecosystem. They see tourists coming in, clearly with money to

SOMEWHERE THE SKY TOUCHES THE EARTH, AND THE NAME OF THAT PLACE IS THE END. (WAKAMBA SAYING)

quirky sense. One hope is that if more park income could be plowed back into villages in the form of water and health facilities, they may in turn be prompted to expose illegal activities. That's not a universally popular idea: It smacks of bribery. Not so much Neighborhood Watch as Neighborhood Snitch.

Any new initiative will take time to prove its worth; if it's shown not to work, it's valuable time wasted with the clock ticking away. Besides, isn't it dangerous to pin hopes on harvesting schemes and tourist revenue when both are such variable commodities, unable to guarantee reliable returns? Conservation and development—they're prickly bedfellows. Yet they have to be united if Kilimanjaro is to be enjoyed by future generations.

MONDAY In the clear of the evening, the dome of Kili reveals itself and the sunset colors are fantastic. Kirimbi selects a grove with a view, and puts up the tents. Only the inner mosquito net of mine is erected so that later I can lie in bed and look up through the acacia lattice at the stars. Little animals trot by all night, and a lion gives a throaty rumble not far away.

spend, but where is this vaunted trickle-down effect? "The rest of the world thinks more about animals than it does of us," they say.

Yet, there is a mood for change, a call for integrated conservation *and* development projects, plans for greater involvement, considerable goodwill. Increasingly, projects are implemented in tandem with local communities, and with a view to these communities seeing a slice of the profits or benefit. Tourists pay Masai to camp on their land; schoolchildren nurture and sell tree seedlings. Other forest products are harvested, but there are mixed feelings about how far you can make natural resources cost effective. Do you allow limited hunting to those with fat wallets in order to pay for environmental work and encourage local people to actively preserve it? The idea is sickening to some, but there are places in Africa where such schemes make

However bleakly I'm painting it, the outlook is not all doom, and not foregone. In many ways it looks better than 20 or 30 years ago. There is greater awareness on all sides, and some genuine goodwill out there. We have to plug away at education, and the steady buildup of trust: That is the greatest tool available for the struggle ahead. I was encouraged in my short visits to see how many trekking companies insisted their employees had a sound knowledge of the mountain's wildlife and environmental problems; that many projects involved local schools and colleges; that some of those starting work as porters and cooks were at the same time paying their way through educational courses to widen their prospects for work in the parks and the tourism industry. And Tanzania's is a young population, eager for a better life. Energy is there. Will it be enough? With enough help, let us hope so.

EPILOGUE

I'D BEEN HOME a few months when, unexpectedly, I was invited to go back to Kilimanjaro. David needed more shots for the film, and several of the team were required to climb the mountain again. What a lark! Once more into the Breach with friends. It proved every bit as enjoyable the second time around and a lot more relaxed. We climbed during the Short Rains, which certainly made things exciting with spectacular storms in the Great Barranco. Up in crater camp, we woke to find everything blanketed in new snow. This was more like it—but a disaster for David, who wanted any footage he took here to match what we had from the previous trip. Hansi was so excited; snow was such a novelty for him. He'd touched the glaciers last time but never made footprints in fresh snow, never seen it fall from the sky. We should have built him a snowman, and I wondered afterward why it didn't occur to us, for we were pinned in that crater for three days and nights. We never did get scenery to match our last visit and only moved on when time ran out, and the porters were getting mutinous at spending so much time up there in the cold. My great personal triumph was that I got to see into the Reusch Crater, which I'd been so disappointed to miss before. Now I stood euphorically on its rim, experiencing its warmth and smell, watching the mountain breathe, watching the wreathing dragon-exhalations issuing from the crater-sides. Oh, Kilimanjaro! There's life in you yet.

5TH CENTURY B.C. The belief that the Nile sprang from snow-clad mountains in equatorial Africa can be traced back to the writings of Aeschylus, who believed that Egypt was "nourished by melting snow." Herodotus depicts the sources of the Nile as three great fountains astride the Equator in what he called the "Mountains of the Moon."

4TH CENTURY B.C. Aristotle alludes to "the so-called silver mountain" to the southwest of the Nile. The legend of a summit strewn with silver persists until the mid-19th century among the coastal Swahilis.

There is a legend in Ethiopia and Tanzania that King Menelik I of Abyssinia, the illegitimate son of Solomon and Sheba, is buried in an ice-cleft on the top of Kibo and King Solomon's mystic ring with him.

1ST CENTURY A.D. Mediterranean merchantmen are trading along the East African Coast, and one Greek, Diogenes, is reported to have traveled inland from "Rhapta" for 25 days, reaching two great lakes and a snowy range of mountains "whence the Nile draws its twin sources." It is unknown exactly where Rhapta was, but it has been suggested it may be identified with modern Pangani or, more likely, Dar es Salaam. In view of the distance described it is possible Kilimanjaro was one of the mountains Diogenes saw.

CA. A.D. 150 The Greco-Egyptian geographer Ptolemy incorporates the "Montes Lunae" into his great Geography. From these Mountains of the Moon, waters are said to flow into great lakes that fed the Nile. Some scholars consider this a reference to Kilimanjaro; to others, the cartographer was clearly indicating the Ruwenzori; whereas Meyer, who leads the first successful climbing expedition to Kilimanjaro, declares categorically that Ptolemy's lunar mountains cannot be identified with any existing equatorial snow-mountain.

Chinese chronicling the 12th and 13th century trade along the East African coast mention "a great mountain west of Zanzibar," which we can take to be Kilimanjaro. In the 13th century, too, an Arab geographer, Abu'l Fida, is said to have told of a mountain that was white in color.

1507 Fernandez de Encisco, a Spanish writer who had visited Mombasa and gained the information from caravan traders, writes that west of Mombasa lies "the Ethiopian Olympus, which is very high, and further off are the mountains of the moon, in which are the sources of the Nile." Again, this has been taken as an early mention of Kilimanjaro (and perhaps the Ruwenzori). Encisco goes on to say that "in all this country are much gold and wild animals, and here devour the people locusts."

Though, according to Meyer, the "Ethiopian Olympus" came and went on subsequent maps, by the 19th century Arab slave traders are regularly telling of a high snow mountain in Chagga country with heavily populated fertile slopes. This would have been known to Rebmann and may well have inspired his explorations (following).

1848 Missionary Johannes Rebmann becomes the first European in modern times to report a snow-capped mountain close to the Equator in Africa. His first sighting of Kilimanjaro takes place on May 11, and he sees it again two days later. Making a second expedition in November of the same year, he reaches the village of Machame and obtains another fine view, enabling him to describe the two main peaks and the saddle-shaped depression between them. Rebmann's findings are reported in the Church Missionary Intelligencer—to be scornfully dismissed by geographers—in particular by the pedant Mr Desborough Cooley, who is devising a map of Africa from his study in England.

1849 April sees the indefatigable Rebmann once more on the road to Chagga. Approaching Machame he considers himself "so close to the snow line that, supposing no impassable abyss to intervene, I could have reached it in three or four hours." He is mistaken of course; it would have taken him as many days.

Rebmann's missionary co-worker Ludwig Krapf gets his first distant look at Kilimanjaro on November 10 and another inspirational sighting on the 16th. In December, he also sees a further high, snow-capped peak which he is told is called "Kenia." (Cooley considers he too is hallucinating.)

1861-63 Baron Carl Claus von der Decken makes the first serious attempt to ascend the peak in August 1861, when he claims to have reached 13,900 feet. His companion, the surveyor R. Thornton, reckons Kilimanjaro's height to be 22,814 feet. Both are over-estimations. The Baron returns to Chagga the following year with Dr. Otto Kersten and reaches an altitude of around 14,000 feet during December.

1871 With his Swahili companion, Tofiki, missionary Charles New climbs to the snow line (probably then approaching 15,000 feet) and ascertains that the white stuff is indeed snow and not silver, as had been rumored. His book is full of interesting details and anecdotes—particularly with regard to the Chagga and Mandara, their chief in Moshi.

1873 New returns to Moshi, hoping to continue his investigations, but Mandara robs him of most of his possessions, including the gold watch given to him by the RGS for his discoveries, and turns him away. Broken in health and spirits, New dies on the way back to the coast.

1883 Joseph Thomson becomes the first European to travel through Masai Land (the title of his book). On the way he crosses the lower slopes of Kilimanjaro (also to be robbed by Mandara); he climbs to 9,000 feet and makes a collection of plants before traveling on. He is the first to see the mountain's northern slopes at close quarters—in fact, during his journeys he practically completes a circuit of the mountain.

Dr. G. A. Fischer passes south of Kilimanjaro and remarks that it seems "well adapted to European settlement."

1884 Harry (later Sir Harry) Johnston leads an expedition funded by eminent British scientific societies. He is away for 5 months, operating from various camps, the first of which, above Moshi, is practically a self-supporting village. From another base at Taveta on the southeast side, he reaches over 16,000 feet on Kibo. He returns with substantial plant and animal collections.

(From lists supplied in his book, we learn that Johnston first collected and named Impatiens kilimanjari; he mentions giant heaths, strange Senecios' and 'the extraordinary' Lobelia deckenii. Subsequently one of these strange Senecios is named for him, as is an Alchemilla (Lady's mantle) and a Begonia.

1885 Bishop Hannington is sent out by the Church Missionary Society to found a mission station at Moshi. He finds time there to make an important botanical collection of Kilimanjaro mosses. Dr. Karl Peters, meanwhile, having founded the GDK (Gessellschaft für Deutsche Kolonisation) travels to mainland East Africa and secures treaties with 12 local chiefs, granting Germany exclusive rights (on paper) to extensive tracts of country, including the fertile area around Kilimanjaro.

1886-87 Following the Berlin Treaty, by which Britain and Germany delineated their spheres of influence around Kilimanjaro, English and American "tourists" begin frequenting the area for sport, at the same time adding their two-pennorth to the scientific knowledge of the region.

1887 An expedition under the Hungarian Count Teleki and Lt. Höhnel explores the Meru area before making a serious attempt on Kilimanjaro and then proceeding to Masai Land. Teleki, following Johnston's route to the summit plateau, climbs to 15,800 feet while his companion takes a series of observations from which a new map is drawn up to include the northern side of the mountain.

Hans Meyer makes the first of his three visits to Kilimanjaro and writes up this year's climb initially as a "first ascent." His high point is probably still 800 feet below the true summit, though close to the crater rim. On Teleki's advice, Meyer approaches from Marangu.

1887-88 Dr. Abbott, an American naturalist, spends a year and a half in the region, exploring the flanks of the mountain to the saddle plateau and making natural history observations. In the autumn of 1888, with Otto Ehlers, Abbott attempts the summit, but abandons the struggle at 17,000 feet (through sickness). Ehlers keeps going and afterwards claims to have reached "the north-western side of the summit" at a height which "could not have been less than 19,680 feet." (Ehler also says he climbed to 16,400 feet on Mawenzi.) Though others seriously doubt him, he does furnish what proves an accurate description of Kibo's crater rim.

An American hunter, W. A. Chanler, walks completely around Kilimanjaro, from Taveta.

Meyer comes again in 1888 with Dr. Oscar Bauman, only to be caught up in an orchestrated insurrection against the new German rule. He fails to reach Kilimanjaro.

1889 First ascent by Meyer with the celebrated Austrian climber Ludwig Purtscheller, approaching by the Ratzel Glacier. They also climb Klute Peak on Mawenzi and then return to the crater rim of Kibo, this time at Hans Meyer Notch. Meyer's book gives abundant detail.

1890 "Heligoland Treaty" between Britain and Germany finalizes East African boundaries and gives Kilimanjaro entirely to what becomes known as German East Africa. Britain controls what is today Kenya (the East African Protectorate). One effect is easier travel around Kilimanjaro for overseas visitors, who no longer have to negotiate with individual chiefs.

1891 An American lady-traveler, May French Sheldon, travels (largely in a palanquin) to Lake Chala and the lower slopes of Kilimanjaro where she meets with local chieftains.

1893-94 The great botanist Georg Volkens spends 15 months in the Kilimanjaro region, studying what he identifies as six separate vegetation zones and making a comprehensive collection of plants, which he divides between the herbariums of Berlin, Kew, and the British Museum. With the geologist Dr. Lent and the zoologist Dr. Kretschmer, Volkens sets up a scientific station above Marangu. Lent and Kretschmer are killed in 1894 by warriors in the Rombo district.

1898 Meyer returns to Kilimanjaro with Ernst Platz for a glacier study and is amazed how the ice has retreated since 1889.

1900 Kilimanjaro is declared a wildlife reservation by the German colonial government. In the first years of the 20th century a number of private scientific explorations are undertaken, notably by the meteorologist Dr. C. Uhlig and geographers Dr. F. Jaeger and E. Oehler.

1909 This is the height of the collecting period of the great scientific establishments of the western world, when animal specimens are being gathered in great numbers. Game hunting is also popular for its own sake as tourism grows. One American expedition from Boston (the MacQueen-Dutkewich expedition) hopes to combine a hunting trip with an ascent of Kilimanjaro, but fails to reach the summit after an accident. At least three porters die of cold.

1912 E. Oehler and F. Klute (German) reach the summit of Mawenzi, calling it Hans Meyer Peak. They also traverse Kibo, making the first ascent of the Drygalski Glacier and descending by the Western Breach. Meanwhile a series of mountain huts are being built along the popular tourist route from Marangu, the first two by an enterprising German planter and hotel-keeper. In December, Dr. Furtwängler and Siegfried König take skis to the summit of Kibo, employing them for a swift descent.

1914 W. C. West of Capetown becomes "the first Englishman" to reach the summit a month before the outbreak of the first world war.

1914-20 Kilimanjaro is the scene of bitter conflict during the

1914-18 war between British and German forces, both of whom rely heavily on native recruitment. It has been said that during the East African Campaign, African deaths built to at least 100,000. A story is told of a German patrol under August Dehnecke, which was cut off behind enemy lines for nearly eight months before surrendering at the Hans Meyer cave on the eastern slopes of Kibo. (Dehnecke dies shortly afterward of the malnutrition sustained during this ordeal.) Following German defeat, in 1920 German East Africa becomes Tanganyika, a "mandated territory" under the protection of Great Britain.

1921 C. Gillman and party reach the crater rim as the first climbers after the mountain comes under British protection. Although they do not cover new ground, Gillman supplies long awaited first-hand information in English. (There has been nothing since the translation of Meyer's book in 1891.) Gillman is commemorated in the mountain's nomenclature—Gillman's Point.

Kilimanjaro's Forest is made into a reserve by British colonial power.

1925 Cameramen from the UFA studio, Berlin, shoot the first film at high altitude on Kilimanjaro, which at last depicts Africans on the crater rim, including the celebrated Chagga guides Msameri (who'd been with Meyer) and his son, Oforo. (Oforo and Jonathan are the first Wachagga known to have reached the summit of Kibo.)

1925-27 Several ascents, including three by the Reverend Dr. R. Reusch, after whom the ash pit of the crater is named. West climbs the mountain again in 1927 with Miss Sheila G. McDonald, the first woman to climb Kibo, and also Mawenzi. In 1926, the mummified leopard, made famous by Ernest Hemingway in "The Snows of Kilimanjaro," is discovered on the crater rim at a place now known as "Leopard Point" by Dr D.V. Latham. It remains there through to the early 1930s.

1929 The Mountain Club of East Africa is founded in Moshi (now the Kilimanjaro Mountain Club).

1930 The doughty British explorer-mountaineers H. W. Tilman and Eric Shipton attempt Kibo from Marangu and in mist trudge around from Gillman's Point to Stella Point but fail to reach the highest point. Tilman is vomiting from altitude sickness and both become snowblind. However they climb Mawenzi before leaving.

Swiss pilots Walter Mittelholzer and Alfred Künzler make the first flight over Kilimanjaro in a 200 h.p. Fokker airplane. Their photographs give the world its first good look into the Reusch crater.

1938 First Kibo Hut is built on Kilimanjaro

1939 Tilman returns and makes a solo climb to the summit of Kibo. He is the first to report fumerole activity in the Reusch crater. Until now the volcano has been thought to be totally extinct.

1938 Purtscheller Peak, the second highest of Mawenzi's four main summits, is climbed by E. Eisenmann and R. Hildebrand.

1947-61 Following World War II, Tanganyika becomes a trust territory under the United Nations with the commitment to lead the people towards self-government and independence, which eventually takes place in December 1961. (Britain continues its guardianship throughout this period.) In 1953 Julius Nyere becomes president of TANU (Tanganyika African National Union), which then has landslide victories in the first democratic elections. Nyerere becomes prime minister before independence; and a year afterwards, when Tanganyika becomes the United Republic of Tanzania (merging with Zanzibar), he is its first president.

1952 K. T. Pugh, Surveyor of the Department of Lands and Surveys, Tanganyika, leads an expedition to determine the height of Kilimanjaro, using predetermined triangulation points. His computations produce an official figure of 19,340 feet, but the altitude continues to vary widely in written references.

1953 Professor C. Downie and Peter Wilkinson of Sheffield University become the first to successfully descend into Mawenzi's Great Barranco as part of a geological reconnaissance.

1955 On May 18, a Dakota of East African Airways crashes into the southeastern slopes of Mawenzi with the loss of all aboard.

An Outward Bound Center is established at Loitokitok on the the Kenyan side of the border, from where regular ascents of Kibo are made by young people from Kenya, Tanzania, and Uganda.

1957 A. Nelson, H. J. Cooke, and D. N. Goodall (British) traverse Kilimanjaro, climbing all three peaks. They make the original route on the Heim Glacier.

1960 Great Penck Glacier is climbed in September 1960 by J. Pike and P. A. Campbell.

1961-62 Tanganyika gains independence in 1961 and its new flag is raised on Gillman's Point as Kibo's summit cannot be reached. In the year following, the flag is raised again, this time on the highest point of Kibo (formerly Kaiser Wilhelm Spitze), which is renamed Uhuru (Freedom) Peak. In that year Tanganyika merges with Zanzibar to become Tanzania.

The steep Kersten Glacier original route is climbed by W. Welsch and L. Hemcarek in September 1962, (a difficult Grade 6 climb).

Three French parachutists break the world record for high altitude landings by dropping into Kibo's crater.

1964 In February Barry Cliff and Rusty Baillie climb Kilimanjaro and Mount Kenya within 24 hours (21 hours 40 minutes. At the time of going to press, the feat has never been repeated.

RAF climbers John Edwards and William Thomson trace the first line up Mawenzi's complex East Face with two bivouacs on the wall—the East Face ice-couloir, otherwise known as "Thompson's Horror."

1968 Ian Howell and Roger "Fred" Higgins force "a more elegant route," with three bivouacs via the Downie Ridge on Mawenzi's stupendous East Face. (The face drops down almost 10,000 feet into two gorges, the Great and the Lesser Barrancos. These gorges are separated by the narrow Downie Ridge, which runs into the East Face of Mawenzi at around 15,000 feet. This point can be reached also by traversing in from the South and North, which is what Edwards and Thomson did when they climbed it.)

1969 Seven blind African climbers reach the summit of Kilimanjaro to raise the profile of the blind in Africa.

1970 Tanzania closes the Loitokitok Route (which starts in Kenya) with the supposed aim of channeling tourists to the Marangu Route. The new Kilimanjaro International Airport is being built.

Fritz Lörtscher (Swiss) traverses Mawenzi's eastern flank with the Chagga guide Fileki (at heights between 12,300 and 14,000 feet).

1971-72 The "innermost facet" of Breach Wall is climbed by Fritz Lörtscher, but the main Wall continues to defeat powerful parties. Lörtscher, who is very active during this period, also solos a new route, which crosses Diamond Glacier and climbs steep rocks to top of Kibo.

1972 A complete traverse of Kibo and Mawenzi is completed by Ian Howell and Phil Snyder over 8 days (up Umbwe/Western Breach, down Downie Ridge and Lesser Barranco to Loitokitok).

A major hut building program begins on Kilimanjaro with development assistance from Norway with Mandara and Horombo huts being reconstructed. (Work continues for several years.)

1974-75 During August a route is claimed on the right hand side of the Decken Glacier by M. Tudo, J. Montford, F. Schock, and J. Kuhn.

D. J. (John) Temple, climbing with Tony Charlton, forces a demanding new route at the east end of the massive Breach Wall, taking in sections of the Balletto Icefield and Heim Glacier. Within months Temple is back on the Breach Wall with Dave Cheesmond, creating a hard new line up the Balletto Icefield and a gully-system above. Temple's description of the huge Breach Icicle connecting the Balletto and Diamond Glaciers does much to attract further aspirants to the Breach Wall.

1975-76 Ian Howell, Bill O'Connor, and John Cleare climb the Kersten Glacier Direct—it involves "spectacular aid-climbing on a hanging icicle (Grade VI; A1)." Paul Fatti and John Moss claim another Grade VI route on the Kersten Glacier, giving a direct start to the above, 1975, route. A few weeks later Iain Allen and Mark Savage create another line on the extreme right hand side of the glacier.

1977 Kilimanjaro National Park is officially opened by President Julius Nyerere.

1978 Rob Taylor and Henry Barber fail to climb the Breach Icicle on Breach Wall after Taylor suffers a severe ankle fracture when an ice pedestal snaps. Barber successfully gets him off the face in a supremely organized rescue, then goes for help. This becomes one of the most controversial of climbing epics, following the publication of Taylor's version of events.

Later that year Reinhold Messner and Konrad Renzler complete the full Breach Wall Direct, including the Icicle.

Heim Glacier Direct Route is climbed by R. Barton and D. Morris over two days in December.

1980 Rudolf Jauk climbs Kilimanjaro in 24 hours from Himo.

1983 Second ascent of Breach Wall by Wes Krause and Scott Fischer.

1984-85 Cousins Richard and Nicholas Crane mountain bike to the top of Kibo following the Marangu Route.

1989 Kilimanjaro National Park becomes a World Heritage Site.

1990-94 Botanist John Grimshaw conducts exhaustive fieldwork in the northern forests of Kilimanjaro, which greatly adds to the knowledge of the mountain's ecology and biogeography.

1995 Kilimanjaro National Park bans risk-sport stunts such as mountain biking, motorbiking, paragliding, hanggliding, etc., which have become regular activities, often associated with sponsored charity climbs. One man even carried his sousaphone to play on the summit, which he did somewhat breathlessly. I doubt that comes under the banned activities.

1999 Kilimanjaro loses 10 feet! Not literally, but in a new survey conducted with the latest satellite technology by scientists from the University of Technology in Karlsruhe.

It was reported in February 2000 (Himavanta) that, using latest satellite technology, a recent German/Tanzanian geological expedition had measured Uhuru, Kilimanjaro's highest point, as 19,330 feet (5891.77 meters). It has long been accepted to be ten feet higher than that.

1999/2000 Mass climb of Kilimanjaro to see in the new Millennium. It's also an excuse to give the mountain infrastructure a facelift.

2001 Large-format film shot on Kilimanjaro by David Breashears and his team.

*Works marked * also carry important bibliographies, which are not reproduced in full here.*
Alexander, Thomas. *Kilimanjaro: New Millenium Guide to Africa's Highest Peak.* (Privately published paperback describing the Marangu and Machame Routes), 1999.

Allan, Iain. "The ice desert of Kilimanjaro." (First ascent of the right hand side of Kersten Glacier), *Alpine Journal* 82, pp 171-3, 1977.

Andersen, P. D. "Heim Glacier." *Climber and Rambler*, August 1976.

Anderson, G. D. *The soil and land use potential of the southern and eastern slopes of Kilimanjaro, Tanzania.* Institute of Resources Assessment, University of Dar es Salaam and International Development Program, Massachusetts, 1982.

Angelakis, Nikolaos. *Mount Kilimanjaro Expedition 1999. GPS Data Processing and Evaluation of the ITRF-Position and Height of Mount Kilimanjaro.* (Paper presented at the First Workshop on GPS and Mathematical Geodesy in Tanzania), 4 October, 1999.

Ardito, Stefano. *Trekking in Africa.* Swan Hill Press, 1996.

*Bailey, Geoff; King, Geoffrey; and Manighetti, Isabelle. "Tectonics, Volcanism, Landscape Structure and Human Evolution in the African Rift." Oxford: *Oxbow*, pp 31-46, 2000.

Balletto, Giovanni. *Kilimanjaro montagna dello splendore. Dai ricordi di un medico alpinista.* Bologna: Tamari, 1974.

Barth, G. "Letter on Kilimanjaro." *Atheneum*, p 149, 1866.

Beard, Peter. *The End of the Game.* San Francisco: Chronicle Books, 1988.

Beck, E. "Plant Life on Top of Mt. Kilimanjaro." *Flora*, 181: 379-381, 1988.

Beck, E., Scheibe, R., and Schulze, E.D. "Recovery from fire: observations in the alpine vegetation of western Mt. Kilimanjaro (Tanzania)." *Phytocoenologia* 14: 55-77, 1986.

Bedale, Julian. "No recognized route," article on the climbing history of Mawenzi East Face. *Mountain Club of Kenya 2000 Bulletin* (Volume 92), 2000.

Beke C. T. "The Discovery of Kilimanjaro." *Atheneum* 1119: 357; 1124: 48, 1849.

Bigger, M. "A Checklist of the Flora of Kilimanjaro." in *Ice Cap 4*, (reprinted with additions as *Some Wild Flowers of Kilimanjaro*, by the Kilimanjaro Mountain Club), 1966.

Bonney, G. F. "Report on Rocks collected by H. H. Johnston from the upper part of the Kilimanjaro Massif." *B.A.A.S.*, pp. 682, 1885.

Brescia, Belo Lionel. *Under Kilimanjaro.* (Book 1 of the Series: "The Shark Teeth Men.") New York: Carlton Press, 1996

Bridges, R. C. *W. D. Cooley, the Royal Geographical Society and African Geography in the 19th Century.* 1976.

Brodie, F. M. *The Devil Drives, Life of Richard Burton*, 1967.

Bruce, E. A. "The Giant Lobelias of East Africa." *Kew Bulletin*, pp 61-88, 1934.

Bull, Bartle. *Safari, a Chronicle of Adventure.* 1988.

Burns, Cameron. *Kilimanjaro and Mount Kenya, A Climbing and Trekking Guide.* The Mountaineers/Cordee, 1998.

Burton, R. F. "Progress of Expedition to East Africa." *J.Roy.Geog.Soc.* 28:188-?, 1858.

--"East Africa Coast Expedition." *Blackwoods Magazine*, 1858.

--"Reports and Comment on East Africa Expedition." *Proc.Roy.Geog..Soc.* 3:115, 116, 208, 211, 213, 304, 306, 1858-59.

--"Report on East Africa Expedition." *J.Roy.Soc.* 29:1-464, 1859.

--"On Cooley and Kilimanjaro." *Atheneum* 1899:407, 1864.

Busk, Douglas. "Kilimanjaro." *Alpine Journal* 60, 1955.

Cane, L.B., "Kilimanjaro," *E.A. Medical Journal*, 21. p 91, 1944.

Carmichael, Stephen W. (and others). *Climbing Mount Kilimanjaro.* 1999.

Cleare, John. *Mountains.* (Chapter on Africa includes description of Heim Glacier ascent.) London: Macmillan, 1975.

"Micro cClimate and Animal Life in the Equatorial Mountains." *Zool. Afr.*4, (2): 101-128, 1979.

Collingwood, Frances. "Portrait of an Empire Builder (H. H. Johnston)." *Geographical Mag* XXXI, No 2, 1958.

Conniff, Richard. "Africa's Wild Dogs." NATIONAL GEOGRAPHIC, 195:5, pp 36-63, 1999.

Cooley, W. D. "The Geography of N'yassi." *Proc.Roy.Geog.Soc.* 15:185, 1845.

--"Kilimanjaro and von der Decken." *Atheneum* 178; 226; 332; 609, 1863.

--"Kilimanjaro and the RGS," *Atheneum*; 84, 1864.

Cordeiro, N.J. "Forest birds on Mt. Kilimanjaro, Tanzania." *Scopus* 17: 65-112, 1994.

Cotton, A. D. "A Visit to Kilimanjaro." *Kew Bull.* 3:97-112, 1930.

Coupland, R. *East Africa and Its Invaders.* 1938.

--*Exploitation of East Africa 1856-90.* 1939.

Crane, Richard and Crane, Nicholas. *Bicycles up Kilimanjaro.* London: Oxford, 1985.

Dainelli, Giotto. "Il kilimangiaro secondo un recente studio." *Rivista Geografica Italiana*, 1902

Dickson, W. L. "The Calculation of the Height of Kilimanjaro." *Empire Survey Review* Vol XII, No 91, pp 206-10, 1954.

Downie, C. "Glaciations of Mount Kilimanjaro." *Geol.Soc.of America.Bull* 75:1-26, 1964.

Downie, C., Humphries D. W., Wilcockson W. H., and Wilkinson P. "Geology of Kilimanjaro." *Nature* 178:828-830, 1956.

Downie, C. and Wilkinson, P. *The Geology of Kilimanjaro.* [The results of the Joint Sheffield University-Tanzania Geological Survey, Expeditions in 1952 and 1957], 1972.

Dundas, C. *Kilimanjaro and Its People.* 1924, reissued 1968.

Edberg, Rolf. *The Dream of Kilimanjaro.* New York: Pantheon, 1976.

Embuscado, M. E., BeMiller, J. N., and Knox, E. B. "A survey and partial characterization of ice-nucleating fluids secreted by giant-rosette (Lobelia and Dendrosenecio) plants on the mountains of eastern Africa." *Carbohydrate Polymers* 31:1-9, 1996.

Engler, A. "Ueber die Vegetationsformationen Ost-Afrikas auf Grund einer Reise durch Usambara zum Kilimandscharo." *Zeitschrift der Gesellschaft fuer Erdkunde zu Berlin*, no 6, Berlin: 1903.

Fantin, Mario. *Kilimangiaro, La Montagna splendente.* Florence, 1962.

--*Kilimangiaro.* Bologna: Tamari, 1963.

--*I tre "Grandi" africani: Kilimangiaro, Kenya, Ruwenzori.* Verona, 1966.

--*Sui ghiacciai dell'Africa.* Bologna, 1968.

Fischer, G. A. "Report of a Journey in the Masai Country." *Proceedings of RGS*, Vol VI, 1884.

Foerster, E. Th. "Vom hoechsten deutschen Gebirge, die touristische Erschliessung des Kilima-Ndscharo." *Muenchner neuste Nachrichten*, 1913.

Gardner, Brian. *On to Kilimanjaro: The Bizarre Story of the First World War in Africa.* 1963.

Geilinger, W. *Der Kilimandjaro, sein Land u. seine Menschen.* Bern/Berlin: Hans Huber, ca.1930.

"The Retreat of the Kilimanjaro Glaciers." *Tanzania Notes & Records* 2:7-20, 1936.

Gilbert, Vernon C. *Plants of Mount Kilimanjaro.* College of African Wildlife Management in Moshi and Office of Environmental Interpretation, US National Park Services, Washington, D.C., 1970.

Gillman, C. "An Ascent of Kilimanjaro." *Geog.Journ.* 61: 1-27, 1923.

Gilseth, Margaret Chrislock. *Home on Kilimanjaro.* 1999

Glassman, Jonathon. *Feasts and Riot: Revelry, Rebellion, and Popular Consciousness on the Swahili Coast, 1856-1888.* History of Africa Series, 1995.

Grimshaw, J. M., Cordeiro, N. J. and Foley, C. A. H. "The Mammals of Kilimanjaro." *Journal of E African Natural History* 84, 105-139, 1995.

*Grimshaw, J. M. *Aspects of the Ecology and Biogeography of the Forest of the Northern Slope of Mt Kilimanjaro, Tanzania.* Unpublished D.Phil. thesis, University of Oxford. 1996.

Grimshaw, J. M. and Grey-Wilson, C. "Impatiens kilimanjari subspecies pocsii." *Curtis's Botanical Magazine* 14: 23-30, 1997.

Grimshaw, J. M., "Disturbance, Pioneers and the Afromontane Archipelago," in: C.R. Huxley, J.M. Lock, D.F. Cutler (eds) *Chorology, Taxonomy and Ecology of the Floras of Africa and Madagascar*, pp 207-220, 1998.

--"The Effects of Disturbance by Large Mammals in an Afromontane Forest Recovering from Logging," in: Timberlake, J. & Kativu, S. (eds) *African Plants: Biodiversity, Taxonomy and Uses*, Royal Botanic Gardens, Kew, pp 65-74, 1999.

--"The Afromontane Bamboo, Yshania Alpina, on Kilimanjaro." *Journal of East African Natural History* 88: 79-83, 1999.

Hamilton W. J. Royal Geographical Society Presidential Address, *Proc.Roy.Geog.Soc.* 19: ix-xvi, 1849.

Hastenrath, Stefan. *The Glaciers of Equatorial East Africa.* Dordrecht: D Reichel, 1984.

--"Glacier recession on Kilimanjaro, East Africa, 1912-1989." *Journal of Glaciology* 43, 455-459, 1997.

Guide to Mount Kenya and Kilimanjaro, Nairobi: Mountain Club of Kenya, 4th edn 1981, and revised 1990, 1998.

Hatchell, G. W. "Queen Victoria, Kilimanjaro and the Kenya/Tanganyika boundary." *Tanzania notes and Records*, 43:41, 1956.

Hedberg, Olov. "Vegetation Belts on East African mountains." *Svensk.Bot.Tid.* 45, 1948.

--"Altitudinal Zonation of the vegetation on the East African mountains." *Proc. of the Linnean Society of London* 165 (1952-53); 2: 134-136, 1955.

--*Features of Afroalpine Plant Ecology.* Acta Phytogeographica Suecica 49: Uppsala, 1964; reprinted 1995.

--"Evolution and speciation in a tropical high mountain flora," *Biological Journal of the Linnean Soc.* 1:135-148, 1969

"Afroalpine centers of biodiversity and endemism." pp 877-882 (vol 2) in: J. H. Seyani and A. C. Chikuni (eds) *Proceedings of the XIIIth Plenary Meeting of AETFAT, Zomba, Malawi, 2-11 April 1991* (2 vols, National Herbarium and Botanic Gardens of Malawi), 1994.

Hemingway, Ernest, *Green Hills of Africa* (Fiction, inspired by his game hunting experiences), 1935.

--*The Snows of Kilimanjaro* (Short story, written in 1936 for *Esquire*. Collected in *The First Forty-nine Stories*, 1939, and regularly every since.)

--*True at First Light*, (A fictional memoir of Hemingway's last African safari, edited and introduced by his son, Patrick Hemingway), 1999.

Hemp, Andreas. "New Fern Records for Kilimanjaro." *Journal of East African Natural History* 86: 37-42,1997.

Higgins, Roger. "The Great Barranco – 1968: the expedition to the East Face of Mawenzi." *Mountain Club of Kenya Bulletin* 67, Feb. 1969.

Hollis, C. "Note on von der Decken." *Tanzania Notes and Records* 50:63-67, 1958.

Hooker, J. D. "On the subalpine vegetation of Kilimanjaro." *J.Linn.Soc.* 14:141-146, 1873.

Hopkins, A. J., *Trail Blazers and Road Makers: A Brief History of the East African Mission of the United Methodist Churches*, 1928.

Howard, J. "The East Face of Mawenzi." *Mountain Club of Kenya Bulletin*, No 71, April 1973.

--"In Memoriam: Arthur Herbert Firmin, 1912-1955." *Alpine Journal*, November 1955.

Howard, Mary Theresa and Millard, Ann V. *Hunger and Shame: Child Malnutrition and Poverty on Mount Kilimanjaro*, New York and London: Routledge,1997.

Howell, I. F. "Kilimanjaro Traverse." *Mountain Club of Kenya Bulletin*, No 70, April 1972.

Huxley, J. "Kilimanjaro volcanic activity." Letter to *The Times*,30 Dec 1942.

IFRA—French Institute for Research in Africa. *Mount Kilimanjaro Land Use and Environmental Management* (Collected reports and papers from 1999 Workshop held in Nairobi by University of Dar es Salaam, University of Bordeaux, the French Institute for Research in Africa, and the Embassy of France in Tanzania), 1999

Illustrated London News. "Active or Extinct? The problem of Kilimanjaro." 202 :80-81,1943.

*Iliffe, John. *Tanganyika under German Rule, 1905-1912*. Cambridge, CUP, 1969.

Ingrams W. H. *Zanzibar. Its History and People*. 1931.

Johnston, Erika. *The Other Side of Kilimanjaro*. (Settler's illustrated memoirs), 1971.

Johnston , H. H. "The Kilimanjaro expedition." *Proc. Roy. Geog. Soc.* 7(3) conf. 137,1885.

"British Interests in Eastern Equatorial Africa." *Scottish Geog. Magazine* i: 5, p 145, also *Journal of the Manchester Geog. Soc.* VI: 12, p 690, both 1885.

The Kilimanjaro Expedition. London: Kegan Paul, Trench, 1886.

Joubert, Jean-Denis and Christin, Eric. *Kilimandscharo Sagenumwobeme Gipfel*. Tanzania: Tanganyika Wildlife Safari, (Editions in German, French and English), 1990s.

Joyce, Jack (ed), *Kilimamjaro Trekking Map*, 1999.

Kapinga, Dr. R., Ngoile, Dr. M., Persha, L., Rodgers, Dr. W.A., and Salehe, J. (eds). *Planning for the Long Term Conservation of the Mount Kilimanjaro Ecosystem*. (Proceedings of a Workshop held at Moshi 27-30 September, 1999), National Environment Management Council with the cooperation of UNESCO and others), 2001.

*Kaser, Georg and Osmaston, H. *The Nature of Tropical Glaciers* "Former Quaternary tropical glaciers; their nature, extent and climates, with special reference to the East African Mountains." Cambridge, 2001.

Kent, P. E. "Kilimanjaro: An Active Volcano." *Nature* 153: 454-5, 1944.

Kersten, O. *Decken's Reisen in Ost Afrika*. 1871.

Kielmeyer, Lieut. "Die Kilimandscharo-Expedition 1893." *Vom Fels zum Meer*, pt 19, 1898.

Kimambo, I. N. and Temu, A. J. (eds). *A History of Tanzania*. 1969, 1997.

Knox, E. B. "The conservation status of the giant senecios and giant lobelias in Eastern Africa." *Opera Bot.* 121:195-216, 1993.

Knox, E. B. and Palmer, J. D. "Chloroplast DNA evidence on the origin and radiation of the giant laobelias in eastern Africa." *Syst.Bot.* 23: 109-149, 1998.

Koenig, S. and Furtwangler, S. Account of their Ascent on Ski. *Norwegian Ski Yearbook*, 1921.

Krapf, Ludwig. *Travels, Researches and Missionary Labours in East Africa*, London: Trubner, 1860. (2nd edition has useful new introduction by R.C. Bridges, London: Frank Cass), 1968.

Krog, John O., Zachariassen, K.E., Larsen, Bjorn, and Smidsrod, Olav. "Thermal buffering in Afro-alpine plants due to nucleating agent-induced water freezing." *Nature*, Vol 282, 15 November 1979.

*Lange, Harald. *Kilimanjaro: the White Roof of Africa*. (Translation from the German, and particularly good for bibliography of German publications), 1985.

Latham, D. V. "Some observations on the physiology of high altitudes in the Tropics." *Geog.Journal* 68, pp 492-503, 1926.

Latham, Gwynneth and Latham, Michael (Eds). *Kilimanjaro Tales: The Saga of a Medical Family in Africa*, 1995.

Lee, Chip. *On Edge: The Life and Climbs of Henry Barber*. Boston: Appalacian Mountain Club, 1982.

Le Roy, Alexandre. *Au Kilima-ndjaro. Histoire de la fondation d'une Mission Catholique en Afrique orientale*. Paris: de Soye, 1893.

Livingstone, D. "On 'snowy' mountains in Africa." *Proc.Roy.Geog.Soc* 1:243, 1856.

Lockall, Simone. "Sleep Walking on the Roof of Africa." *BMC Summit* 19, pp38-40, 2000

Lörtscher, Fritz. "Kilimanjaro: first ascent of the Northern Ice-field." *Alpine Journal* 78, pp166-7, 1973.

Lovett, Jon C. and Uronu, Ludovick O. N.. *Draft Field Guide to the Forest Trees of Kilimanjaro*. Botanical Museum, Copenhagen, 1994.

Lovett, Richard. *History of the London Missionary Society*, London, 1899.

Loxton, John and Campbell, Peter, "Mawenzi from the North." *Mountain Club of Kenya Bulletin* 36, December 1955.

Lucas, C. P. *The Partition and Colonization of Africa*. 1922.

Maddox, Gregory; Giblin, James; Kimambo, Isaria N. (eds)

*Malisa, Elia, *Geology of the Tanzanite Gemstone Deposits in the Lelatema Area, NE Tanzania*. Helsinki, 1987.

McKinder, H. J. *The First Ascent of Mt Kenya*. (edited with introduction by K. Michael Barbour, has useful references to early E. African exploration.) Ohio University Press, 1991.

MacQueen, Peter. *In Wildest Africa: The Record of a Hunting and Exploration Trip Through Uganda, Victoria Nyanza, the Kilimanjaro Region and British East Africa, With an Account of an Ascent of the Snowfields of Mount Kibo, in East Central Africa, and a Description of the Native Tribes*. Boston: L. C. Page, 1909.

Marchal, Michel and Robino, Gilbert. *Kenya, Kilimandjaro, Ruwenzori "Les Montagnes la lune."* Chamonix: ENSA, 1975.

Marimonti, Lorenzo and Merendi, Romano. *Ruwenzori, Kenya, Kilimanjaro*. Bologna, 1959.

Martin, David [not directly attributed]. *Kilimanjaro [Africa's Beacon]: Land, People History*. Harare/Arusha African Publishing Group/Tanzania National Parks (TANAPA), undated, c.1999

Mathew, G. "The Periplus of the Erythrean Sea." *East Africa and The Orient*, 1975.

Matthiessen, Peter, *An African Trilogy*. (Comprising *The Tree where Man was Born*, 1972; *African Silences*, 1991; *Sand Rivers*, 1981.) London: Harvill, 2000.

Maxon, Robert M. *East Africa: An Introductory History*. Nairobi: E. African Educational Publishers, 1986. Reprinted West Virginia University Press, 1994.

Mazrui, Ali. *The Africans, a Triple Heritage*. (BBC book in conjunction with TV series), 1986.

Messner, Reinhold. *Free Spirit, a Climber's Life*. (Chapter on his climb of Breach wall with Konrad Renzler.) London: Hodder & Stoughton, 1991.

Meyer, Hans. *Ostafrikanische Gletscherfahrten*. Leipzig, 1890.

--*Across East African Glaciers: the first ascent of Kilimanjaro*. London: G. Philip & Son, 1891.

--*Zur Kenntnis von Eis und Schnee des Kilimandscharo*. In Verhandlungen der Gesellschaft f.Erdkunde zu Leipzig, 1891.

-- "Gletscher des Kilimandsharo." (Report of his new Kilimanjaro expedition), *Geographische Zeitschrift* 5: heft 4, 1899.

--*Der Kilimandjaro, Reisen und Studien*. Berlin: Reimer, 1900.

--*Hochtouren im Tropischen Afrika*. Leipzig: Brockhaus, 1925.

*Miller, Charles. *The Lunatic Express, the Magnificent Saga of How the White Man Changed Africa*. 1971.

--*Battle for the Bundu: the First World War in East Africa*. 1974.

Mitchell, John. *Guidebook to Mt Kenya & Kilimanjaro*. Nairobi: Mountain Club of Kenya, 3rd ed., 1971.

Mittleholzer, Walter. *Kilimandjaro Flug* (the first flight over the mountain, which revealed the inner crater), Urich: Orell Fuessli, 1930.

Moorhouse, Geoffrey. *The Missionaries*. London: Eyre, Metheun, 1974; Readers Union, 1975.

Moreau, R. E. "Pleistocene Climatic Changes and the Distribution of life in East Africa." *Journ.Ecology* 21:415-435, 1933.

--"A contribution to the ornithology of Kilimanjaro and Meru." *Proc. Zool. Soc. London*, 1935: 843-891, 1936.

Murchison, R. I. "Livingstone, and comment on Kilimanjaro discovery." *Proc.Roy.Geog.Soc* 1:243-4, 1856.

--"On Kilimanjaro and Burton expedition." *Proc.Roy.Geog.Soc* 1:450, 1857.

--"On von der Decken expedition to Kilimanjaro." *Proc.Roy.Geog.Soc.* 8:2, 1863.

Needham, J. and Gwei-Djen, Lu. "The earliest Snow Crystal Observations." *Weather* 16(1961)10:319-327, 1961.

New, Charles. "Letter to Dr Kirk." *Proc.Roy.Geog.Soc* 16:161, 1872.

--"Account of Kilimanjaro ascent." *Alpine Journal* 6:51, 1872.

--*Life Wanderings and Labours in East Africa*, London: Hodder & Stoughton,1873. Reprinted 1874.

Newmark, William D. (ed) *The Conservation of Mount Kilimanjaro*. (important papers, including by: D.M. Gamassa, T. Pocs, S.B. Misana, C.A.H. Foley and J.M. Grimshaw, W.D. Newmark, etc.) IUC—The World Conservation Union,1991.

--*"Conserving Wildlife in Africa: integrated Conservation and Development Projects and Beyond," in *BioScience*, July 2000.

O'Connor, Bill. "Kersten Glacier Direct." *Climber and Rambler*, August 1976.

Oehler, E. "Von einer Forschungsreise am Kilimanjaro." *ZDOA*,46, PP 124-156, 1915.

Oliver, D. and Hooker, J. D. "Plants collected by Thomson J. in East Africa." *J.Linn.Soc*.21:392-406, 1885.

Oliver, R. *The Missionary Factor in East Africa*. 1951, reprint 1965.

--*Sir Harry Johnston and the Scramble for Africa*. 1957.

--*The African Experience*. London: Weidenfeld & Nicolson, 1991. Phoenix paperback, 2000.

Packenham, Thomas. *The Scramble for Africa*. London: Weidenfeld & Nicolson, 1991.

Petermann, A. "Letters on Kilimanjaro." *The Atheneum* 1348, 1853 & 194; 298, 1862.

Peters, Carl. *New Light on Darkest Africa*. 1891.

Pfisterer, Gary. "Unwitting Variations on the Heim." *Seven Summits*, 2000.

Pocs, Tamas. "The Altitudinal Distribution of Kilimanjaro Bryophytes." From J.H. Syani & A.C. Chikuni *Proceedings XIIIth Pleanary Meeting AETFAT*, Malawi, 2: 797-812, 1994.

Pugh, K. T. "The Height Determination of Mount Kilimanjaro, Tanganyika, East Africa: August-September 1952." *Empire Survey Review* Vol XII, No 91, pp 194-206, January 1954.

Purtscheller, L. "Die Ersteigung des Kilimandscharo." *Mitteilungen des D.Oe. Alpenvereins*, pp 85, 1890.

Rebmann, Johannes. Journal and letters in Church Missionary Society Archives, 1845.

--"Journey to Jagga, the snow country of East Africa." *Church Missionary Intelligencer* 1, 1849.

Rebmann, J. and Erhardt, J. "Map of the East African Interior." (the Slug Map). *Proc.Roy.Geog.Soc*. 1856.

*Reader, John. *Kilimanjaro*. London: Elm Tree Books, 1982.

Reusch, R. Report of Kilimanjaro ascents, *Tanganyika Times* 10 February, 1928.

*Rheker, J.R., Taiti S.W., and Winiger, M. *Bibliography of East African Mountains*. Kenya: Privately printed, 1989.

Richard, J. J. "Volcanic observations in East Africa." *J. East African Nat. Hist. Soc* 18: 1-12, 1945.

--"Kilimanjaro crater fumaroles and seismic activity during 1942-45." *Nature* 156:352-4, 1945.

Richards, C. G. *Krapf, Missionary and Explorer*. ca. 1950.

Richards, Charles (ed.). *Some Historic Journeys in East Africa*. London: Oxford University Press, 1961.

Richards, P. W. *The Tropical Rainforest*. 1952.

Ridgeway, Rick. *The Shadow of Kilimanjaro: On Foot Across East Africa*. London: Bloomsbury, 1998.

Riwkin-Blacjk, Anna (photos) and Lindgren, Astrid (text). *Sia Lives on Kilimanjaro*. NT: Macmillan, 1959.

Robinson, John. *Kilimanjaro Burning*. Birchbrook Press, 1998.

*Rosqvist, Gunhild. "Quarternary Glaciations in Africa." *Quarternary Science Reviews*, Vol 9, pp 281-297, 1990.

Rotberg, R. I. *Joseph Thomson and the Exploration of Africa*. 1971.

Ruddiman, W. *Earth's Climate. Past and Future*. New York: W. H. Freeman & Co., 2001.

Saburi, J., Angelakis, N., Jaeger, R., Illner, M., and Jackson, P. (with K. T. Pugh). "Height Measurement of Kilimanjaro." In *Survey Review*, Vol 35, No 278, pp 552-562, October 2000.

Salisbury, Geoffrey. *The Road to Kilimanjaro*. (Work with the blind in Africa, culminating in a Kilimanjaro ascent.) London: Minerva, 1997.

*Salt, G. "The Shira Plateau of Kilimanjaro." *Geog. Journ*. CXVII, Part 2, pp 150-166, 1951.

--"A Contribution to the Ecology of Kilimanjaro." *J.Ecol*. 42:375, 423, 1953.

Sampson, D. N. "The Geological Survey of Kilimanjaro." *Mountain Club of Kenya Bulletin* 56, 1963.

Savage, Mark. *Kilimanjaro 1:500,000 Map and Guide*. 1988, completely revised 1992, frequently reprinted.

Shulman, Neville. *On Top of Africa: the Climbing of Kilimanjaro and Mt Kenya*. Shaftesbury: Element, 1995

Sinclair, P. J. "Kilimanjaro active." letters to *The Times* 24 Dec 1942; 5 May 1943.

Smith, Antony. *The Great Rift, Africa's Changing Valley*. New York: Sterling, 1988.

Smyth, W. F. "Presidential Address. " *Proc.Roy.Geog.Soc* 20: ix, 1850.

Spear, Thomas & Waller, Richard. *Being Masai, Ethnicity and Identity in East Africa*. London: James Currey (also Dar es Salaam, Nairobi, and Athens, Ohio), 1993.

Spink, P. C. "Volcanic activity on Kilimanjaro." Letters to *The Times* 24 April 1943; 18 Aug 1943.

--"Glaciers in the Kilimanjaro crater." *Quart.J. Roy. Met. Soc*.,1943

Stahl, K. "Outline of Chagga History." in *Tanganyika Note and Records*, pp 35-49, 1965, reprinted 1974.

--*History of the Chagga People of Kilimanjaro*. The Hague: Mouton, 1964.

Stambach, Amy. *Lessons from Mount Kilimanjaro: Schooling, Community, and Gender in East Africa*. New York/London: Routledge, 2000.

Stock, Eugene. *History of the Church Missionary Society*. London (4 vols), 1899.

Stringer, Chris and McKie, Robin. *African Exodus, the Origins of Modern Humanity*. London: Cape, 1996; Pimlico, 1997.

Stuart-Watt, Eva. *Africa's Dome of Mystery*. London: Marshall, Morgan & Scott, ca.1930.

TCCIA. "Corruption and drug trafficking in Tanzania: a socio-economic analysis: a research study by the Tanzania Chamber of Commerce, Industry and Agriculture (TCCIA) and Workshop on Corruption and Drug Trafficking in Tanzania." Held at the Kilimanjaro Hotel, 12 October, 1994.

Tanzanian Notes and Records, Vol 64: Commemorative Issue on Kilimanjaro, reprinted and revised 1974

Taylor, Rob. *The Breach: Kilimanjaro & the Conquest of Self*. New York: Coward, McCann & Geohegan, 1981.

Temple, John. "Breach Wall." *Climber and Rambler*, August 1976.

Tenderini, Mirella. *Le Nevi dell Equatore: Kilimanjaro, Kenya, Ruwenzori*. Centro Documentazione Alpina, 2000.

Thesiger, Wilfred. *My Kenya Days*. London: Harper Collins, 1994; Pimlico paperback, 1995.

Thomson, Joseph. "Notes on the Geology of East Central Africa." *Nature* 1880:102.

--*Through Masailand: A Journey of Exploration among the Snowclad Volcanic Mountains and Strange Tribes of Eastern Equatorial Africa*. London: Sampson Low, Marston, 1885.

Thornton, R. "Journey to Kilimanjaro." *Proc.Roy.Geog.Soc*. 9: 15-16, 1864.

--"Notes on a Journey to Kilimanjaro with von der Decken." *J.Roy. Geog.Soc*. 35: 15, 1865.

Tichy, Herbert. *Auf fernen gipfeln: abenteuer auf dem Dach der Welt*. Vienna etc: Fritz Molden, 1976.

Tilman, H. W. *Snow on the Equator*. London: Bell, 1937; New York: Macmillan, 1938.

Tombazzi, Giovanni. *New Map of the Kilimanjaro National Park*. Hoopoe Adventure Tours, Tanzania, and Nature Discovery Ltd., 1998.

Tremonti, Marino. *Il Kilimangiaro: Monografia Geografico Alpinistica*. Bologna: Tamari,1964.

Truffaut, R. *From Kenya to Kilimanjaro*. Hale, 1957.

Uhlig, C. "Vom Kilimandscharo zum Meru: Vorlaeufige Mitteilungen ueber eine Forschungsreise." Part 2, from *Zeitschrift des Gesselschaft fuer Erdkunde zu Berlin*, No 10, 1904.

Vavra, Robert. *The Unicorn of Kilimanjaro*. New York: Morrow, 1988.

Volkens, Georg. *V.G.E.*, 22, pp 152-73, 1895.

--"Exkursionen am Kilima-Ndjaro." *Verhandlungen der Gesellschaft fuer Erdkunde zu Berlin*, Band 22 no.3, 1895.

--"Der Kilimandscharo: Darstellung der allgemeineren Ergebnisse eines fuenfzehn-monatigen Aufenthalts im Dschaggalande." Berlin: Reimer, 1897.

von der Decken, C. C. *Reisen in Ost Afrika in 1859-1879*. (In 4 volumes, edited by O. Kersten), Leipzig, 1879.

--"On the Snowy Mountains of East Equatorial Africa." *Proc.Roy.Geog.Soc*. 8:5, 1886.

von Lettow-Vorbeck, General Paul. *My Reminiscences of East Africa, the Campaign for German East Africa in World War I*.

Warburton-Lee, John. *Roof of Africa*. Shrewsbury: Swan Hill, 1992.

Ward, Clive, Boy, G., and Allan, I. *Snowcaps on the Equator: The Fabled Mountains of Kenya, Tanzania, Uganda and Zaire*. London: The Bodley Head, 1988.

Webb, G. "Top Dog." *Africana* 2:21,1962.

Western, David. *In the Dust of Kilimanjaro*. Washington DC: Island Press/Shearwater, 1997.

Whittow J. B. and Osmaston H. A. *The Deglaciations of the East African Mountain*. Occasional paper 3 of the Brit. Geomorphological Research Group, 1966.

Willock, Colin and Time-Life editors. *Africa's Rift Valley*. Amsterdam: TimeLife (World's Wild Places), 1974.

Willoughby, J. C. *East Africa and its Big Game*. London: Longman, 1889.

PHOTOGRAPHY AND ILLUSTRATIONS CREDITS

ACKNOWLEDGMENTS

I NEVER EXPECTED to go to Kilimanjaro, and the experience was for me an exciting voyage of discovery, both at the time and since. So my first fat thank you goes to David Breashears for the invitation to take part in his film. The climb reawakened my youthful passions for plants, animals, and rocks and I have had enormous fun following up on these since, during the writing of this book. I owe deep gratitude to all those I badgered endlessly with questions, and who always have answered promptly and with great patience. In particular, I acknowledge Henk Beentje, Roger Bilham, John Grimshaw, Ian Howell, Moses Kazimoto, Freddie Munna, Henry Osmaston, Alan Rodgers, Gunhild Rosqvist, Canute Temu, and Buck Tilley. And I am grateful to Eric Knox for explaining the amazing mechanics of Kilimanjaro's monstrous lobelias, to Henry Barber for sharing his recollections of the Breach Wall on Kilimanjaro in 1978, and to John Edwards for recording (at long last) his memories of the first ascent of Mawenzi East Face in 1964.

The generosity of so many scientists, historians, climbers, and friends in responding to my approaches both surprised and touched me. I am thinking here of Iain Allan, Geoff Bailey, Julian Bedale, Edwin Bernbaum, Peter Cattermole, Robert Caukwell, Eric Christin, Geoffrey Clarfield, John Cleare, Barry Cliff, Tom Dunkel, Ian Evans, Charles Foley, Polly Gillingham, Lindsey Gillson, Jonathon Glassman, James Grove, Susan Gruber, Geoff King, Sabine Kohler, Helen Leavesley, Phyllis Lee, Ian McMorrin, Atwitye Makwetta, Jim Milledge, William Mziray, William Newmark, Roland Oliver, Brian O'Shea, Louise Pirouet, David Pluth, Tamas Pocs, Scott Ransom, Chris Stringer, John Temple, Peter Wilkinson, and Pamela Willoughby.

Help, too, came from many organizations. I thank Margaret Ecclestone of the Alpine Club Library; Michael Albrecht and Paul Jenkins of Mission 21 in Basel; and Mary Ingoldby, the Oral History Coordinator at the British Empire and Commonwealth Museum in Bristol. At the Royal Geographical Society, I was helped by Clive Coward, Francis Herbert, and Eugene Rae. Information also came from the Church Missionary Society Library and Archives, from the *Illustrated London News*, from the School of Oriental and African Studies, and from Michelle Hawkins at Lonely Planet Publications.

Very warm thanks go to fellow members on the Kilimanjaro trips, film crew, "talent," and Tanzanian helpers, who made the whole experience so lively and memorable. The children, Hansi and Nicole, deserve special mention for being such good troupers; as do Arabella Cecil and Monica Martin for looking after us and all arrangements so efficiently throughout. I want, too, to record my appreciation to Adamson Eliau who carried more than his share of my luggage up and down the mountain; and to Kirimbi and Amiri of Sokwe, Ltd, who showed me the Masai steppe.

As always, I thank my husband Peter Salkeld for his unselfish support—and for keeping me supplied with bookshelves as my collection of Africa books just kept on growing. And, finally, I acknowledge the unstinting encouragement and help I have received from Kevin Mulroy, Johnna Rizzo, Sadie Quarrier, and all the good folk at National Geographic. Thank you all.

KILIMANJARO FILM ACKNOWLEDGMENTS

MOUNTAIN FILM TEAM
David Breashears: Director, Producer, Cinematographer, Boston, MA; Arabella Cecil: Co-producer, Oxfordshire, England; Jack Tankard: Cinematographer, Whittier, CA; Robert Schauer: Cinematographer, Graz, Austria; Scott Ransom: Videographer, Telluride, CO; Dave Ruddick: Sound Recordist, Freeland, WA; Ace Kvale: Still Photography, Ophir, CO; Buck Tilley: Camera Assistant, Arusha, Tanzania; Douglas Neithercut: Rigger, Boulder, CO; Joey Papazian: Production Assistant, Snowbird, UT

TREK TEAM
Heidi Albertsen: Fashion Model, Copenhagen, Denmark; Roger Bilham: Geophysicist, Boulder, CO; Jacob Kyungai: Mountain Guide, Arusha, Tanzania; Hans Mmari: Student, Arusha, Tanzania; Audrey Salkeld: Author, Cumbria, England; Rick Thomson: Business Owner, Watertown, MA; Nicole Wineland-Thomson: Student, Watertown, MA

MOUNTAIN LOGISTICS
Allan Phillemon and Corbett Bishop Safaris: Arusha, Tanzania

SHERPA CAMERA TEAM
Wongchu Sherpa: Chyangba, Nepal; Lhakpa Gelje Sherpa: Thapting, Nepal; Kami Sherpa: Bakam, Nepal; Nawang Phuri Sherpa: Thapting, Nepal

TANZANIAN CAMERA TEAM
Shafael Mboya, Machame; Exaud Nkya, Machame; Goodluck Swai, Machame; Julius Nkya, Machame; Estomy Nkya, Machame; Goodluck Wilson, Machame; Reinatus Mjombaa, Arusha; Bob Massawe, Machame

LOCATION MANAGERS
Damian Bell: Arusha, Tanzania; Sanyula Kabisa: Arusha, Tanzania

USA PRODUCTION TEAM
Truett Latimer: Executive Producer; Charlotte Lazenberry: Film Distributor; William A. Anderson and Julie Wai-Sum Yuen: Editors; Mose Richards and Janna Martin: Writers; Alan Williams: Composer; Monica Martino: Production Coordinator; Kevin Anderson: Assistant Production Manager; Scott Swofford and Myles Connolly: Production Consultants; Leah Carey and Rachel Clift: Assistants to the Producers

ADVISORS TO THE KILIMANJARO EXPEDITION
Dr. Henk Beentje: Botanist; Dr. Roger Bilham: Geophysicist; Dr. Douglas Hardy: Climatologist; Dr. William Mziray: Botanist

SPECIAL PRODUCTION ASSISTANCE
John K. Boyer; David Fanning; Walter Scott, Jr.; Sokwe, Ltd.; Gijs & Monica De Raadt; Moivaro Coffee Plantation; Northern Air; Peak Promotion; Newtonville Camera; Wesley Krause; Thomson Safaris; Tim Mangini; Wilson Chao; Derrick Ashong; David Boyden; Reggie Heyworth; Kurt Papenfus; Howard Donner

STAFF CREDITS

Kilimanjaro
Audrey Salkeld

Published by the National Geographic Society
John M. Fahey, Jr., *President and Chief Executive Officer*
Gilbert M. Grosvenor, *Chairman of the Board*
Nina D. Hoffman, *Executive Vice President*

Prepared by the Book Division
Kevin Mulroy, *Vice President and Editor-in-Chief*
Charles Kogod, *Illustrations Director*
Marianne R. Koszorus, *Design Director*

Staff for this Book
Kevin Mulroy, *Project Editor*
Johnna M. Rizzo, *Editor*
Sadie Quarrier, *Illustrations Editor*
Carol Farrar Norton, Brian Noyes, *Art Directors*
Martha Martin, *Researcher*
Carl Mehler, *Director of Maps*
Joseph F. Ochlak, *Map Researcher*
Gregory Ugiansky, Tibor G. Tóth, *Map Production*
Gary Colbert, *Production Director*
Lewis R. Bassford, *Production Project Manager*
Janet Dustin, *Illustrations Assistant*
Melissa Farris, *Design Assistant*
Connie Binder, *Indexer*

Manufacturing and Quality Control
George V. White, *Director*
John Dunn, *Manager*
Phillip L. Schlosser, *Financial Analyst*

One of the world's largest nonprofit scientific and educational organizations, the National Geographic Society was founded in 1888 "for the increase and diffusion of geographic knowledge." Fulfilling this mission, the Society educates and inspires millions every day through its magazines, books, television programs, videos, maps and atlases, research grants, the National Geographic Bee, teacher workshops, and innovative classroom materials. The Society is supported through membership dues, charitable gifts, and income from the sale of its educational products. This support is vital to National Geographic's mission to increase global understanding and promote conservation of our planet through exploration, research, and education.

For more information, please call 1-800-NGS LINE (647-5463) or write to the following address:

National Geographic Society
1145 17th Street N.W.
Washington, D.C. 20036-4688 U.S.A.

Visit the Society's Web site at
www.nationalgeographic.com.

Library of Congress Cataloging-in-Publication Data

Salkeld, Audrey.
Kilimanjaro : to the roof of Africa / Audrey Salkeld ; introduction by David Breashears.
p. cm.
Includes bibliographical references and index.
ISBN 0-7922-6466-5 (hard)
1. Mountaineering--Tanzania--Kilimanjaro, Mount. 2. Kilimanjaro, Mount (Tanzania)--Description and travel. I. Title.

GV199.44.T342 S35 2002
796.52'2'0967826--dc21   2001052171

Major funding for
Kilimanjaro: To the Roof of Africa was provided by the

Houston Museum of Natural Science

and Omaha's Henry Doorly Zoo
Museum of Science, Boston
Denver Museum of Nature & Science
Fernbank Museum of Natural History
Fortworth Museum of Science and History